INDIGENOUS PEOPLES
AND THE MODERN STATE

CONTEMPORARY NATIVE AMERICAN COMMUNITIES
Stepping Stones to the Seventh Generation

Acknowledging the strength and vibrancy of Native American people and nations today, this series examines life in contemporary Native American communities from the point of view of Native concerns and values. Books in the series cover topics that are of cultural and political importance to tribal peoples and that affect their possibilities for survival, in both urban and rural communities.

SERIES EDITORS:

Troy Johnson, American Indian Studies, California State University, Long Beach, Long Beach, CA 90840, trj@csulb.edu

Duane Champagne, Native Nations Law and Policy Center, 292 Haines Hall, Box 951551, University of California, Los Angeles, Los Angeles, CA 90095-1551, champagn@ucla.edu

BOOKS IN THE SERIES

EDITORIAL BOARD

INDIGENOUS PEOPLES
AND THE MODERN STATE

EDITED BY
DUANE CHAMPAGNE,
KAREN JO TORJESEN, AND
SUSAN STEINER

A Division of Rowman & Littlefield Publishers, Inc.
Walnut Creek • Lanham • New York • Toronto • Oxford

ALTAMIRA PRESS
A division of Rowman & Littlefield Publishers, Inc.
1630 North Main Street, #367
Walnut Creek, CA 94596
www.altamirapress.com

Rowman & Littlefield Publishers, Inc.
A wholly owned subsidiary of The Rowman & Littlefield Publishing Group, Inc.
4501 Forbes Boulevard, Suite 200
Lanham, MD 20706

PO Box 317
Oxford
OX2 9RU, UK

British Library Cataloguing in Publication Information Available

Library of Congress Cataloging-in-Publication Data

Indigenous people and the modern state / edited by Duane Champagne, Karen Jo Torjesen, Susan Steiner.
    p. cm. — (Contemporary Native American communities ; 10)
    Includes bibliographical references and index.
    ISBN 0-7591-0798-X (cloth : alk. paper) — ISBN 0-7591-0799-8 (pbk. : alk. paper)
    1. Indians of North America—Politics and government. 2. Indians of North America—Government relations. 3. Indians of North America—Social conditions. 4. Self-determination, National—North America. I. Champagne, Duane. II. Torjesen, Karen Jo, 1945– III. Steiner, Susan. IV. Series.

E98.T77I53 2005
323.1197'07—dc22   2004029088

Printed in the United States of America

♾™ The paper used in this publication meets the minimum requirements of American National Standard for Information Sciences—Permanence of Paper for Printed Library Materials, ANSI/NISO Z39.48-1992.

CONTENTS

Preface

THE GROWING VISIBILITY, activism, and internationalization of indigenous peoples call for greater engagement with the concerns of native peoples and the complexities of their relationships to the modern state. The need is all the more urgent in these closing years of what the 1993 United Nations' resolution pronounced as the International Decade of the World's Indigenous People. Indigenous peoples are seeking to retain a distinctive cultural and political identity while participating in national and economic life, to resolve problems that exist between them and state governments, and, generally, to raise international awareness of the diversity and value of their cultures and social organizations. In the spring of 2002, Claremont Graduate University convened a conference on "Indigenous Peoples and the Modern State: Comparative Perspectives from Canada, the United States, and Mexico" with the support of a grant from the Canadian government.

What made this conference unique was the comparative perspective. The relationships between indigenous peoples and their national governments had never been examined by Canadian and American scholars working together. Social, environmental, economic, ethnocultural, political, and international issues do not exist in a vacuum. They exist within particular nation-states, with distinctive histories and different political institutions. Canada and the United States, unlike many other nations, have a history of treaty making with indigenous peoples, recognizing forms of indigenous sovereignty through treaties. This they have in common; however, the issues of sovereignty differ. In the United States, issues of sovereignty mark the recent debates on casinos, "the new buffalo for Native Americans, and a new source for prosperity." In Canada, issues of sovereignty range from transport of nuclear waste through reserves and settlements to the conflicts between tribal and state systems of justice. A comparative approach was able to bring into sharp relief the distinctiveness of the situation of the indigenous peoples in Canada and the United States. This comparative perspective was further enhanced by including the issues of indigenous peoples in Mexico.

The issues of sovereignty are shaped quite differently in Mexico than in Canada or the United States. For the indigenous peoples of Mexico, autonomy has become subject to profound misrepresentation. Autonomy does not mean sovereignty; rather, it implies being part of the larger political and institutional structures of Mexico. The Zapatistas claim not to be another nation but to be Mexican and Chamula, Tzeltal, or Tzotzil: that is, ethnic groups from Chiapas, wanting the right to their ethnic normative systems and styles of conflict resolution. They want to be able to negotiate with the modern state, not to be separated from it. As in many other countries, indigenous peoples of Mexico see their rights, as set forth in the United Nations' document referred to above, as being constantly violated by the Mexican state.

Indigenous knowledge—indigenous approaches to social, environmental, political, and economic issues—often differ from those of the nation-states—hence the need to bring together the indigenous and nonindigenous activists, politicians, and scholars from across the disciplines to bring into sharp relief the way indigenous peoples themselves approach what concerns and what defines them, and to provide a context in which to negotiate questions of policy and trade that cross the national boundaries of Canada, the United States, and Mexico.

The conference was organized into three panels: Indigenous Identity and the State, Culture and Economics, and a Trilateral Discussion: Canada, the United States, and Mexico. Each of the panels engaged a set of issues from a comparative perspective. The first two focused on Canada and the United States, exploring governmental policies toward indigenous peoples and the differences in the issues raised by First Nations and Native Americans. All panels represented a transdisciplinary approach with experts trained in different fields, such as law, anthropology, history, economics, and politics.

The few academic conferences on indigenous peoples have concentrated on a single issue, such as environment, language, land, rather than, as with this conference, on the multiple perspectives that comparison and transdisciplinary approaches allow. The tendency in the few academic programs dealing with indigenous issues is to focus on traditional disciplinary distinctions, such as cultural anthropology, art, or health, rather than on multiple methodologies. In bringing together scholars and activists who span cultural, political, and legal expertise, the conference on "Indigenous People and the Modern State" both mirrors the way indigenous peoples themselves approach what concerns and what defines them, and also provides a useful model and a valuable context in which to probe questions of policy and trade that cross the national boundaries of Canada, the United States, and Mexico.

One of those conceptual terms that tends to enter the academic vocabulary before it has had a chance to acquire the "solidity of specification"—*transdisciplinary*— describes, in the simplest historical sense, that process by which new fields and subjects of study become wrenched from the existing ones. Law, American literature, education, and management are only four examples of established concentrations that have leapfrogged existing organizations of knowledge to come into existence. In this same way, indigenous peoples are, in effect, creating new fields of political philosophy and political economy through self-determination movements and interactions with nation-state governments. Because their critiques and formulations exist largely in oral traditions and do not conform to typical Western patterns and theories, indigenous peoples are also contributing new approaches and methodologies to the questions of creating political power and authority through different models of social organization.

The first panel, on Indigenous Identity and the State, dealt with topics of cultural identity, land, sovereignty, and concerns for the environment within Canada and the United States. The U.N. Working Group on Indigenous Populations has used a working definition to indigenous: peoples maintaining a historical continuity with preinvasion and precolonial society for whom the preservation and transmission of their ancestral territories is essential to their continued existence as peoples who seek to maintain their own cultural patterns, social institutions, and legal and political systems. Concern for the land and its biodiversity places indigenous peoples within the environmental justice movement. Among the issues specific to them are the protection of timber and concerns over uranium mines, oil pipelines, and fishing rights.

The second panel, on Culture and Economics, dealt with intellectual property, education and language, art, and commerce. Articles 7, 8, 12, 14, and 15 of the U.N. Draft Declaration on the Rights of Indigenous Peoples deal with cultural integrity, identity, culture, spiritual and religious traditions, and language. Inherent in every one of the rights mentioned are the discussions and conflicts now going on within Canada and the United States. Issues of intellectual property are particularly thorny at the intersection of oral cultures and cultures of the published word. Largely preserved in oral traditions, the knowledge and wisdom of indigenous peoples—in this case, the healing powers of plants—is transmitted across generations within family and apprenticeship relations. Presently, pharmaceutical companies, often the very constituencies who devalue this knowledge, are making enormous profits, while indigenous peoples remain unrewarded. Many consider the patenting of indigenous knowledge or "biopiracy" a double threat, first of creativity and innovation, and second, of stolen knowledge and economic profit.

In issues of education, primary emphasis was placed on the problems and conflicts indigenous peoples face in perpetuating their cultural heritage and the pressure on them to assimilate into the larger society. Some discussion was directed toward indigenous studies programs and the level of attention to Canadian indigenous peoples in American university programs. Since the 1960s, indigenous studies departments have emerged throughout North America; Canada has led the way with the first such department at Trent University in 1969. A central question, however, persists: how to link indigenous communities to the culture of universities; how to interweave traditional indigenous paradigms into the classroom, journal articles, and other "spaces" so different from what exists in indigenous communities.

In regard to the first issue, a complicating factor is the diversity of indigenous cultures and languages, and a major concern is the pattern of general language loss. The U.S. Indian Nations at Risk Task Force in 1991 recommended the promotion of tribal language and culture; in 1992, the White House Conference on Indian Education recommended the amendment of the Bilingual Education Act to support Native American languages. Since 1969, over twenty-five tribal colleges have been developed. Questions remain: how do these institutions, conscious as they are of indigenous cultures, become truly reflective of the culture? In addition, the attitude in the Untied States towards bilingualism has changed radically since the 1960s. Canada offers some models in the Canadian commitment to bilingualism and the establishment of such institutions as the Institute for Indigenous Government in 1991, the first autonomous and indigenous-controlled public postsecondary institution.

The third panel—Trilateral Discussion: Canada, the United States, and Mexico—offered a three-way comparison on issues discussed in the first and second panels, which focused exclusively on Canada and the United States. This trilateral comparison brought activists and scholars of Mexican and indigenous peoples into the discussion with Canadian and American representatives. Many of the comparisons discussed above were explored, adding issues concerning indigenous people of Mexico.

As in other countries, indigenous peoples of Mexico see their rights as set forth in the United Nations' document referred to above as being constantly violated by the Mexican state. On the issue of biopiracy, international corporations (Monsanto, for example) are "patenting" a type of corn grown in Mesoamerica for thousands of years. The patent is to be their property, and indigenous peoples will have to "buy" the right to continue planting it.

The disappearance of native languages and culture are likewise concerns in Mexico, as indigenous populations are being transformed into cheap labor forces for industries. Increased environmental pollution, the loss of forests, and the rise of tourism threaten indigenous cultures as international corporations and state governments develop regions that are home to indigenous peoples for profit. Discussion among the entire populace is crucial to begin to find solutions that enable indigenous and other social organizations to participate fully and constructively in negotiations with the state.

The comparative approach of the conference brings into sharp relief the distinctiveness of the situation of the indigenous peoples in Canada, contrasting Canadian governmental, economic, educational, and cultural policies toward First Nations with those of their neighbors to the south. The boundaries of these contiguous nation-states impact differently on the tribes whose territories have been bisected by the borders of the nation-state. For example, the Inuit live across Canadian and U.S. borders. In such cases, the same indigenous group is impacted by very different policies. Although the first two panels were dedicated to the comparison between Canada and the United States, the discussion period following each panel expanded into a trilateral discussion of the issues raised. This trilateral discussion has been captured through a synopsis of the ensuing discussion and is presented following the papers for that panel.

The organizers of this conference want to express appreciation to the Canadian Consulate for their commitment to a deeper understanding of the relationship between governments and their indigenous peoples. Through a grant from the consulate, it was possible to initiate this collaboration between Canadian, American, and Mexican scholars and indigenous activists. Special thanks goes to Pam Johnson, the cultural affairs advisor, who provided guidance, counsel, and support at each step of the way. The participation of Canadian Consul General Colin Robertson and his support were deeply appreciated. The production of this volume was a collaborative project between the Claremont School of Religion and the Native Nations Law and Policy Center of UCLA, and the editors wish to express their thanks to both schools. Very special thanks goes to Susan Graham for her excellent organizational work during the conference and for her invaluable help in coordinating with the editors and contributors in the production of this volume.

INDIGENOUS IDENTITY
AND THE STATE

I

Rethinking Native Relations with Contemporary Nation-States

I

DUANE CHAMPAGNE

CONTEMPORARY NATIVE IDENTITIES are to a large extent based on relations to nation-states. While native peoples have identities that predate the formation of nation-states, and many aspects of these pre-state identities continue to persist and make their weight felt in everyday life, native identity is largely defined in relation to colonizing cultures and state governments. Native communities are generally relegated to the margins of contemporary nation-states and their issues often seen as problems of incorporation, integration, civilization, and modernization. Native communities are seen as "other" groups that must ultimately be brought within the pale of the national community and culture. Some nation-states are working to include racial and ethnic minorities within the scope of a more diversified national community. Diversity, multiculturalism, and racial tolerance are often viewed as positive trends within nation-states or multicultural nation-states. While many countries still face extreme differences among ethnic groups and submerged nations, often leading to violence and possible separatism, the ideal form of nation-state includes diversity, democracy, and equal opportunity for most citizens regardless of class, race, gender, or ethnic group. The ideal of a diverse or multicultural nation-state is a goal for most nation-states, and is the image that most modernists, postcolonial and postmodernists, present as the desirable trend in the future.[1]

The multicultural or diverse nation-state, however, does not work well with the aspirations, values, cultures, and institutions of native or indigenous communities. Native communities predate the formation of modern nation-states and predate the arrival of settler colonists by thousands of years. Native communities have governed themselves from time immemorial and have maintained independent institutions, cultures, and territories. Native peoples seek to preserve their territory and rights to self-government, and want to continue and develop their institutions, culture, religion, and governments. Native communities have found it difficult to follow the usual paths of assimilation and integration chosen by most immigrant settler communities. Native peoples insist on rights to land and self-government that are highly unusual and outside the theory of the formation and growth of nation-states. The treating of indigenous peoples as ethnic or racial groups ready for nation-state assimilation and integration has resulted in considerable abuse and much resistance from native peoples. Much of this resistance continues in both overt and less visible means and ways, and is largely an expression of different values and goals between nation-states and indigenous communities.[2] Nation-states, with their strong policies of assimilation, integration, and sometimes incorporative multicultural diversification and inclusion, have policies and values that run counter to indigenous values and goals. This process is often called nationalism.[3]

There is no place either in the nation-state or the multicultural state for the point of view of native peoples, and consequently native peoples are at odds and in coercive participation, even in the most liberal and democratic visions of the diversified and inclusive nation. Nation-states tend to assume a common social and political culture, but more recent challenges have asked them to open to gender, racial, and ethnic inclusion and participation, but no such hand is extended to the issues presented by indigenous peoples around the world and within specific nation-states.[4] The usual nation-state policy is to ask indigenous peoples to assimilate socially, politically, and economically, often within extremely unfavorable conditions.[5]

Unless the state governments of the future are willing to take seriously the viewpoints and values of indigenous nations, the possibility of building state governments based on consensus, justice, mutual understanding and respect, noncoercion, and diversity is not possible. Ethnic and racial groups have been able to modify the relatively singular emphasis on national culture and community, and have expanded the discussion to include multiple races and ethnicities. These forms of diverse inclusion have the hope of creating more equal and just national communities, and strengthen the range and possibilities of the nation-state, but these changes, while satisfying the majority in many instances, do not satisfy the demands on indigenous communities and submerged nations. The forms of institutional organization and values in native communities are alien to those used to construct contemporary nation-states, bureaucracies, and capitalist markets. Native peoples represent alternative claims to government, land ownership, land and resource management, community organization and identity, and different institutional patterns for achieving ends. The nation-state and the multicultural nation-state both are not well suited to meet the democratic and consensual needs of indigenous peoples for inclusion within the state. Any state fully capable of rec-ognizing the long-standing issues of indigenous peoples will need to recognize their claims to land; their different understandings of land, community, and gov-ernment; their different institutional relations of community and government; and their different cultures and values. Only a state that can include and respect the native rights to land, self-government, and culture without direct coercion can achieve the goal of an open and democratic state. Nation-states and multicultural nation-states do not extend their definitions of inclusion to bring in native com-munities in a voluntary manner, and therefore continue to deny the foundation of consensual inclusion critical to the definition of a democratic state.[6] Such a state must be defined as a *multinational state*, where indigenous rights are recognized; their institutions, claims to territory, and cultures are respected; and they are allowed a mutually agreed measure of self-government according to their own understand-ings. Such a multinational state would better achieve the consensual basis of soci-ety of all groups—indigenous, immigrant, ethnic, gender, and racial—and would better achieve the ideal of a democratic and consensual-based state government.[7]

In the literature on indigenous peoples, there is much discussion of their col-onization, assimilation, and the adaptation to nation-state policies. There is a gen-eral agreement or understanding that native communities, which are generally small and powerless, must make accommodations to present circumstances of gov-ernment.[8] Indigenous peoples will make accommodations to changing systems of nation-states, globalized markets, information, and technology. The national com-munities of nation-state governments that encompass indigenous peoples need to recognize and respect indigenous rights and cultures. Indigenous peoples cannot realize their rights and views under the present arrangement of nation-states or contemplated multicultural states; a new regime of government is required wher-ever indigenous peoples are found, and this institutional order must include and recognize the rights and views of indigenous peoples. Such a state structure I am calling a multinational state, and will discuss its implications in more detail below.

The Stateless Indigenous Identity and Community

The ultimate claims to native identity and nationality do not derive from con-temporary nation-states.[9] Native nationality is not a grant from the nation-state for limited rights to territory or self-government, and does not derive from colo-nial legal proclamations or the legal decisions of courts, either national or in-ternational. Native identity and nationality derive from their occupation of the land and from their self-government according to their own way developed over the years. Natives have lived in the Western Hemisphere for more than twelve thousand years, and that long occupation gives them the rights to territory and self-government that long precedes the formation of nation-states over the past two hundred years.

Even though the long occupation of the Western Hemisphere gives natives precedence, natives generally have creation stories that outline the formation of the world, and the place where people are placed on the land, as well as their relation to the land. The creation stories provide many social, political, and cultural institutions, which are often upheld and kept through ceremony and tradition as part of the cosmic order. Many native communities have migration stories that depict movement from west to east in addition to creation stories. Why a particular people might live in a specific territory may depend on stories, a migration legend, or a creation story. In all of these cases, the people live in a particular place, with specific institutions and ceremonies, and with particular forms of government and community organization that are often believed to be the gift and hand of the Creator or spiritual intermediaries.[10] The land, the families, clans, bands, villages, government, and ceremonies are generally seen as gifts from the Creator, and therefore have a sacred and spiritual dimension. The gifts must be honored and maintained in order for the native people to show their thanks and remain in good standing with the order and purpose of the cosmos as given by the Creator. Most native communities believe they have a special purpose and task to perform within the grand plan of the cosmic order. The people have a special relation to the Creator and only through honoring and obeying the sacred order of the cosmos through individual and community actions, ceremonies, and moral relations with human and spiritual beings will the native individuals and community perform their spiritually given tasks and purposes. Consequently, many native communities have strong investments in maintaining their way of life, beliefs, ceremonies, and institutions, because they believe they are gifts from the Creator, and their future, as well as the well-being of the world, may depend on their upholding covenant relations with the Creator. Some communities believe that if they do not perform their ceremonies and maintain their way of life, the world will be destroyed or corrupted.[11]

Native relations between community, land, and spirituality are not well understood by nonnative communities and officers in nation-states. The land is given by the Creator, and the social and political institutions are given, and therefore they must be honored. Not to honor the will of the Creator is to disrupt the sacred order of the cosmos, and will bring imbalance and destruction onto the perpetrators. In the view of many native communities, the cosmos is filled with many powerful beings who can harm people if they are not respected and honored. Plants, animals, elements, rocks, humans, fire, water, earth, and wind are often seen as powerful forces that must be accommodated and respected.[12] Natives do not see the world as one where only humans have agency or soul. The native world is full of forces that have agency, soul, or spirit. Humans have a role to play in the cosmic drama, but not necessarily a central role or an exclusive role. Upsetting or disrespecting the powers of the cosmic order will lead to retaliation and restoration of order. Humans seek a balance of powerful forces in order to live their lives and achieve their assigned life and community tasks within the cosmic community. The native view of cosmic order and community includes the powerful forces of the cosmos; sometimes clans or societies are named after powerful beings in an effort to seek their approval and blessings. Individuals seek visions in many cultures in order to find their life task and seek powerful spirit allies to aid them in their life activities. The land, plants, animals, and elements such as fire, wind, water, and earth had specific powers, and humans have specific relations to the powers and must honor and respect those relations in order to maintain well-being and balance for living a fruitful and honorable life.

The native conception of community and relation to nature varies considerably from the Western Enlightenment view. Attitudes toward land and nature are fundamentally different form Western rationalist views, which often inform the creation of nation-states. Land is given as a sacred gift and a sacred stewardship. People do not own land, but must care for the land as part of their sacred task within the purpose and direction of the cosmic order. The Western emphasis on land as a resource that must be exploited and transformed into cultural and valuable goods is very different. The world as resource for the work of humans to transform into increasingly more productive and useful things is wholly foreign to native interpretations of nature and their place within the cosmic order. These fundamental differences in cultural epistemology are at the root of conflict between nation-states and native communities. The two different cultural epistemologies indicate two very different views of the order and purpose of nature, and the relation of humans within the cosmic order. Nevertheless, if states and their national communities are willing to address the issues of multiculturalism, it must not be only with the cultural views that are generally compatible with their own; native views present entirely alien values and goals to Western national communities. Honoring native values and epistemologies is a first step toward a multicultural state. Honoring native understandings of land, government, and community institutions are steps toward developing a democratic and consensually based multinational state.

Native institutional relations often involve understandings of relations of groups to powerful beings, such as animals and plants. Native institutional relations are not seen as unique and separate from the cosmic order of life and change, but are part of the cosmic order, embedded within the cosmic order, and reflective of cosmic order and direction. Native institutions are seen as part of the sacred plan and purpose of life and the cosmos set by the Creator. Thus native institutional, ceremonial, social, and political relations are seen as part of the sacred order set by the Creator or intermediaries. Humans must respect and honor the social and political institutions and groups that make up the native community. Again, the cosmic tie of native community institutions to cosmic beings and powers puts native understandings of community and institutions at a different order than those provided by contemporary nation-states. These sacred and cosmic relations of native communities, institutions, and ceremonies do not find direct counterparts in the secular nation-states of the contemporary period. Native communities are made up of families, kinship groups, clans, villages, bands, and regional and tribal groupings. Furthermore, native communities and their institutional relations are tightly overlapping, meaning that ceremonial, kinship, leadership, and economic relations are closely interrelated, with little specialized division of labor that characterizes the Western capitalist market economy or bureaucracy of the nation-state.[13] Native social and political institutions are very different from those of contemporary nation-states, and any attempt to create a multinational state must be willing to accommodate the differences in cultural epistemologies and institutional relations.[14]

Native identity within precontact society, as well as to a large extent during the present, is also very different from the national community of the nation-state. National loyalties and identities characterize the nation-state, but in native communities identities are often not tribalwide and are definitely not ethnic in the sense of pan-Indian identities. Native social and cultural institutional arrangements are local and specific. Unlike what is commonly understood by national communities, natives do not form a single ethnic group, nor do they form an ethnic identity. The identity and identification as "Indian" or as a tribe is created through the process of colonization.

Natives hold their own identities within their communities and cultures. There are thousands of native communities within the Western Hemisphere. Native nations have very specific creation stories, institutional relations, cultural epistemologies, and community relations. Each is unique in its combination of cultural belief, political relations, land, and community relations. In each case, the identities are created through the specific relations of creation stories, kinship, and territoriality. Native identities are specific and diverse and are different within each tribal community. Since there are thousands of native communities in the Western Hemisphere, there are thousands of native identities. For example, among the Creek Confederacy, a person belongs or identifies with his or her mother's clan and the sacred square or village where his or her mother and her clan kinspeople live. Similarly, a person might say he or she is a Crow, but his or her personal identity will belong to a specific clan whether that clan belongs to a mountain or prairie band. Native identity is subtribal and specific, often with no national or tribal-level identities. These native identities need to be respected within any multinational state, and as I will argue later, natives have developed numerous extensions of their community identities within the nation-state, and have created identities that will allow them to manage relations within a state structure. Nevertheless, native identities are very different from national community identities and any consensually based multinational state should be able to accommodate non-Western identities, although loyalties and participation in a multinational state on the part of natives will require changes and extensions of traditional community specific identities.

Native communities did not form nations or states in the contemporary sense of nation-state. The institutional and cosmic relations and epistemologies were extremely different from Western understandings. To this day, native institutions and community values are not well understood by nation-state officials or the mainstream national communities. Native issues, identities, and community organization are often assumed to be similar to ethnic groups; hence, natives are not believed to have any more rights or powers than other ethnic groups within the nation-state. Instead, natives have very specific and numerous identities, communities, and cultural epistemologies that provide them with values and direction in their lives. Many native communities believe that they have as individuals and communities a specific purpose and role to play in the cosmic order, and they strive to honor and play out those roles in world history and within the cosmic order. Native cultural epistemologies, values, and institutional relations are alien to those of the West and to the logic and history of nation-states. To a large extent, nation-states have ignored native communities and their ways because they made little sense within—and have little compatibility with—national community cultures and nation-states. However, ignoring native values and communities will not make them go away.

If one can make a single generalization about native communities over the past five hundred years of colonization, it is that they have persisted. Native communities continue to strive to preserve their cultures, communities, self-government, and territories. Nation-states have tried to assimilate and integrate natives, but with limited success. The persistence of native institutions, cultural epistemologies, communities, and identities requires that any state wanting to create a consensual political order must take the indigenous viewpoint into account; otherwise, natives are left out of the nation-state, and will persist in their ways and suffer continued political and cultural oppression.[15] Native rights have been ignored, and native peoples have not been invited to join as partners in nation-state communities. Natives are given the choice of abandoning their cultures and heritage in order to gain full citizenship within the nation-state. This is a price that many native communities are not willing to pay, and they therefore demand a democratic method of joining the national community, while retaining native rights to land, cultural heritage, self-government, and community organization.

Colonization and Contemporary Nation-States

The policies of nation-states have generally focused on assimilation of native peoples. Even in the United States where the "Self-Determination Policy" has been in effect for over thirty years, there are deep trends of assimilation. Nation-states, those with strong nations and relatively unified cultures, promote the incorporation and assimilation of indigenous and other peoples into the mainstream. The U.S. civil rights movement is largely focused on gaining access to equal opportunity and full economic and social equality or citizenship. Recent policies of multiculturalism allow those from different races or ethnic groups the capacity to assimilate and incorporate into U.S. society, but at the same time allow groups and peoples to retain a sense of racial, ethnic, or cultural identity. All these policies are geared to promote participation and inclusion into mainstream society, but not necessarily, in more recent versions, to obliterate cultural and historical heritages.

Nation-states have treated indigenous peoples in a variety of different ways. In the United States, native peoples are recognized to have land and limited rights to self-government based on treaties and laws developed since the beginning of the colonial period. One of the first policies for managing native issues in the United States was premised on the belief that native peoples would have to be educated and turned into small farmers. Native peoples would be assimilated and brought into the social and economic life of the United States. Native peoples, however, resisted quick and easy assimilation, and by the 1820s and 1830s, U.S. policy turned toward removal. Assimilation practices did not change native peoples quickly enough to enable them to be accepted by Americans, and the natives generally preferred to live in their own communities, within their own cultures, and on their own land.[16]

In the United States, natives are not parties to the Constitution and were not citizens until a congressional act in 1924. U.S. natives are granted citizenship, but these rights do not impair or supersede native rights granted by the tribe. In effect, native peoples in the United States have dual citizenship, with the United States and with their native nation. Many native people opposed the Indian Citizenship Act, but all natives are now citizens of the United States according to U.S. law and government policy. Issues of jurisdiction and citizenship rights continue to be hotly contested in the United States. U.S. policies continue to be assimilative, and the citizenship act was one step toward incorporating natives into the U.S. nation and society.

In Canada, natives were granted gradations of citizenship with the Indian Act of 1876. Those natives who chose to be Indian were allowed to live on native reserves, but with limited and restricted rights in Canadian society. Canadian reserve Indians were not allowed to vote, and were under the civil control of Indian agents. Similar to the arrangement in the United States, the Canadian plan is highly assimilative. The act encouraged natives to abandon reserve life and take up life as full Canadian citizens.[17] However, in Canada, one is either a citizen of Canada with full legal rights, or a reserve Indian with restricted rights but retaining native rights. Natives who become Canadian citizens forfeit all native rights and claims and assume full rights and obligations as Canadian citizens. The fundamental theme in the Indian Act and much of Canadian Indian policy is to assimilate and enfranchise native people into mainstream Canadian society.

These basic policies remain in force today, although there has been much controversy and numerous revisions in the Indian Act, especially as it applied to women. Women who married Canadian citizens were granted full citizenship but lost their native rights. A nonnative woman marrying a native man became native and claimed native rights.[18]

In Mexico, natives are granted full citizenship but there is no recognition of native rights to land, self-government, or cultural preservation. Native rights in Mexico are not legally or formally recognized. The tactic of granting full citizen rights to all the peoples, including natives, obliterates the political and cultural autonomy of native peoples in Mexico and throughout much of Latin America. Mexico does not recognize an "Indian problem" although millions of native peoples in Mexico do not speak Spanish. The nation-state that ignores indigenous rights by granting full citizenship does not recognize the social and cultural history of indigenous peoples and is not predisposed to recognize their rights to land, self-government, and cultural autonomy.[19] The Mexican relation to the native peoples and native rights is more akin to those found throughout the world than are the institutions of native rights and recognition found in the United States and Canada.

Why are native rights in North America, or more specifically, the United States and Canada, so different from the rest of the world?[20] The methods and histories of colonialism in North and Latin America provide a basis for understanding assimilation and identity of the native peoples and their nation-states. In Mexico, Cortés and Indian allies defeated the Aztec Empire and the Spanish assumed the powers of the empire. That meant rights over labor, a form of taxation, assumed rights over territory, and the right to spread Christianity. The Spanish claimed conquest, and although recognizing the independence of the native nations in the 1500s and 1600s, soon reduced the status of Indians to individuals and ignored the powers and rights of leaders and communities to manage land and other assets. Indians were relegated to the lower rung of a caste system, and were incorporated into the Spanish colony and Mexican states as individuals with formal legal rights, but with few social and political rights or powers within the colonial and nation-state formations. The Spanish Empire and Mexican nation-states formally obliterated native rights to self-government, land, and cultural autonomy, although many native communities continue to pursue their native traditions, languages, and social and political identities.

The colonial history of North America north of the Mexican border is very different from the colonial experiences of native peoples in the rest of the world. In North America, many European nations entered into competition for land, trade, and strategic advantage. The French, Spanish, British, Dutch, and Swedes all formed colonies and competed for territory, land, trade, and native alliances. During the 1500 to 1820 period, European nations were frequently at war over territory, religion, trade, and diplomatic advantages. The warring states of Europe were translated into warring conditions among the colonies of North America. The native peoples were drawn into trade and trade dependencies, as well as alliances with one or more of the European colonies. Wars were fought more cheaply if native warriors could be purchased to fight. Many native nations were allied to one or another of the European colonies in order to ensure continued trade and to maintain diplomatic ties. In this situation of competing European colonies, native nations had diplomatic and political leverage. No one European colony dominated North America for long until after 1820, and the Indian nations held leverage, which resulted in hundreds of treaties of peace and friendship, trade, diplomatic, and military alliances with European powers. In the treaties, the Europeans recognized native rights to territory, government, and culture.[21]

Hundreds of treaties were negotiated in the early colonial period. The United States negotiated over 800 treaties, although ratifying only about 370.[22] Treaties in such abundance are very rare in world history. Only a few places in the world even have a few treaties between colonizers and natives. There are a few treaties in Mozambique and India, and one treaty in New Zealand. In North America, treaties were instruments that memorialized agreements and provided the natives with recognition of political and economic powers. In both the United States and Canada, treaty making continued into the nation-state period, ending in the United States in 1871 and in Canada about 1921, but has been renewed again in the 1990s in settlement of numerous land claims in British Columbia.[23] After 1871, the United States continued to make agreements with native communities through congressional acts and executive orders by the president.

Treaties forced the colonizers and nation-states to recognize native nations with rights to territory, self-government, and cultural autonomy. During much of the colonial period, native nations were in a position to protect their national claims from colonizing forces. After 1820, the period of European colonial competition was over, and the Canadian and U.S. states increasingly placed the native people in a weaker political position; finally, the natives were clearly brought under the powers of the nation-states by the end of the nineteenth century. The nation-states, while having a history of treaties and native recognition, embark on assimilation policies designed to obliterate native rights by including the natives as full citizens. Many native individuals and communities are reluctant to accept assimilation, and work hard to preserve native lands, language, political rights, and culture.

The present-day complexities of native identity in the United States and Canada derive to a large extent from the conflicting forces of nation-state assimilation and the cultural and community forces of native identity. Through five hundred years of colonialism, native communities have sought to preserve community and identity, and this persistence is no accident.[24] The forces of nation-state assimilation are found in education programs, land redistribution or allotments, enfranchisement, and efforts to incorporate natives into markets or economic self-sufficiency within reservation or reserve locations. U.S. boarding schools or Canadian residential schools were designed to teach mainstream values and lifestyles, and encouraged abandonment of native cultures, values, and ways of life. Allotments were designed to enable natives to become self-sufficient economically and then take on U.S. citizenship, while abandoning tribal membership and community participation. Native language, culture, religion, and values were discouraged, and Western culture encouraged. Nation-states worked hard to change values and identities among native peoples and assimilate them.[25]

Native communities had long ceased to be monocultural and became multicultural as many people adopted some or all of the new values and ways of life. Native identities on reservations and reserves became complex and multidimensional. Despite the significant efforts of nation-states to assimilate natives and dissolve native cultures and identities, many native peoples retain significant aspects of a native or tribal identity. Native peoples continue to defend their native rights and try to protect their land, preserve their cultures, and exercise self-government. New Western values are often adopted, but native or tribal identities persist side by side.[26]

Tribal identities continue to play a major part of native identities. A native who has a tribal community connection will most often identify through this tribal affiliation, such as Crow or Ojibway. Tribal identity and membership rules vary from tribe to tribe. Current U.S. federal law allows tribes to maintain their own criteria for tribal membership. The Oklahoma Cherokee have a very broad definition of tribal membership and require that citizens trace their lineage to an ancestor on one of the Cherokee census rolls. The Cherokee argue their membership rules are based on national affiliation rather than by race or other criteria. Many tribes have adopted blood quanta as a means to determine tribal membership. Some have set the bar of blood quantum very high, such as 50 percent. Native communities did not use blood quantum as a criteria for group membership in precolonial days. The racialization of native community membership is a legacy from the Bureau of Indian Affairs (BIA), which uses blood quanta to determine eligibility for program benefits. The racialization of tribal membership rules is an adoption of nation-state criteria for membership or access to tribal benefits.[27]

Pan-Indian identities are also products of the national community of the nation-state, since the mainstream society creates and upholds the generic term of *Indian*. Used in this way, *Indian* appears as an ethnic group designation, and for most people in the mainstream, Indians are seen as a homogenous ethnic group. But Indians or natives are composed of hundreds of cultures, languages, communities, and institutional patterns. Each native community has a tribal or subtribal identity, and most community-based natives identify first through their tribal or subtribal identity. The subtribal identities can be villages, a sacred square or site, family, band, clan, or region. Pan-Indian identities emerged within urban areas and at universities, and were a response to the generic use of *Indian* as an ethnic group. Native peoples, or Indians, found themselves identified as the same, and treated similarly in law and public relations. Native peoples organized national groups to defend their similar interests and to take action in American society where large groups are more effective. The National Congress of American Indians (NCAI) is formed by hundreds of native nations, each with one vote regardless of land or population size. Native respect for tribal identity and autonomy is preserved in the NCAI. Pan-Indian identities were useful when collective orientations or actions were necessary, often in the political and social movement arenas. Nevertheless, pan-Indian identity did not supersede tribal identities, and were often preserved within the pan-Indian movements such as the American Indian Movement and NCAI.[28]

Pan-Indian and tribal identities are used situationally. Among fellow natives, most will use their tribal or subtribal identity. Among non-Indians, the native individual will often say he or she is Indian, and leave it there, because he or she does not expect non-Indians to understand tribal or subtribal identities. Natives use these identities situationally because knowledge and understanding of native peoples and identities is not well known outside native communities.

Native identities are not just oppositional to understandings and views created by the national community or the nation-state. Most natives have a direct and important identification as American or Canadian citizens, and will perform many of the obligations and exercise the rights of nation-state citizens. Many natives serve in the armed forces, and are proud of that service and identification. Veterans are highly honored within contemporary native communities and are granted special privileges and honors at powwows and community events. Serving in the armed forces does not mean that the native people have assimilated or surrendered their identity.[29] The U.S. or Canadian nation-state is the holder of various treaty rights and recognition of native rights, and defending the nation-state is also a defense of the nation-state's recognition of native rights to territory, cultural autonomy, and self-government. Native peoples are often aware of the rights and obligations of nation-state citizens, and exercise those rights and enjoy their benefits. Native rights and obligations are not given up. In the United States, natives exercise both rights as native and nation-state citizens, and sometimes these are in conflict. In Canada, natives must choose between native rights and Canadian citizenship. In Mexico, there is no choice or dual citizenship, since all natives are considered citizens and there is no nation-state recognition of native rights to land, culture, or self-government. Natives are well aware of the rights and obligations of nation-states citizenship, and often exercise those rights and fulfill the obligations, but at the same time, native rights, struggles, and identities are preserved and exercised in appropriate times and places.

Native Rights and the Nation-State

There are at least two arguments for why nation-states seek to absolve indigenous rights and identities. First, nation-states seek to develop unified national communities that support the institutions, values, and commitments of the state. Unified national communities are seen to be more easily mobilized to support the state, when most citizens share a common culture and similar values. Most nation-states try to homogenize and assimilate their populations, immigrants, and citizens in order to gain voluntaristic service from their citizens. This ideal arrangement is seen to support and mobilize the national community for state goals such as economic development, common internal markets or economic exchange, and military defense. In the unified nation-state model, individuals or groups who are not participant within the national community or culture are seen as potentially disruptive and disloyal, or perhaps as inefficient participants in national political and economic life. A strong nation-state often seeks to develop homogenous culture among its citizens through schools and state organization of social and political life.[30]

Indigenous peoples living under a state with the unified nation-state model will often be subject to strong programs of assimilation and incorporation. The nation-state will attempt to culturally assimilate the group through education programs and other forms of socialization. Such programs are coercive, since native peoples are often insistent on preserving their own cultures, although during periods of forced acculturation such views may go underground and be hidden from state officials and members of the national community. The United States during the 1870–1960 period, and Canada during the 1870–1970 period, fit the unified nation-state model very well. Both nation-states had extensive and often coercive programs of cultural assimilation and economic incorporation of Native Americans. Retaining native cultures and identities was underemphasized.

In more recent years, both Canada and the United States have given way to more multicultural models of national culture and community, but the emphasis is still on acceptance and participation in nation-state culture, political institutions, and laws. For many ethnic groups, minorities, and racial groups, assimilation and incorporation into national community and cultural life are long-term goals, and the openness of the multicultural nation-state is tested by its willingness to accept racial and ethnic minority cultures. Ethnic study is generally the study of how ethnic, minority, and racial groups negotiate assimilation and incorporation into the nation-state's culture, economy, and political institutions. Many modernization theorists measure a nation-state's progress and long-term institutional stability by how successful they incorporate multicultural groups into their national community and culture.

The values and institutions of indigenous peoples, however, are generally ignored in the unified and multicultural nation-state models. In both models, indigenous peoples are asked to abandon their land and self-government for citizenship within the national community of the nation-state. Native peoples, however, with their cultures, institutions, and territories, are asked to abandon those traditions for assimilation and incorporation into the nation-state. Neither unified nor multicultural nation-states have a place for indigenous rights to land, self-government, and cultural preservation. Since the native views and interests are not protected or recognized within the nation-state model, then native peoples are generally coerced into cultural, political, economic, and social assimilation. Nation-state policies are often seen as favorable and beneficial to native people by granting them enfranchisement within the nation-state and the rights and opportunities that are afforded by national citizenship. Native peoples face long struggles to preserve land, self-government, and culture within the hostile hegemonic culture and polity of the nation-state. Native rights are not recognized or protected within the framework of most nation-states, but are protected only through political process and extranational instruments such as treaties in the United States and Canada. Native groups must work through nation-state institutions and international fora in order to gain recognition for their rights and views. Nation-states and national communities are often not aware or often unwilling to recognize native claims. Native peoples struggle to protect and preserve their land, self-government, and cultures within nation-states that are predisposed to dissolve their communities and assimilate the people as individuals into the national community.

A second argument made to explain the marginalization of indigenous peoples and nonrecognition of indigenous rights is that most nation-states throughout the world are inherently unstable, and therefore are reluctant to recognize groups or rights that challenge the central principles of the nation-state.[31] In the past several decades, native peoples around the globe have pursued their issues and rights within international fora. Many claim significant progress; in the 1970s, they were barred from U.N. activities behind barricades, while at the beginning of the twenty-first century they are allowed to enter into discussion about their issues and have been granted nongovernmental organization (NGO) status.[32] Native peoples have been active in pursuing ratification of their rights through a series of articles in the United Nations' Draft Declaration on the Rights of Indigenous Populations. Many of the leading nation-states, notably the United States and Canada, have declined to ratify or approve the indigenous articles proposed for the draft declaration. In both the United States and Canada, many of the points in the U.N. Draft Declaration on the Rights of Indigenous Populations are already recognized in one form or another, and indigenous peoples are often looking to the United States and Canada to take the lead in the recognition of indigenous rights at the international level. Both Canada and the United States, however, have not been forthcoming in the international recognition of indigenous rights, and are extremely reluctant to approve or ratify the over fifty articles affirming native views and rights within the proposed U.N. Draft Declaration on the Rights of Indigenous Populations.[33]

Neither Canada nor the United States provides official reasons for their reluctance; both nations continue to say they are favorably disposed toward and want to continue to revise language of the draft declaration. Diplomats informally conjecture that the reluctance of the United States and Canada to reaffirm international indigenous rights is related to the United States' concern that affirming rights to land, self-government autonomy, cultural autonomy, and other indigenous rights may well create considerable instability among many nation-states that are already fragile democracies and unstable state government structures. Affirming indigenous rights to land and government autonomy will destabilize many nation-states. The unified nation-state model is considered the ideal within these discussions, and the United States views their position as one where it is in U.S. interests to preserve the nation-state status quo in order to help ensure political stability around the world. Affirming and implementing native rights will lead to greater difficulty in preserving the present status quo of nation-states and international markets. Other ethnic groups, minorities, racial groups, or submerged nations seek autonomy from existing nation-states, which could possibly destabilize the present arrangement of nation-state relations and the international markets that they support. Consequently, both the United States and Canada seek to preserve and support the present arrangement of nation-state political and economic relations above their support for indigenous rights and political autonomy, since such an affirmation may be destabilizing and disruptive of present nation-state relations.

The arguments of assimilative pressures from strong nation-states and the threats from the assertion of native rights within weaker nation-states present complementary arguments for understanding the difficulties of asserting indigenous rights in the present world order of nation-state relations.

Constructing a Multinational State

Native rights will not prosper within an international system of nation-states, whether strong or weak. Weak nation-states see indigenous rights as a threat to order, and seek to repress native views. Relatively strong nation-states, like Canada and United States, have moved in limited ways to recognize indigenous rights, as long as those rights do not challenge the fundamental or constitutional laws of the nation-state. Mexico and many Latin American nation-states simply refuse to acknowledge indigenous rights, but must suffer their exercise below the surface of official state policy and relations. The unified nation-state model, however, remains deeply and fundamentally embedded in efforts to create a culturally and socially homogenous national community. The unified nation-state model assumes that there must be consensus at the foundation of the constitution or formation of the nation-state. This model, like that of the United States, assumes a unified cultural community, or in the multicultural variation of the model, a underlying consensus about political unity or participation.[34] For a relatively homogenous national community or a community of immigrants who are seeking religious or political freedoms, the idea of national consensus on the unified institutions of the nation-state is generally reasonable. The consensus underlying both the unified nation-state and the multicultural nation-state do not apply to indigenous peoples who have had governments, institutions, culture, and land that predate the formation of the nation-state. Indigenous peoples are either not parties to the formation of the nation-state or are unwilling participants forced into citizenship. In both cases, the indigenous people are coerced into participation in the nation-state that, in many cases, does not recognize most issues of importance for the indigenous peoples.

The nation-state is inherently unstable because it cannot achieve the consensus that is required to support the national community and state structure. Groups such as indigenous peoples, whose values, institutions, traditions, and land claims are not incorporated as part of the original act of nation-state creation and consensus, are left with relatively coerced cultural, institutional, and political participation in the national community and nation-state. Coercive measures for participation and incorporation of native peoples do not create voluntary participation but only compliance and the informal pursuit of native rights within national or international arena. The nation-state model will pit indigenous peoples, submerged nations, and some minority and gender groups against the cultural and legal hegemony of the nation-state, and will not lead to full participation or recognition of rights and citizenship. Granting of full citizenship merely abstracts and legally absolves the rights and values of indigenous peoples, and forces indigenous peoples to pursue alternative, non-nation-state avenues of securing their rights and values.

The fundamental flaw of the unified or multicultural nation-state is that it assumes all peoples are in agreement with the consensual principles of nation-state organization and participation. If a group (such as indigenous peoples) is not in agreement with the fundamental organization and rules of participation of the nation-state, then it is encouraged and forced to participate under alien rules. Such forced and nonconsensual participation breaks the basic principles of consensual participation in the nation-state and leads to cultural, political, legal, and territorial hegemony by the national community and nation-state, and the conscious subordination of rights, values, institutions, self-government, and territorial claims. The continued nonrecognition of indigenous rights to land, self-government, cultural autonomy, and consensual participation will lead to inherent social, political, and legal conflicts that may not be solvable under the unified or multicultural nation-state models.

An advantage of a multinational state model is that it can recognize a variety of institutional, cultural, political, land, lifestyle, and national arrangements and try to develop a consensual basis for social and political participation in a multinational community and multinational state. A multinational state structure would more effectively recognize the social, political, territorial, cultural, and lifestyle powers of its constituent national community than do the unified or multiethnic state models. If the values and institutions of a nation-state do not implicitly represent the social and political powers of their national community, then it will be inherently unstable.[35] Many contemporary nation-states suffer from inherent instabilities as they try to forge unified national communities and nation-states over communities that are not consensually, socially, institutionally, culturally, or territorially incorporated for participation or representation. A multinational state would recognize the social, institutional, territorial, and political powers and values of its constituents, and create a consensual basis for participation in the multinational community and multinational state.

The nation-state must recognize ethnic, religious, or racial differences, but those are not the only criteria through which groups form and exercise their values.[36] Indigenous groups have their own forms of community, culture, institutional relations, self-government, and territory. Indigenous peoples will not consensually participate in a state that does not recognize their inherent and immemorial rights. Any multinational state that can extend its scope of incorporation to include not only religion, ethnicity, and race but also nationality, lifestyle, and indigenous rights will have a better chance to create a consensual basis for participation in a multinational community and multinational state. Nation-states that continue not to recognize indigenous rights will continue to coerce assimilation and incorporation—thus engendering subtle, if not overt, conflict, and will either maintain a form of cultural and political hegemonic coercion, or will suffer from the dysfunctions of inherent absence of institutional cultural consensus at the base of the national community and nation-state institutions. Stable nation-states will not be achieved through the paths of coercion and domination, since such regimes engender resistance and subtle forms of nonparticipation, which disrupt political, social, cultural, and economic relations.[37]

The path to nation-state stability rests upon recognition and incorporation of social and political powers inherent within the peoples who compose the national community. Those communities such as indigenous peoples, who have significantly different cultures, religions, institutional formations, governments, and territorial claims, must be recognized and brought within a consensual and mutual institutional framework within an inherently multinational nation-state. The concept of a multinational state expands the current understandings of assimilation and incorporation, and requires rethinking of the forms of consensual participation. Non-Western religions and institutional orders must be recognized, respected, made lawful, and protected, in order that indigenous peoples will have the freedom to pursue their values and cultures without coercive repression and domination from the national community or nation-state. Recognizing and incorporating indigenous interests, values, and communities into a multinational state is a form of incorporation that grants consensual participant status to the indigenous peoples, and encourages the long-run stability and cooperation within the multinational community and multinational nation-state. Because they will have a broader consensual foundation, nation-states will be more enduring, more stable, and more harmonious after they recognize, protect, and respect the rights and institutions of indigenous peoples.

Notes

1. Kate Nash, *Contemporary Political Sociology: Globalization, Politics, and Power* (Malden, MA: Blackwell, 2000), 156–272.

2. Clifford Geertz, "The Integrative Revolution: Primordial Sentiments and Civil Politics in the New States (1963)," in *Nations and Identities*, ed. Vincent P. Pecora (Malden, MA: Blackwell, 2001), 279–91.

3. Anthony D. Smith, "The Origins of Nations," in *Nations and Identities*, ed. Vincent P. Pecora (Malden MA: Blackwell, 2001), 335, 341–49.

4. Ernest Gellner, "Nations and Nationalism," in *Nations and Identities*, ed. Vincent P. Pecora (Malden, MA: Blackwell, 2001), 304–8.

5. Taiaiake Alfred, "From Sovereignty to Freedom," in *A Will to Survive: Indigenous Essays on the Politics of Culture, Language, and Identity*, ed. Stephen Greymorning (Boston, MA: McGraw-Hill, 2004), 118–23; Moana Jackson, "Colonization as Myth-Making: A Case Study in Aotearoa," in *A Will to Survive: Indigenous Essays on the Politics of Culture, Language, and Identity*, ed. Stephen Greymorning (Boston, MA: McGraw-Hill, 2004), 95–108.

6. Donald S. Lutz, *The Origins of American Constitutionalism* (Baton Rouge: Louisiana State University Press, 1988), 5–69.

7. Duane Champagne and Ismael Abu Saad, "Concluding Comments and Conference Declaration: A View toward the Future," in *The Future of Indigenous Studies: Strategies for Survival and Development*, ed. Ismael Abu-Saad and Duane Champagne (Los Angeles: UCLA American Indian Studies Center, forthcoming); Susan Mendus, "Losing the Faith: Feminism and Democracy," in *Democracy: The Unfinished Journey, 508 BC to AD 1993*, ed. John Dunn (New York: Oxford University Press, 1992), 207–19; Nash, *Contemporary Political Sociology*, 221–71.

8. In the United States, owing to income from gaming, a small number of native nations have gained considerable access to political influence. The large majority of U.S. native communities, however, do not have similar influence, although they are often indirect beneficiaries of the political engagement of the more influential gaming nations. See Carole Goldberg and Duane Champagne, "Ramona Redeemed? The Rise of Tribal Political Power in California," *Wicazo Sa Review* 17 (spring 2002): 43–64.

9. For an introduction to issues of native identities, see Joane Nagel, *American Indian Ethnic Renewal: Red Power and the Resurgence of Identity and Culture* (New York: Oxford University Press, 1996); Stephen Cornell, *The Return of the Native: American Indian Political Resurgence* (New York: Oxford University Press, 1988); Devon A. Mihesuah, "American Indian Identities: Issues of Individual Choices and Development," in *Contemporary Native American Cultural Issues*, ed. Duane Champagne (Walnut Creek, CA: AltaMira Press, 1999), 13–38; Ward Churchill, "The Crucible of American Indian Identity: Native Tradition versus Colonial Imposition on Postconquest North America," in *Contemporary Native American Cultural Issues*, ed. Duane Champagne (Walnut Creek, CA: AltaMira Press, 1999), 39–67.

10. See, for example, Chahtaimmataha in "History of the Chahta Nation," ed. Gideon Lincecum, as told by Chahtaimmataha, in the Gideon Lincecum Papers (Austin, TX: Eugene C. Barker Texas History Center, University of Texas at Austin, 1861); Edward Benton-Benai, *The Mishomi Book: The Voice of the Ojibway* (Hayward, WI: Indian Country Communications, 1988); George Dorsey, *The Mythology of the Wichita* (Norman: University of Oklahoma Press, 1995), 25–30; Emily L. Smith, "Ma-Ona and the Creation of the World," in *Folklore of the Winnebago Tribe*, ed. David Lee Smith (Norman: University of Oklahoma Press, 1997), 25–30; and Paul G. Zolbrod, *Dine bahane: The Navajo Creation Story* (Albuquerque: University of New Mexico Press, 1984).

11. Frank Waters, *Book of the Hopi: The First Revelation of the Hopi's Historical and Religious Worldview of Life* (New York: Penguin, 1977), 334; Jean Chaudhuri and Joyotpaul Chaudhuri, *A Sacred Path: The Way of the Muscogee Creeks* (Los Angeles: UCLA American Indian Studies Center, 2001), 114.

12. Rebecca Tsosie, "Land, Culture and Community: Envisioning Native American Sovereignty and National Identity in the 21st Century," *Hagar: International Social Science Review* 2, no. 2 (2001): 183–200; Chaudhuri and Chaudhuri, *Sacred Path*, 95–116.

13. Max Weber, *Economy and Society*, vol. 1, ed. Guenther Roth and Claus Wittich (Berkeley: University of California Press, 1978), 160–66; Max Weber, *General Economic History* (New Brunswick, NJ: Transaction, 1981), 275–78, 352–69; Max Weber, *Max Weber on Capitalism, Bureaucracy, and Religion*, ed. Stanislav Andreski (London: George Allen and Unwin, 1983), 21–29.

14. Kenneth Morrison, "Native American Religions: Creating through the Cosmic Give-and-Take," in *The Native North American Almanac*, ed. Duane Champagne (Detroit: Gale Research, 1994), 633–41; Huston Smith and Reuben Snake, eds., *One Nation under God: The Triumph of the Native American Church* (Santa Fe, NM: Clear Light, 1996), 16–20; Rodney Frey, ed., *Stories That Make the World: Oral Literature of the Indian Peoples of the Inland Northwest* (Norman: University of Oklahoma Press, 1995).

15. Amnesty International, *Human Rights Violations against Indigenous Peoples* (New York: Amnesty International, 1992); James W. Zion, "The Relevance of the U.N. Process for Indigenous Self-Determination, and Traditional Indian Law in the Administration of Self-Governance," unpublished manuscript (Window Rock, AZ: Navajo Supreme Court, 2003), 3, 7.

16. Leroy Eid, "Indian Geographic Distribution, Habitat, and Demography during the Nineteenth Century," in *The Native North American Almanac* (Detroit, MI: Gale Research, 1994), 206–9.

17. J. R. Miller, *Skyscrapers Hide the Heavens: A History of Indian-White Relations in Canada* (Toronto: University of Toronto Press, 1989), 108–15.

18. Katherine Beatty Chiste, "Aboriginal Women and Self-Government: Challenging Leviathan," in *Contemporary Native American Issues*, ed. Duane Champagne (Walnut Creek, CA: AltaMira Press, 1999), 76–81; Vice Chief Mary Jane Jim, "Racism and the Alteration of the Role of Indigenous Women in Decision-Making," in *Indigenous Peoples, Racism and the United Nations*, ed. Martin Nakata (Sydney, Australia: Common Ground Press, 2001), 123–30.

19. Stefano Varese, "The Territorial Roots of Latin American Indigenous Peoples' Movement for Sovereignty," *Hagar: International Social Science Review* 2, no. 2 (2001): 201–17.

20. Jackson, "Colonization as Myth-Making," 95–108; Varese, "The Territorial Roots," 201–18; Richard Howitt, "A Nation in Dialogue: Recognition, Reconciliation and Indigenous Rights in Australia," *International Social Science Review* 2, no. 2 (2001): 261–76.

21. C. A. Weslager, *The Delaware Indians* (New Brunswick, NJ: Rutgers University Press, 1972), 121; Paul Wallace, "The Iroquois: A Brief Outline of Their History," in *The Livingstone Indian Records 1666–1723* (Gettysburg: Pennsylvania Historical Association, 1956), 19; Paul Phillips, *The Fur Trade*, vol. 1 (Norman: University of Oklahoma Press, 1961), 314, 464, 500–504, 553–54; Paul Phillips, *The Fur Trade*, vol. 2 (Norman: University of Oklahoma Press, 1961), 20–26, 69, 80, 197–208; and Wilbur Jacobs, "Diplomacy and Indian Gifts: Anglo-French Rivalry along the Ohio and Northwest Frontiers, 1748–1763," *History, Economics and Political Science* 6 (1950): 44–55. See also Otto Hintze,

"Military Organization and the Organization of the State," in *The Historical Essays of Otto Hintze*, ed. Felix Gilbert (New York: Oxford Press, 1975), 183; and Theda Skocpol, *The State and Social Revolutions* (London: Cambridge University Press, 1979), 19–24.

22. Russel Barsh, "The Legal Significance of U.S. Indian Treaties," in *The Native North American Almanac* (Detroit, MI: Gale Research, 1994), 461–71.

23. Miller, *Skyscrapers*, 152–69.

24. Duane Champagne, "The Cultural and Institutional Foundations of Native American Conservatism," special issue on "North American Indians: Cultures in Motion," ed. Elvira Stefania Tiberini, *L'Uomo: Societa, Tradizione, Sviluppo* 8, no. 1 (1995): 17–43.

25. Thomas Biolsi, *Organizing the Lakota: The Political Economy of the New Deal on the Pine Ridge and Rosebud Reservations* (Tucson: University of Arizona Press, 1992), 3–60; Miller, *Skyscrapers*, 99–115, 189–207.

26. Mihesuah, "American Indian Identities," 23–31.

27. Churchill, "Crucible," 45–52.

28. For information on NCAI, see www.ncai.org/main/pages/ncai_profile/history.asp.

29. Kenneth R. Philp, ed., *Indian Self-Rule: First-Hand Accounts of Indian-White Relations from Roosevelt to Reagan* (Salt Lake City, UT: Howe Brothers, 1986), 105.

30. See, for example, Michel Foucault, *Discipline and Punishment: The Birth of the Prison*, trans. Alan Sheridan (New York: Vintage Books, 1979); Michel Foucault, *The History of Sexuality, vol. 1: An Introduction*, trans. Robert Hurley (New York: Vintage Books, 1980); Anthony Giddens, *The Nation-State and Violence* (Berkeley: University of California Press, 1987).

31. Russel Barsh, "Indigenous Peoples in the 1990s: From Object to Subject of International Law?" *Harvard Human Rights Journal* 7 (1994): 33–86; Russel Barsh, "The Aboriginal Issue in Canadian Foreign Policy," *International Journal of Canadian Studies* 12 (1995): 107–33; Russel Barsh, "Indigenous Peoples and the UN Commission on Human Rights: A Case of the Immovable Object and the Irresistible Force," *Human Rights Quarterly* 18, no. 4 (1996): 782–813; Russel Barsh, "Aboriginal Peoples and Quebec: Competing for Legitimacy as Emerging Nations," *American Indian Culture & Research Journal* 21, no. 1 (1997): 1–29.

32. Personal communication, Oren Lyons, November 2001, Santa Fe Conference for Honoring Nations.

33. William Jonas, "Setting the Scene," *Indigenous Peoples, Racism and the United Nations*, ed. Martin Nakata (Sydney, Australia: Common Ground, 2001), 35–47.

34. Alexander Hamilton, James Madison, and John Jay, *The Federalist Papers*, ed. Benjamin F. Wright (New York: Barnes & Noble, 1996), 89–97; Dave R. Palmer, *1794: America, Its Army, and the Birth of the Nation* (Novato, CA: Presidio Press, 1994), 87–93.

35. Anthony Orum, *Introduction to Political Sociology*, 4th ed. (Upper Saddle River, NJ: Prentice Hall, 2001), 77–87, 96–100.

36. Carole Goldberg, "Descent into Race," *UCLA Law Review* 49, no. 5 (June 2002): 1373–76, 1388–94.

37. See, for example, Eugene Genovese, *Roll Jordan Roll: The World the Slaves Made* (New York: Vintage, 1976); Talcott Parsons, "On the Concept of Political Power," in *Class, Status, and Power*, ed. R. Bendix and S. M. Lipsett (New York: Free Press, 1966), 240–65.

Border Crossings/Crossing Borders: Native Americans and the Issue of Border Crossing

2

STEVEN J. CRUM

SINCE TIME IMMEMORIAL, and well before the arrival of the Europeans, Native American tribal peoples have created territories whose boundaries followed certain geographic features, such as rivers and valley regions. Many of the tribes made certain that their territories encompassed more than one life zone. They did this so that if the natural food supply failed within one zone, the people could easily shift to another zone within the territory.

However, with the coming of the Europeans, many tribes found their ancestral homelands divided and split by the creation of newly established political entities. For example, in 1848, with the end of the so-called Mexican American War and the signing of the treaty of Guadalupe-Hidalgo, the United States acquired from Mexico a huge area of today's Southwest. A short time later, in 1853, the United States secured more land from Mexico in the Gadsden Purchase, which added the area of southern Arizona to the United States. With these land acquisitions of the mid-nineteenth century, the 1,952-mile international border that separates the United States from Mexico came into existence.

Not only did the U.S./Mexican international border split more than one aboriginal tribal territory, it also split the people themselves. Some became labeled as Mexican Indians and others as U.S. Indians. The divisions became evident among several tribes, including the Tohono O'odham (formerly Papago) of southern Arizona, and the Kumeyaay of southern California.

The splitting of tribes also became reality further north with the creation of the international border between the United States and Canada. That border came into existence at different points in time. The first was in 1783 after the United States had won its independence from Britain with the conclusion of the Revolutionary War. With the signing of the Treaty of Paris, the United States acquired the land south of the St. Lawrence River, and Britain maintained the area north of the river, which eventually became Canada. Some years later, in the Webster-Ashburton Treaty of 1842, the United States and Britain determined the boundaries along the 49th parallel from the east coast to the Rocky Mountains. Finally, in 1846 in the Oregon Treaty, the United States and Canada determined the international boundary as the 49th parallel from the Rocky Mountains to the Pacific Coast. These treaties divided the homelands of several tribes, including the Iroquois of New York, the Ojibwa of the Great Lakes, the Dakota of the northern Great Plains, the Blackfeet people of Montana, and the Salish people living in the Pacific Northwest.

This chapter takes a look at four tribes split by modern-day international boundaries: the Kumeyaay of southern California, the Tohono O'odham of Arizona, the Iroquois of New York, and the Blackfeet of Montana. The argument of this chapter is that these boundaries or these borders have negatively disrupted the lives of the above tribes in more than one way, and my chapter discusses some of those disruptions.

The Kumeyaay

The first tribe to be addressed is the Kumeyaay of southern California. The aboriginal homeland of the Kumeyaay lies fifty miles north of today's international border and fifty miles south in the area now labeled Baja California in Mexico. As already mentioned, the international border came into existence in 1848, which immediately divided the homeland of the Kumeyaay. From the mid-nineteenth century forward, tribal members could not easily cross the border because the United States frowned upon and discouraged the movement of native people. The Bureau of Indian Affairs (BIA) wanted U.S. Indians, including those in California, to become sedentary reservation individuals. The BIA regarded Indian travel or migration within a tribal territory as "nomadic," which needed to be eliminated if tribes were to become civilized.[1]

In short, the Kumeyaay of Mexico and the United States found themselves cut in half both physically and psychologically. The life of Delfina Cuero, a Kumiai (Mexican spelling), is typical of Kumeyaay individuals for most of the twentieth century. Born around 1900, Cuero spent most of her adult life in Mexico. But as an elder, she finally entered the United States and died in this country in 1972. On the other hand, her two daughters continue to reside in Mexico to this day.[2] Here is a case of one family being divided by the international border.

Although some Kumeyaay most likely found ways to cross the border, they could not do so easily, especially when the United States cracked down on border crossing at different points in time. The first instance was in the 1950s during the Cold War when the United States was concerned about the communist threat both internally and externally.[3] More recently, in the 1980s and 1990s, the United States controlled the international border even more because of the "war on drugs." With the construction of miles of fences along the border and with increased militarization, Kumeyaay people of more recent years found it impossible to keep in contact with family, relatives, and tribal members on both sides of the border. Lack of contact prevents the people of the same tribe from knowing about each other. Anselmo Dominguez Ortiz, a Kumiai in Mexico, stated that he "knows almost nothing about the other half of his tribe."[4]

However, within the last four years, both the Kumiai of Mexico and the Kumeyaay of the United States have been working hard to persuade the United States to allow Kumeyaay to cross the border so that the tribe can maintain contact. In 1998 alone, tribal members held four meetings with U.S. officials on this issue. The last meeting took place on the Viejas Reservation in San Diego County, which was attended by thirty Kumiai from Mexico. These meetings made it possible for Mexican Kumiai in 2000 to secure "laser visas" to cross the border and to remain in the United States for seventy-two hours and to travel twenty-five miles north of the international border. To secure these temporary visas, the Kumiai can show a baptismal certificate and not a birth certificate, because many of them don't have birth records from Mexico.[5] Most recently, with the laser visas, a busload of Kumiai from Mexico crossed the border at Tecate in January of this year to visit the Kumeyaay on the Viejas Reservation.[6] Despite these positive outcomes of the last four years, the tribe still remains split and will remain so because of the heavy policing of the international border by the United States.

There are some visible differences between the Kumiai of Mexico and the Kumeyaay of the United States. In some ways, the Kumiai has been able to hold onto certain traditional practices more so than the Kumeyaay in the United States. The reason is that the Mexican government has largely ignored rural Indian people of Mexico over the years, and the Kumiai essentially remained unrecognized and lived in isolation for decades. This reality enabled them to preserve various native ways, including the making of basketry and pottery.[7] In contrast, the Kumeyaay have been subject to various forms of acculturation experiences over the decades. They were subject to the earlier Spanish Indian mission policy from 1769 to 1833, which did not impact more inland and rurally isolated tribal peoples in Baja California in the area we now call Mexico. Later, in the late nineteenth century and into the twentieth century, the BIA carried out a national campaign to assimilate tribes, including the Kumeyaay and other southern California tribes. The young students were sent to the Sherman Indian School in Riverside, California, to become "Americanized." The BIA labeled the Kumeyaay and other tribes of southern California as the "Mission Indians." It was not until recently, after the BIA had muted its earlier assimilationist policies, that the Kumeyaay and others would reassert their indigenous tribal names.[8]

The Tohono O'odham

The experiences of the Tohono O'odham (Desert People) in nearby southern Arizona are similar to the Kumeyaay of southern California. The Tohono O'odham also had their tribal territory split by the international border. Currently, approximately 23,000 live in the United States on the Tohono O'odham Reservation, whereas 1,400 continue to reside south of the border in Mexico. Like the Kumeyaay, the O'odham made efforts to communicate with each other over the years despite the border. In fact, in 1984, the U.S. Tohono O'odham allowed some 250 Tohono O'odham of Mexico to become tribal members.[9] But with the war on drugs and the militarization of the border in the 1980s, Tohono O'odham communication has been difficult to maintain after U.S. officials built a barbed wire fence along the ninety-mile distance that the Tohono O'odham Reservation shares with the border. The border crackdown has made the O'odham highly critical of U.S. policy. One tribal member stresses, "we are Indian but we are treated like illegals."[10] Henry Ramon, chairperson of the Tohono O'odham in the United States, asserted, "We didn't cross the border—the border crossed us."[11]

To maintain ties with families on both sides of the border, the Tohono O'odham have inaugurated various actions. In July of 1989 they asked the United Nations' Subcommittee for Indigenous Rights to examine the United States' policy of not allowing tribal people to cross the border even though their aboriginal land lies on both sides.[12] Like the Kumeyaay, the O'odham in 1999 and in 2000 convinced U.S. officials to grant laser visas so that O'odham of Mexico could cross the border and temporarily visit relations in the United States. Most recently, in 2001, the O'odham are trying to convince U.S. officials to allow the O'odham of Mexico to become U.S. citizens. To them, the freedom to cross is a matter of preserving identity.[13]

The Iroquois

In moving northward, there are also a number of tribes who are split by the U.S./Canadian border. Unlike the southern tribes, the northern tribes can argue that the right to cross the international border is based on treaty rights. Specifically, the Iroquois, whose homeland exists both in northern New York and the province of Quebec in Canada, point out that two historic treaties grant them the legal right to cross. The Jay Treaty of 1794, negotiated between the United States and Britain, included the following provision: "Indians dwelling on either side of the said boundary line, freely to pass and repass by land or inland navigation."[14] In essence, this treaty allowed the Iroquois and other Indians of the region to cross. Some years later, the Treaty of Ghent of 1814 reaffirmed this crossing provision of the Jay Treaty. Based on these treaties, the Iroquois have had a long history of moving back and forth to maintain kinship linkages.[15]

But as the years went by, both the United States and Canada began to restrict Iroquois border crossing. One of the earliest instances occurred in the 1920s after the U.S. Congress passed the Immigration Act of 1924. What this act did was to exclude Indians from Canada from entering the United States based on the earlier treaty rights. In one particular instance, Baptist Iroquois from Canada were prevented from entering the United States to attend a Baptist evangelistic service on the Tuscarora Reservation in New York.[16] Clinton Rickard, a prominent Tuscarora, played a leading role in publicizing the above injustice. In imparting his views, he stated, "I did not consider that there was any such thing as 'Canadian Indian' or United States Indian.' All Indians are one people. We were here long before there was any border to make an artificial division of our people. . . . It was our belief that the white man's border should never be used to separate our people."[17]

To fight for the right to cross the border, Rickard carried out two courses of action. The first was the creation of an organization called the Indian Defense League of America, which was opened to Indian people who wanted to fight the cause. His second move was to take the above matter to a U.S. federal district court in 1927. In *McCandless v. United States*, the district court upheld the earlier treaties and asserted that Indian people had the right to cross the international border. This lower court decision was upheld one year later by the 3rd Circuit Court of Appeals. In essence, Rickard and other Iroquois had to fight to have the United States recognize earlier treaty rights.[18]

However, the positive steps taken in the 1920s would not have a lasting effect. Years later, in the 1950s, both the United States and Canada built roads leading to the Cornwall International Bridge which crosses the St. Lawrence River, connecting the United States and Canada. This bridge crosses Mohawk Reservation land located on both sides of the border with the Saint Regis Reservation lying on the U.S. side. In addition to the road, Canadian officials also constructed a tollgate and a customhouse on Cornwall Island, which is part of the Mohawk Reservation on the Canadian side. Without informing the Iroquois, the Canadian government expected the Indians to pay duties for any goods taken over the international bridge. In response to this action, John Sharrow, a Mohawk leader from Canada, stressed that the Mohawks would block the bridge unless Canadian officials agreed to pay the Mohawks $45,000 for rent for the placement of the immigration facilities. Canada took this threat seriously and backed away from its policy of duties. Additionally, it paid the Mohawks the rental fee.[19]

Ten years later, in 1968, the Canadian government again resorted to having Indians pay duties on goods that had a value of more than five dollars. Again, the Mohawk people took action. Approximately one hundred tribal members conducted a "sit-in" on the bridge and also blocked it with twenty-five cars. Finally, in February 1969, the officials backed away from their position and allowed the Indians to take goods across the bridge duty-free. One of the noted leaders involved in this struggle was Mike Mitchell.[20]

However, Canada continued to alternate its policies toward Indian people. In 1988 Mike Mitchell, grand chief of Akwesasne, took a truckload of goods into Canada. Immediately Canadian officials maintained that he owed the government $361.64 in payment for duties. Mitchell took his case to court, and a federal district court in Canada ruled in his favor, that Indians have the right to cross the border without impediments. But the Canadian Supreme Court overturned this lower-court decision of the 1990s in 2001 when it ruled that Mohawks do have to pay duties to transport goods across the border. The court used the argument that the Mohawks had no continuous "pre-contact north-south trade" route before the arrival of the Europeans. By making this decision, the court devalued the earlier treaty rights, and it also made itself an authority on precontact Iroquois cultural practices.[21]

The Blackfoot Confederacy

Another northern tribe split by the international border is the Blackfoot Confederacy. There are four historic Blackfoot bands: the Blackfeet tribe, which lives in Montana, and the Blood Tribe (Kainai), the Peigan Nation, and the Siksika Nation, all whom live in the province of Alberta in Canada. Like the other tribes, the Blackfoot have had their share of problems with the border. At times, border officials harass Indians. They open up medicine bundles which spiritual leaders use in ceremonies on both sides of the border. Additionally, gifts that Blackfoot secure from traditional "giveaways" are subject to customs duties at the border. At different points in time—1980, 1982, 1989, and most recently 2002—the Blackfoot people have expressed deep concern of the insensitivity of border agents.[22] At a large conference held in Great Falls, Montana, in June 2002, over three hundred individuals of the Blackfoot Confederacy held their second annual gathering to discuss border issues. Susan Webber, of the Blackfeet tribe in Montana, asserted that "there's a lot of us on the border that have been artificially broken up. . . . We have [to] come up with some kind of solution that will be reasonable for everyone, the governments and us."[23] The participants want both the United States and Canada to hire Indian people who can educate non-Indian border patrol agents about native practices. This would make the agents culturally sensitive to the native people who carry ceremonial items across the border for religious purposes. The conference participants gave the example of one native leader not being permitted to bring a headdress for ceremonial purposes from Canada into the United States. The Indians want both nations to develop "crossing protocol" for indigenous peoples.[24]

Despite the problems, the Blackfoot people, divided by the international border for over a hundred years, revived their earlier confederacy in 2000. Bill Old Chief, chairperson of the Blackfeet in Montana, commented about the border, "It's separated us physically, but it couldn't separate our hearts."[25] The various bands have worked in different ways to maintain ties with each other. For example, in the 1980s, officials of the Red Crow Community College (created by the Blood Tribe of the Blood reserve in Canada) started holding meetings with Blackfeet leaders of the Blackfeet Community College on the Blackfeet Reservation in Montana. Tribal educators of the two tribal-run colleges discussed important issues such as accreditation. More important, the dialogue was still another way of the people of the Blackfoot Confederacy to solidify traditional ties.

International borders have clearly impacted various Native American tribes over the years. Tribes whose lands have been divided by these borders have been holding meetings to make their concerns known to the larger public. In June 1994, various tribal leaders held a meeting at Tecate, along the U.S./Mexico border, and participants "demanded the right to cross freely [the international border] for ceremonial and religious purposes."[26] Nothing resulted from this meeting. Four years later, in August 1998, a larger number of tribes held a gathering in Albuquerque, New Mexico. One of their major goals was "the right to freely cross the border without toll charges."[27] Again, nothing resulted from this meeting with respect to U.S. governmental legislative action.

In retrospect, tribal people have always expressed their concern about the creation of political boundaries that have split native realities. Perhaps George Manuel, a Shuswap tribal leader of Canada, said it best in his book, *The Fourth World*, when he wrote, "the boundary . . . bore no relation to the realities of the great North American Plains. Neither the Indian people nor the buffalo had ever seen the invisible boundary that now cut through the hearts of many nations."[28]

Notes

1. G. Phillips, *The Enduring Struggle: Indians in California History* (San Francisco: Boyd and Fraser, 1981), 57–60.

2. B. Ortiz, "Kumeyaay Borderlines," *News from Native California* 14, no. 14 (summer 2001): 12–13.

3. F. Shipek, "Kumeyaay," in *Native America in the Twentieth Century: An Encyclopedia*, ed. Mary B. Davis (New York: Garland, 1994), 296–97.

4. C. Barfield, "A People Divided," *San Diego Union Tribune*, January 24, 1999, A1.

5. C. Barfield, "Kumeyaay Seek End to Border as Barrier," *San Diego Union Tribune*, December 28, 1999, B1.

6. C. Barfield, "Baja Indians Seek Help with Border Documents," *San Diego Union Tribune*, January 17, 2002, B8.

7. "U.S.–Mexico Border Divides Kumeyaay Peoples," *Yakama Nation Review*, January 29, 1999, 12.

8. Phillips, *The Enduring Struggle*.

9. "Once Divided: Indigenous Peoples in the U.S. and Mexico United across the Border," *Abya Yala News* 9, no. 1 (1994): 10–11.

10. "Ranchers Form Vigilante Posses along Border," *Indian Country Today*, May 10, 2000, A1.

11. V. Talisman, "Borders and Native Peoples," *Native Americas: Hemispheric Journal of Indigenous Issues* 18, no. 1 (spring 2001): 12.

12. "Once Divided," *Abya Yala News*.

13. "Agreement Eases O'odham U.S.–Mexico Border Crossing," *Yakama National Review*, March 31, 2000, 14; "Tohono O'odham Targeted in Border Zone Seek Citizenship," *Indian Country Today*, June 13, 2001, A1–A2; "Legal Residency Asked for Tohono O'odham," *Indian Country Today*, August 8, 2001, A3.

14. R. Osborn, "Problems and Solutions Regarding Indigenous Peoples Split by International Borders," *American Indian Law Review* 24, no. 2 (1999–2000): 472.

15. D. Evans, "Superimposed Nations: The Jay Treaty and Aboriginal Rights," *Dollhouse Journal of Legal Studies* 4 (1995): 218–22; S. O'Brien, "The Medicine Line: A Border Dividing Tribal Sovereignty, Economics and Families," *Fordham Law Review* 53, no. 2 (November 1984): 315–50.

16. B. Graymont, *Fighting Tuscarora: The Autobiography of Chief Clinton Rickard* (Syracuse, NY: Syracuse University Press, 1973), 65–85.

17. Graymont, *Fighting Tuscarora*.

18. Graymont, *Fighting Tuscarora*.

19. L. Hauptman, *The Iroquois Struggle for Survival: World War II to Red Power* (Syracuse, NY: Syracuse University Press, 1986), 146–49.

20. Hauptman, *The Iroquois Struggle*.

21. P. Barnsley, "High Court Puts Native Rights in Doubt," *Windspeaker* (July 2001): 3; D. Bonaparte, "Border Struggles," *Native Americas* 17, no. 1 (Spring 2000): 36.

22. "Position Paper on Bloods' Border Issues," *Kainai News* (August 1980): 8, 11; "Blood Indians Make Unsuccessful Attempt to Cross Illegally at Customs Border," *Kainai News* (June 1982): 6; "U.S.–Canada Border Issues Committee," *Kainai News* (August 1989): 7.

23. "Border Laws Hamper Travel for Blackfoot Confederacy Members," *Indian Country Today*, June 26, 2002, B1.

24. Barfield, "A People Divided"; Barfield, "Kumeyaay Seek End."

25. R. Selden, "Invisible Line Couldn't Separate Blackfeet in Their Hearts," *Indian Country Today*, May 17, 2000, A2.

26. "Once Divided," *Abya Yala News*.

27. Talisman, "Borders and Native Peoples."

28. G. Manuel and M. Posluns, *The Fourth World: An Indian Reality* (New York: Free Press, 1972), 23.

Status Indian: Who Defines You? 3

L. JAMES DEMPSEY

FROM A CULTURAL PERSPECTIVE, every society in human history has defined who its members were and were not. This process may have been formally created and recognized or informally done; however, the result was the same: individuals knew what groups they were a part of and why. For the Indian tribes of Canada, the Canadian government circumvented this process in 1876 with the passage of legislation known as the Indian Act.

Sections of the act dealing with who was legally recognized by the government as an Indian remained virtually unchanged until the act was amended in 1985; these changes have become popularly known as Bill C-31. This chapter looks at two unique issues that have arisen since the amendments were passed. The first deals with Indian reactions and problems with Bill C-31, and the second examines some of the effects that over one hundred years of an imposed definition have had on Indians as they take control over defining themselves.

Historical Background

For the Indian tribes that would ultimately come under Canada's jurisdiction, their ability to define their membership was not jeopardized until 1850. It was at this time that the four British colonies that would form Canada began to pass legislation allowing each colony to deal with the Indians and the lands they occupied within the colony's borders. In order to achieve this agenda, the colony had to define who was an "Indian" and therefore subject to this legislation. These initial attempts used cultural, ethnic, and blood quantum measures to define who was an Indian and therefore affected by this legislation. In 1867, the new Dominion of Canada inherited this practice, although they would define

Indian identity in a traditionally "British" manner. This meant tracing inheritance and heritage through the male line.

The Canadian government's policy toward Indians has been one of protection, civilization, and assimilation. This meant protection of Indians from the negative influences of Canadian society; while being protected, Indians would be educated in the values and ways of Canadian society. Once deemed suitable for citizenship, Indians would be assimilated into Canadian society. This process was known as enfranchisement, which meant that an Indian was legally a ward of the government (a *status Indian* as defined in the Indian Act) until "civilized," at which time he or she would be given all of the benefits of citizenship and be removed from the restrictions of the Indian Act and become a *non-status Indian* (enfranchised).[1]

Over the years, this voluntary enfranchisement policy did not prove to be successful; therefore, the government introduced a number of ways involuntary enfranchisement could achieve the same result. The Indians affected by these policies are the ones Bill C-31 was designed to reinstate. Most notable of this group were Indian women who had been removed from government band lists upon marriage to a person who did not have status. The section of the Indian Act pertaining to women had been introduced in 1869 and had its origin in the British legal system, where women were not perceived to be persons as defined by the law because they could not own land. This section of the act was imposed on Indians, even though many tribes in eastern Canada and British Columbia traced ownership of family property through females rather than males. It also was believed in 1869 that women, once married, became a part of their husband's culture; therefore, it was expected Indian women would join the dominant culture and not need the protection of the Indian Act.

The years 1920 to 1922 created another large group of individuals who were involuntarily enfranchised. During this period, the superintendent general (Minister of Indian Affairs) was given the power to declare "any Indian, male or female, over the age of 21 fit for enfranchisement."[2] In addition, some Indians who served with Canada in the two world wars or received university degrees were enfranchised.

Legal challenges to these discriminatory sections of the Indian Act were launched in the 1970s and, though defeated, they did establish that the federal government would have to deal with the issue. With the passing of the Canadian Constitution in 1982, section 3, part 3(C) of the Indian Act came into direct conflict with the provisions in the Charter of Rights and Freedoms, which prohibited discrimination based on gender.

During the 1984 federal election, the Conservative Party made a promise that, if elected, the controversial section would be amended. In early 1985, after being elected, the Conservatives presented their amendment to Parliament; the bill was introduced and went through the required three readings in just three months. This effectively prevented any organized protests by bands or Indian organizations.

In June 1985, the Canadian Parliament passed a series of amendments to the Indian Act, which has become popularly known as Bill C-31. The bill was designed to bring the Indian Act into accord with the provisions of the Canadian Charter of Rights and Freedoms. According to the government:

> Bill C-31 removed sex discrimination clauses from the Indian Act and abolished the concept of enfranchisement. Bill C-31 also provided for the restoration of Indian status and band membership to individuals who had lost them as a result of the discriminatory clauses. Bill C-31 allowed for their children to be recognized as status Indians. In addition, Bill C-31 enabled bands to determine their own memberships rules and thus take an important step toward self-government.[3]

The initial purpose of the bill was twofold: firstly, to reinstate those Indians who had lost their "Indian status" as defined by the Indian Act because they had been enfranchised, and secondly, to allow each reserve in Canada to formulate its own band membership code. As a result, persons who lost or were denied status because of discriminatory sections in the previous act became eligible to apply for registration and, if approved by the government, would be reinstated on their respective band lists. Specifically, these people are:

- women who lost status through marriage to a non-status person;
- individuals who lost or were denied status through other discriminatory clauses in the Indian Act;
- individuals who lost status through enfranchisement;
- children of persons in any of the above categories.[4]

The second aspect of the bill was to allow bands to create their own membership rules that would define who was and who was not a band member. Once completed, the Department of Indian Affairs would turn over its band list to the band in question, ending over one hundred years of government definition and control of band membership.

The Controversy

Why has a controversy arisen from what initially appeared to be a straightforward action by the government to correct a historic injustice? Native reaction to the government's policy has been anything but one of unqualified acceptance and has resulted in much misunderstanding and bitterness on the part of Indians and many bands. In fact, the number of bands that have submitted their membership rules or accepted those who were reinstated varies from province to province.[5] To add to the confusion, three Alberta bands have been involved in a court case to have Bill C-31 declared null and void because they believe the bill overrides their aboriginal rights. This action puts the whole process virtually on hold until the case is decided.[6]

Indian reactions to the bill centered on the perception that the government was defining Indian status without consulting Indians. On the other hand, the government believed it was returning that right to Indians in the form of band membership codes and at the same time correcting the involuntary removal of status from Indian women and men. Many bands were also concerned that reinstated individuals would return to the already overcrowded reserves, a fear that has not materialized. Most of the individuals affected by Bill C-31 just want what had been taken from them.

The Controversy Today

Depending on the outcome of the legal challenge, Bill C-31 could be declared unconstitutional or within the jurisdiction of the federal government. If the former occurs, then the government would have to reconsider the issue; however, if Bill C-31 is held to be legal, then bands would have to create a membership code and accept those individuals who were at one time band members.

It should be pointed out that some bands have created a membership code. However, it is important to understand that under Bill C-31 band membership and status are not always the same. A band code, for example, could accept a former band member and his or her non–band-member spouse and children as band members; however, the federal government would not recognize the spouse's status as an Indian because under the bill no person can gain or lose status through marriage. The government would recognize the children since the provisions of the bill extend to the first generation. Another scenario could see a band accept the former band member but not the spouse or children. In this case, the children would have status but not band membership. To address this possibility, a general list has been created by the government that includes all Bill C-31 Indians who have not been accepted onto a band list.

The onus of providing proof that one is entitled to be reinstated lies with individuals, and if they or their ancestors were involuntarily enfranchised prior to 1951, they may discover that providing the evidence will prove to be difficult. The Department of Indian Affairs did not maintain efficient records until 1951. An even more difficult case arises for those who were adopted by non-status parents or were in foster care, because provincial records can be hard to obtain. As of December 1993, there were 170,000 applications of which 113,000 have been ac-

cepted by the government.[7] These figures show that the government grossly un-
derestimated the number of applications, which they believed would total 60,000.[8]

The second controversy is a direct result of the first and pits Indian against
Indian. While the numbers of those being reinstated are considerable and have
caused the Department of Indian Affairs many headaches trying to process them,
the number of bands that have finalized their membership codes remains under
40 percent. Only a minority of the completed codes accept Bill C-31 applicants
as full band members. Prior to 1985, Indians were legally defined as status (recognized as Indians by the government) or non-status (not recognized as Indians
by the government), but the separation of status and band membership under the
bill has, in effect, created four groups of Indians:

- those who have Indian status and band membership;
- those who have Indian status but do not have band membership;
- those who have band membership but do not have Indian status;
- those who do have Indian status or band membership (non-status).

Modern social changes have also affected Indians, the most notable being the
acceptance of gender equality by Indian women. However, the majority of those
who have been reinstated are women and their children, yet many bands refuse to
accept them onto their lists; this has led to a perception of gender discrimination.
A number of reasons are given, such as being married to a non-Indian and moving off the reserve, which has led to these women being "assimilated" and resulted
in them losing their traditional heritage—an interesting statement considering
that many of these same people acknowledge that cultural traditions are passed
down to children via their mother. There is also a widespread fear by band members that "Bill C-31s" will take over the reserve if given band membership, or at
least tax reserve resources to the limit. In fact, the desire by the majority of those
reinstated is not to return to their reserve but to simply have what they deem to
be a part of their identity given back to them. Regardless of these views, reinstated
Indians believe it is now the bands that are preventing their "rights" from being
returned, rather than the government. "Bill C-31s" have carried out various forms
of protests such as sit-ins and roadblocks of band offices, but for the most part
these tactics have been unsuccessful in changing the position of band councils. In
addition, the government has been very wary of putting pressure on bands to com-
plete their codes, much less accept those who have been reinstated, mainly due to
the pending court case.

Another area of perceived inequality for all "Bill C-31s" is that they are
"second-class" Indians since, prior to 1985, status guaranteed the right to membership in a band and the concomitant rights to vote for chief and council, to

run for public office on reserve, and to receive all the benefits accorded all band members. While these rights still exist for those granted status under the bill, they are not necessarily guaranteed, as they are now dependent on membership and often residency requirements that are now decided by bands.

One other area is the belief that assimilation is still the goal of the Indian Act and only the blatant process of enfranchisement has been removed. Under section 6 of the bill, an individual who has only one parent entitled to reinstatement is classified under section 6(2). Due to the provisions under this section, the individual can only transmit status to succeeding generations if his or her spouse is a status Indian also. It is believed that this would eventually result with the elimination of status Indians.

The irony of the debate is that even though terms like "traditional" and "aboriginal rights" are used in the discussion of who has the right to define who is a status Indian, it is the Indian Act's definition that in fact is being debated.

Generally speaking, prior to 1985, no bands had legally questioned the Indian Act's definitions and national Indian organizations did not make it an issue. In fact, during the national conference of the Native Indian Brotherhood (now Assembly of First Nations) in the late 1970s, the chiefs walked out of a presentation made by the Minister of Indian Affairs because it raised the question of how changes to the Indian Act's Indian definition should be handled.

Bill C-31 has truly had an effect on Canada's Indians by polarizing them in favor or against the amendment and this split has placed many Indians in limbo until the court challenge establishes a final decision.

Notes

1. For an overview of this period see, John Tobias, "Protection, Civilization, Assimilation: An Outline History of Canada's Indian Policy," in *As Long as the Sun Shines and Water Flows*, ed. Ian A.L. Getty and Antoine S. Lussier (Vancouver: University of British Columbia Press, 1983).

2. For an overview of this period, see John Taylor, *Canadian Indian Policy during the Inter-War Years, 1918–1939* (Ottawa: Queen's Printer, 1983).

3. Indian and Northern Affairs Canada, *Report to Parliament: Implementation of the 1985 Changes to the Indian Act* (Ottawa: Queen's Printer, 1987), i.

4. Indian and Northern Affairs Canada, *Report to Parliament*, 6.

5. As of September 1995, 240 of Canada's 608 bands have control over their band membership. *Financial Post*, October 7, 1995.

6. In 1995 these three bands lost their case; however, they appealed the judge's ruling. They proved that the judge was overly biased and the case is now being tried again.

7. Statistics obtained from John Dempsey, Indian Oil & Gas, September 2002.

8. Indian and Northern Affairs Canada, *Report to Parliament*, 4.

Discussion of Indigenous Identity and the State

PANEL MEMBERS: DUANE CHAMPAGNE, STEVEN CRUM,
AND JAMES DEMPSEY; MODERATOR: ANN TAVES

*T*HE DISCUSSION FOLLOWING PART I *began with a request that L. James Dempsey expound on his discussion of bands.*

Dempsey: I mentioned three bands that were challenging the court, all of them from Alberta. Their reserve is oil rich, and the band is small; but they not only challenged Bill C-31, they came up with their own band code, which, surprisingly enough, in many instances, was excluded from the position they took in court. One example is the traditional, ancestral idea of women marrying nonstatus men [see below]. My point is, whatever the challenge, the band sets its own way of defining band membership. In practice, it sometimes excludes as members those you would think should be included.

A series of questions followed that focused on precisely that topic: claiming Indian status.

Dempsey: There is the practical and there is the psychological side to claiming status. People who have been reinstated, especially older people who once lost their status, talk about different, past situations, such as: "My brother married a non-status woman, and she became Indian. My sisters and I married non-status men; we became non-Indian." This particular issue is especially important in regard to treaties. The non-status woman who became Indian through marriage received an annual treaty payment of $5 a year. The Indian women who married non-status men got no treaty payment. Their brother's wife, by the way, never learned to speak whatever language the tribe spoke.

On the practical side, therefore, there are the benefits. Aside from treaty payments, the two dominant ones are health and education. The number of reinstated people has exploded and the government just wasn't ready for it.

On the psychological side, the women who married non-status men felt something had been taken from them. From their point of view, their status was their birthright; yet, it was now being given back. One might argue, however, that their birthright also came from a special government definition.

Champagne: In most Indian communities, clans adopt individuals coming into the family; those who belong to the family belong to the community. In other communities, status is based on race rather than on family traditions. The BIA also imposed a blood marker to prevent those who dropped below quarter-blood content from getting services from the BIA, such as medical, health, and education. For the BIA, it was a matter of budget.

Some communities have adopted a strategy to preserve the community and keep people around who are living in the neighborhood. One can have, for example, a partial sort of blood marker and the percentages may vary from community to community. In some, status is marked by having 50 percent or even higher. The problem here is that over time, future generations are so diluted, they are no longer members of the tribe.

Some tribes have begun to rethink the entire marker issue. Other tribes have abandoned the marker entirely. The Cherokee, for example, argue a national position. Their point is that as a nation, Cherokee, like any other nation, can choose to adopt or to take in anybody they want. They define membership largely from descent. If you have any ancestor, regardless of how remote, if you have any ancestor on any Cherokee official roll—there are perhaps five or six rolls—then you can claim membership in the Cherokee nation.

Crum: Some tribes do not recognize genealogy at all. There is a famous case of a woman who, biologically, was a member of Santa Clara Pueblo—she was born and raised and lived there all her life. She married a non-status Navajo man. Traditionally, Santa Clara Pueblo was probably a matrilineal community with descent reckoned through the mother. Over time, the community became Christianized; and the clan became patrilineal, with descent or clan membership reckoned through the father. Thus, when the woman, a long-time member of the community, married a Navajo, an outsider, and not a member of the clan, she and her children were excluded from clan membership. She sued in court; the United States government ruled that the Santa Clara Pueblo, and all tribes, have the right to decide criteria for membership. Simple genealogy does not adequately cover all the ways or all the possibilities of defining Indian.

Champagne: Again, on the issue of blood content, the U.S. government institutionalized blood content for Native Americans, beginning in 1920, with passage of the congressional Snyder Act. One-quarter or more of a given tribal blood entitled you for services. If you were less than one-quarter, you were not entitled. This measure became a BIA regulation in 1924, and lasted until 1986, when a court position in California denied a student from the Pomo tribe a BIA grant to go to college because she was less than one-quarter. The student took her case to court and won. As a result, from 1986 on, the one-quarter blood content was essentially eroded as a criteria. The real question, however, is why, in 1924, did the BIA start using the policy in the first place? I believe the reason has a lot to do with the kind of racial thinking prevalent at the time. Look at the 1924 Immigration Act, which was really racist. Essentially, the act told the world who could come into the United States and who couldn't. Some could come in larger numbers; others, in smaller numbers. If you had ancestors here, you could come in larger numbers; but if you were from Africa, in some instances, you were barred. If you were from any Asian country, except for the Philippines, you were barred.

Crum: Another example of the psychological implications of identity is the notion that Native American people are "casino rich." Only 148 tribes have casinos. The vast majority do not; but the impression held by the larger American public, in general, is that we are all wealthy. We're not; and this perception really does a tremendous injustice to the larger Native American population. Most of the tribes can never get into gaming, because we can't compete against the Nevada gaming establishment. As a matter of fact, the most money I myself have ever received from my government is a $24 check in 1973, when I was an undergraduate at college. It's painful for me, then, when people on the UC campus where I work say, "You guys are okay financially."

Champagne: I can add more to that. Of the 148, or maybe 200, tribes that have some sort of gaming establishment, only about 15 are doing extremely well. The vast majority are very small operations. Those doing extremely well are located near big cities. Pequots, for example, have a monopoly in the Northeast; they do quite well, as do a few places in Minnesota and in Michigan. Some of the groups in California do quite well because they're in the radius of Los Angeles and San Diego; but these are exceptions. Places in the Great Plains, like the Chippewa at Turtle Reservation—a small place in North Dakota—or casinos in the Lakota Mountains are very small. They might gross maybe $20 million in a year and maybe $2 million is profit. The small casinos employ forty to sixty people, but the amount of money they generate is not very significant and has no major impact on the community. They are more just like another business in the community.

One psychological impact of successful casinos is that people who lived in poverty for so many years, all of a sudden, have a lot of money; and they don't know what to do with the money. How to spend it? They don't know anything about investments.

A certain percentage of gaming funds, according to law, has to be redistributed either through per capita payments or through investments in the community infrastructure. That's what makes Indian gaming different from gaming in Nevada. I think the percentage of redistributed funds is 70 percent of the profit. There is a tremendous amount of pressure to redistribute per capita, rather than make capital investment, probably because so many members of the community are extremely poor. However, different groups distribute funds differently. One important criticism of gaming is that only a few people make these decisions. In an egalitarian society, all people want to have a share in the decision making. All also want to share in the money and see immediate benefit, but redistributing per capita is not necessarily a good long-term strategy because gaming is not going to last forever. The tribes really have to diversify. Gaming can be an economic building project if tribes take the capital and invest it in something more enduring.

The final set of questions for Part I centered on whether people can decide identity for themselves, whether they can choose the tribe to which they say they belong.

Dempsey: Native identity is very complex, but ultimately it refers to tribal, not personal, identity. If you ask someone who he or she is, the answer will be Ojibwa, or, maybe, it will be the name of a specific band or clan. Band or clan identities are sometimes stronger than the general Ojibwa identity. Ojibwa people, moreover, are all Canadian, or they are little essential groups.

In spite of identities for native peoples being tribal or subtribal, however, the larger society considers Indians to be homogeneous, somewhat like an ethnic group. Even the law mentions "Indians"; it doesn't mention tribes. Identity, in these cases, is defined externally. It is situational.

It is too complicated for mainstream society to talk about different tribal identities. For them, a shorthand is necessary, a single key definition. But that single definition (i.e., Indian) is way too simplistic and doesn't get at the diversity and richness of the communities.

I'm part Indian. If I say "I'm part Ojibwa," no one knows what I mean, but every Indian I know has a tribal background and understands tribal identity. I'll say "I'm Ojibwa"; he'll say "I'm Tonkan." Identity also depends on the context one uses. Ultimately, a person will identify primarily with his or her community.

Champagne: In Indian country today, there is a resurgence of community identity and effort to restore culture in community as well as self-government. Tribes are pressing these issues now much more than they did thirty or forty years ago. The world has also changed, thus making these efforts possible. In the United States, the struggle has been longer and deeper than in Canada. Tribes want to become economically self-sufficient. To a certain extent, gaming is an effort to achieve economic self-sufficiency. Ideally, the point is not to make any single person rich, but to reinvest in preserving culture and community. I would argue that native culture is not capitalistic; it doesn't support individual capitalism. Individual capitalism breaks the rules of social conduct; when an individual accumulates capital, classes are created, which breaks down social structure. Native culture supports a form of collective capitalism, the model for gaming in which the tribe controls the establishment. The entire community benefits.

I think the tribal structure is in resurgence; but if the tribes do not meet the challenges of global competition, they may in effect be worse off than they have been. Even if tribes have had more or less effective policies, market forces are not government policies. They are forces of social and political arrangements that could be even more powerful and potentially more insidious to native communities than government policies have been. Tribes have to meet the challenge of binding and controlling those forces to protect their interests in this new world. At the same time, they must preserve the core values of community. Those communities will be different from what they were a hundred years ago, or even twenty or thirty years ago; but the question remains: can native communities, while meeting the challenges of the global economy, maintain those core values that are indigenous or that identify them as a community of native people?

Each community will accept the challenges on its own terms and within its own cultural frameworks. What the Iroquois decide to do is going to be very different from what the Navajo decide, because of their different histories and cultures. Some communities will reject the challenge completely. Some will move at much slower rates than people think they should, but the end game is to preserve community and not take on anything that will destroy it.

Dempsey: In Canadian First Nation communities, a lot has survived, but certainly not in the same form as it was 200, 300, 400, 500 years ago. Even without the European contact, change is part of time. Indian ideas and beliefs also have become enculturated or integrated with other aspects of the new society. After contact, natives rode horses; prior to contact, they had not done so, but horses are now so associated with natives, they are both nontraditional and traditional at the same time.

Crum: Years ago, I took some elders to a prison where they performed rituals, and also, in the ceremony, prayed the Hail Mary. The inmates ended up very confused. The next week, they questioned me as to how could the elders be considered elders when they had prayed the Hail Mary. I told the inmates the elders had integrated the Hail Mary into their own traditional belief system. One has to remember that to integrate something doesn't mean not to do something else. If you use a computer now, it doesn't mean you don't use a pencil anymore.

CULTURE AND ECONOMICS II

The Culture of Leadership: North American Indigenous Leadership in a Changing Economy 5

BRIAN CALLIOU

The Need for Leadership

INDIGENOUS PEOPLES have taken steps to improve the world's economy despite being among its most impoverished. Notwithstanding the foreign economic and legal systems imposed upon them, North American indigenous peoples have never entirely acquiesced to settler rule.[1] They have resisted the imposition of cultural and institutional structures of the settler state and attempted to retain their autonomy.[2]

North American indigenous peoples[3] have historically adapted to change. Environmental, economic, social, or cultural change has led indigenous peoples to adapt to the circumstances. North American indigenous people have continually adapted and have been involved to varying degrees in the development of the North American economy. They were involved in the fur trade,[4] agriculture,[5] and the extraction of natural resources.[6] They often maintained a dual economy that included their traditional pursuits of hunting and gathering and took part in the new economy developed by the settlers.[7] Aboriginal peoples were active participants until the settler societies began to marginalize them from the economy.

Commentators trying to explain North American Indians' lack of participation in the economy took an assimilationist approach.[8] They argued that aboriginal peoples' cultural traits would cause them to fail in the modern economy. They would only be successful in the modern economy if they accepted Western European training and education. Modernization theory reflects this assimilationist attitude by arguing that industrialization and technological progress was inevitable and that traditional economies and traditional values would perpetuate underdevelopment.[9] Unless aboriginals dropped their old ways, they would not succeed and would only have themselves to blame. Thus, many of the earlier studies on economic development viewed aboriginal cultures and traditions as impediments to successfully participating in a capitalist economy. However, there is now a growing body of literature that supports the utilization of traditional aboriginal forms of governance and traditional principles of leadership as the basis for economic and community development. For example, Dean Howard Smith argues that tribal economic development can only be successful when built upon a strong indigenous cultural identity.[10]

Furthermore, North American indigenous peoples have returned[11] to their aboriginal identity, cultures, and traditions and established renewed pride in their "Indianness."[12] Many have taken steps to develop their communities to integrate into national and global economies. Indeed, many tribes have assumed control over aspects of their communities and many have established competitive and successful economic enterprises.[13] In Canada, for example, land-claim settlements and treaties form the basis for increasing powers to self-govern.[14] Economic benefits are flowing from land-claim settlements, government agreements, and various industries exploiting the natural resources on traditional Indian lands.[15] Dealing in these arenas is new for many aboriginal leaders and managers, who are assuming significant responsibilities in these areas.

This paper explores the use of traditional principles and concepts of leadership and governance as a basis for economic development and community growth. I argue that aboriginal leaders today need to revitalize traditional principles and concepts of leadership and combine them with the modern competencies, knowledge, and skills required of mainstream managers and leaders. This combined approach to leadership development will better prepare aboriginal leaders to direct their communities, organizations, and businesses successfully into the new economy. In addition, the nation-building model provides a basis for this combined approach to economic and community development for North American indigenous leaders to set the community's own strategic direction. The combined approach will ground North American indigenous peoples in their own identity and values, thus allowing them to better deal with continual change and with any crisis that may arise.

As the business world becomes more competitive, the economy becomes more global, and change becomes constant, tribal leaders and managers must acquire and exhibit modern leadership and management competencies, capabilities, and skills to deal effectively with industry, business, and government leaders. To understand the knowledge, skills, and competencies required by North American indigenous leaders we must discuss what is meant by leadership.

Leadership

Leadership literature is vast.[16] In trying to categorize the enormous amount of leadership literature, Keith Grint discusses the development of leadership studies and describes the ensuing debate.[17] He isolates four main themes in the study of leadership: the trait approach, which is essentially the "hero" or "great man" approach; the situational approach; the contingency approach; and the constitutive approach.

The trait approach essentially viewed leaders as heroes who had the "right stuff" to lead through a variety of challenges. The studies of these great men focused on personal attributes of these leaders and their individual characteristics such as family background, education, and experiences through life. It is thought that this leader is able to lead under any circumstances.

The situational approach, on the other hand, viewed the circumstances or situations the leaders faced as being the more important factor in the emergence of the great leaders. Thus, according to the situational approach, unless the right situation arises, a leader of great potential may never have the opportunity to excel.

The contingency approach looks at the essence of the leader but also takes into account the context or situation. If the context aligns with the leader's strengths, then he or she will lead effectively and efficiently in that situation. However, if the leader's strengths do not align with the situation, then he or she should step aside and allow the best leader for that particular situation to take control. Continual self-awareness and situational analysis are required for the contingency approach. The leader must know and acknowledge his or her limitations and be prepared to let someone else take the helm.

The constitutive approach is a "pro-active affair for leaders."[18] Leaders in the constitutive approach actively shape the groups' interpretation of the environment or context. The leaders also try to persuade the group that their interpretation is the truth. Thus, leaders must interpret each context or situation they face and then convince others. Although they must respond to organizational culture, they also have the opportunity to shape that culture. The constitutive approach questions the objectivity of the situation or conditions and holds that such conditions are in fact contestable. What leaders do is essentially an interpretive affair, says Grint. He argues that "leadership is firmly within the arts, not the sciences."[19] Nevertheless, historically, leadership and management were studied scientifically.

After studying leaders as heroes or great men, leadership and management progressed to the study of management as science.[20] These early studies heralded the "command and control" method of leadership and management. The objective of scientific management was to obtain maximum efficiency from workers. Frederick Taylor studied the workplace through the science of movement.[21] He studied and timed workers' precise movements to find ways for them to become more efficient. Henri Fayol studied managerial activity relating to organizational research.[22] His analysis considered the functions or elements of management to include planning, organizing, coordinating, and controlling production and the workplace. He set out managerial principles that included division of work for specialization of tasks for greater efficiency and productivity, a clear chain of command, clearly de-fined authority and responsibility, and the subordination of personal interest in relation to the general interests of the organization. Fayol emphasized the univer-sal functions and principles of management and believed that any political, reli-gious, or other organizational leader could apply his principles. Max Weber studied bureaucratic rationality in the 1800s and saw it as an ideal mechanism for harnessing the manpower and resources of the industrial revolution.[23] Weber saw parallels between the mechanization of industry and the growth in bureaucratic forms of organization. He noted that the process of administration became rou-tinized, the same as machines routinized production. Weber provided a definition of bureaucracy as a "form of organization that emphasized precision, speed, clar-ity, regularity, reliability, and efficiency achieved through the creation of a fixed di-vision of tasks, hierarchical supervision, and detailed rules and regulations."[24]

A new approach to leadership and management emerged that empowered rather than controlled the workers. Max Dupree, like Grint, argues that leadership is not so much a science as it is an art.[25] He says leaders help people be all they can be. They essentially empower people, develop them, and unleash their pro-ductive and creative potential. Dupree argues that success is measured as a social achievement—as a team effort, not as an individual achievement. Leaders essen-tially mobilize and motivate their team players to achieve a common goal. Thus, Dupree argues that the signs of outstanding leadership appear not within the leader but with the followers. He asks: Are the followers reaching their full po-tential? Are they learning and growing? Are they achieving the desired results? Do the followers change with grace?[26] Dupree states that leaders are servants to the followers and ask how they can help followers to be more successful.[27]

Warren Bennis and Burt Nanus's definition of leadership says, "Leadership is what gives an organization its vision and its ability to translate the vision into re-ality."[28] They argue that the new leader is a transformative leader; that is, he or she can transform a vision into reality. Furthermore, they state that effective leader-ship can "move organizations from a current state to a future state, create visions of potential opportunities for organizations, instill within employees commitment to change, and instill new cultures and strategies."[29] Bennis and Nanus make a dis-tinction between leaders and managers. They say, "Managers are people who do things right and leaders are people who do the right thing."[30] In other words, man-agers have the technical skills to ensure the organization functions smoothly and efficiently. Leaders are concerned with whether what the organization does is the right thing—does it coincide with the vision and values of the organization or should a new path be charted to take advantage of new trends? Although there is a clear distinction between managers and leaders, many commentators now advo-cate that managers must learn to be leaders.[31]

This literature review illustrates a brief overview of the thinking in regards to leadership and management and that there has been a clear shift in the thinking from the "command and control" form of leadership to the "stewardship" form of leadership where leaders empower their followers to unleash their creative and productive potential.

Indigenous Leadership

North American tribal leadership literature is not extensive but a few studies have been conducted on the historical leadership among North American Indians.[32] However, there have been a number of biographies[33] and profiles of tribal chiefs[34] and other North American indigenous leaders.[35] Literature on current tribal leaders is scant but growing.[36]

Scholars writing on North American indigenous leadership are increasingly arguing that the effects of colonization and the oppression suffered by indigenous peoples must be overcome through revitalizing some of the traditional values and principles. For example, Manley Begay, a Navajo with the University of Arizona, has studied U.S. tribal leaders and argues that Indian leaders have the enormous task of overcoming the effects of the oppression suffered in Indian country. He says, "Native leaders have become responsible for the tasks of rebuilding, reuniting, reshaping, and revitalizing these nations. Foremost among those leaders who have taken on the nation-building challenge is the Native chief executive."[37] In Canada, sociologist Menno Boldt, from the University of Lethbridge and Mohawk political scientist, and Taiaiake Alfred, from University of Victoria, have taken critical perspectives on contemporary Indian leadership in Canada.[38] Both argue that today's chiefs seem more accountable to the Department of Indian Affairs than they are to their own people. They both argue that the effects of colonialism, especially of the imposed laws, political, and economic structures, have resulted in a substantial loss of traditions and governance structures. Boldt argues that Indians can only survive "as Indians" if they reclaim their traditional governance structures and leadership.[39] Alfred also argues that First Nations must revitalize their traditional values to serve as mechanisms for reestablishing governments and forms of leadership that preserve their nationhood.[40] Alfred uses the Mohawk's model of traditional governance as a guideline for leadership. In my argument, I do not mean indigenous leaders need to go back and recapture some pristine form of leadership practices. Rather, I am arguing that indigenous leaders need to be grounded in their culture, traditions, and history, which may have been dormant or practiced only underground. They need to revitalize these and come to a collective agreement, within their own nations, on their values and principles as a community so that they are better able to adapt, deal with change, and grow. Culture and traditions are not static, but rather are fluid. Throughout history, North American indigenous leaders have had to deal with changes in the environment and with other groups and constantly adapted to such changes with a view to the survival of their peoples.

I recognize that there are diverse cultures and traditions among the indigenous leaders and their communities of North America.[41] However, I do see many similarities and am going to make some broad generalizations, which we must recognize have limitations. I have reviewed a considerable amount of the literature on North American indigenous leaders, especially the biographies and histories of chiefs and political leaders that tend to illustrate certain characteristics of great indigenous leaders.[42] Firstly, these great chiefs, warriors, and medicine men had a strong sense of their identity and knew themselves as a part of their culture. For example, they had a strong sense of their history and culture as learned through stories, oral traditions, and ceremonies as well as a strong spiritual upbringing. Secondly, these great Indian leaders were visionaries. They did not make short-term decisions. They looked far into the future and had a vision or strategic direction of where they wanted their communities to go. For example, during treaty negotiations, these leaders were looking to do the best they could for the generations in the future, often looking seven generations out. Thirdly, these aboriginal leaders were action-oriented people. They did not just talk—they took action. Their followers could see they worked hard to carry out their visions for the community. For example, when a hunt or a raiding party was planned, these leaders ensured the plans were carried out, often leading the venture. Fourthly, these great aboriginal leaders were sharing individuals and respectful of their followers. They provided for their families and for their communities and shared what they could to do their best to ensure that no one went without. An example of this is the potlatch and other giveaway ceremonies where leaders shared their material or food wealth. Fifthly, these aboriginal leaders generally sought the council of others. They shared decision-making powers with others and encouraged open dialogue. They sought some degree of consensus for decisions. These broad generalizations are a sampling of the leadership qualities expressed through action by the traditional North American indigenous leaders.

Despite these traditional characteristics being practiced by the great leaders in the recent aboriginal history, many of these traditions were suspended or only practiced underground due to colonialism and its imposed laws and governing systems. However, these traditional leadership characteristics were not entirely lost. Our leaders can revitalize and relearn them along with the contemporary competencies required for the modern, fast-paced, global world. These characteristics of traditional North American aboriginal leaders are needed by today's indigenous leaders, in combination with modern leadership and management competencies. As Smith, Begay, Boldt, and Alfred argue, there is a need for indigenous leaders to revive the governance and leadership principles, based on traditional values, to "survive as Indians."

North American indigenous leaders who have taken this combined approach of being versed in both traditional teachings and modern management principles have tended to be among the most economically and socially successful. Indeed, the Harvard Project on American Indian Economic Development's research and publications bears this out.[43] Indigenous leaders, therefore, not only need the competencies, skills, and knowledge of their traditions and values along with the modern competencies of managers—a foot in both worlds, so to speak—they also need to be able to lead their nations to take control of their own strategic direction. One approach for moving in that direction is the nation-building model.

Nation-Building Model

The nation-building model evolved from research undertaken by sociologist Stephen Cornell, political economist Joseph Kalt, and education scholar Manley Begay Jr. as part of the Harvard Project.[44] This is a groundbreaking study that is ongoing to the present and is still very relevant. The Harvard Project began in the mid-1980s and continues today. It examined economic development on American Indian reservations and asked the question: why were some tribes economically successful, despite having less land or natural resource base, than other tribes that might have more resources and land available? They asked what successful tribes did to give them sustainable economies on their reservations, which resulted in reduced social problems associated with poverty and unemployment.

The Harvard Project findings illustrate that successful Indian tribes exercise de facto sovereignty over themselves and their resources by establishing effective institutions that match their culture, set a strategic direction, and take concrete action in the achievement of their goals. The conclusions reached by the Harvard Project on American Indian Economic Development are for American indigenous tribes, but there is nothing to say that these conclusions might not work for Third World countries. The Harvard Project has more recently carried out their research model with the Canadian First Nations with similar findings.[45]

Before explaining each of these concepts, we first review what Cornell and Kalt call the traditional approach to tribal economic development used by the Bureau of Indian Affairs, and which is generally agreed to have been a failure. The traditional approach to tribal economic development is essentially short-term and nonstrategic.[46] This traditional approach does not focus on the fundamental issues such as "What kind of a society are we trying to build?" Rather, its emphasis is on short-term strategies like starting more businesses, building more industrial parks, and creating more jobs. Long-term strategic thinking is discouraged and little or no concern is given to whether the new businesses are sustainable, whether there is a market for more industrial parks, and whether the jobs being created are jobs the tribal members are interested in or qualified to do. The traditional approach also tended to let others, such as the Bureau of Indian Affairs, set the agenda rather than allowing the tribe to do it.[47] Tribes essentially followed the strategies set by the Bureau of Indian Affairs or state agencies with available funding. The traditional approach to tribal economic development also viewed economic development as primarily an economic problem.[48] Attention is paid to narrow economic variables with little attention paid to the political environment in which development is to proceed. Finally, the traditional approach to tribal economic development viewed indigenous culture as an obstacle to development.[49] This view reflects the modernization theory and its attempts to assimilate and acculturate indigenous peoples into Western European culture and values.[50] Modernization theory sees no intrinsic value in indigenous cultures—maybe only for purposes of tourism or arts and crafts production. The sad results of the traditional approach to tribal economic development are reflected in many failed tribal enterprises, continued poverty, and a politics of spoils where tribal leaders or managers milked any short-term benefits for all they could.[51] The outside world's perception of tribal peoples was one of incompetence and chaos. Such public perceptions undermined any claims to self-government by tribal groups.[52]

In comparison to the traditional approach to tribal economic development, the Harvard Project team concluded that the nation-building approach was to be the basis for the economically successful tribes in the United States. The Harvard Project found that with the nation-building model, tribal economic development was first and foremost a political problem.[53] The characteristics of the nation-building model are political, not economic. Indeed, the Harvard Project on American Indian Economic Development summarizes its key findings from their research as follows: "Successful Native Nations assert the right to govern themselves and exercise that right effectively by building capable governing institutions that match their culture."[54]

The first concept of the nation-building model is exercising de facto sovereignty. By exercising de facto sovereignty, the Harvard Project researchers meant that tribes assert their local autonomy through the "assertion of self-decision making, self-government over the key economic development decisions on the reservation."[55] In other words, they take ownership and control over their local decision making and practice self-government in fact. Joseph Kalt describes a story of the White Mountain Apache tribal chairman (chief) who told the Bureau of Indian Affairs agent that he would not be needed at their meetings any more and that they would call him if they needed him.[56] From that day forward, the White Mountain Apache made their own decisions. They asserted de facto sovereignty.

The second concept that the Harvard Project team found necessary for successful aboriginal economic development was the establishment of effective institutions that match the culture.[57] By effective institutions, the Harvard Project researchers meant that tribes could not assert de facto sovereignty successfully unless they first established effective institutions that could provide the following: stable institutions and policies, fair and effective dispute resolution, separation of politics from business management, a competent bureaucracy, and a cultural match between their modern governance structure and their traditional forms of leadership and values.[58] For example, an effective institution in the tribal community includes the establishment of unbiased tribunals or courts following clear rules of law that would make investors more comfortable about investing in development projects on the reservation should disputes ever arise. This holds for both outside investors and for investors from the reservation. Investors would not risk their money in ventures where inefficient institutions increase their risk and cannot protect their investments. Professionally run tribal regulatory or zoning departments following clearly expressed guidelines to assure investors and reduce the risk they would otherwise face.

Effective governments carry out three primary functions: they operate effective and capable day-to-day bureaucracies, they provide for the settlement of disputes (especially over capital assets), and they separate politics from business.[59] They maintain stability through these effective institutions and processes. Many successful tribes have established independent boards, usually incorporated separate from the tribal government, to run the tribal enterprises and assets. The Harvard Project found that the likelihood of having a profitable enterprise increased fivefold if tribal leaders were not serving as directors of the board for the enterprise.[60] Effective institutions create a stable tribal environment and are more likely to attract investors than those without this stability.

Effective institutions may not be enough to be successful if they are not culturally appropriate. There must be a match between the modern governance structures and the traditional beliefs and values.[61] Imposing or copying institutions that are not culturally appropriate would likely be unsuccessful, according to the Harvard Project study. Some tribes have government structures that reflect traditional decision-making structures such as the Cochiti Pueblo who have a "pure theocracy form of government" where the religious tribal leader (the *cacique*) annually appoints the tribal politicians.[62] They have no written constitution.

In essence, the effective institutions of self-government must "match the underlying cultural norms of legitimacy."[63] Institutions need to be something the tribe can accept as their own. However, this does not mean that all tribes must rediscover the historically accurate traditional governance structures. The Flathead Tribes of Montana were culturally diverse when they were placed together on a reservation by the Bureau of Indian Affairs. Here, one traditional form of government structure is unlikely to be acceptable by the other cultures. Thus, a written constitution based somewhat on the Constitution of the United States was acceptable to the various tribes that constitute the Flathead of Montana.[64] Cultural match means that each tribe must find institutions and structures that match their culture to some degree and are acceptable to them.

The third concept of the Harvard Project findings was to set a strategic direction for the tribe.[65] This involves setting a vision of the community and planning for the long term. Along with setting a vision, tribes might establish a mission statement and expressly state the values they want to live by in their communities. Decisions such as whether a ski resort should be built on their mountains take into account their values, vision, and mission, and their long-term plans. Thus, the White Mountain Apache in Arizona decided their strategic direction would involve building a ski resort while the Yakima tribe in Washington decided that building a ski resort did not fit within their strategic plan because doing so conflicted with their values of viewing the mountain as sacred. Each tribe has to make these decisions themselves. Strategic plans and visions assist them in making such decisions. Setting strategic direction is long-term, visionary thinking. It is proactive rather than reactive thinking. It takes into account a broader perspective on community building rather than narrowly focusing on just economics.

The final concept of the Harvard Project findings is taking concrete action through strong leadership.[66] Leaders of organizations or tribes often spend time setting out strategic plans, visions, and missions, and then set them on shelves to collect dust. Those leaders, tribes, and organizations that take concrete action actually carry out their visions, their goals, and their plans. They make the decisions to act and they take immediate action. Successful tribes set out plans of actions with timelines to ensure planning targets are being met. They also evaluate their performance on an ongoing basis to see if their actions are achieving the goals they set. If not, they adjust as required. Nevertheless, they do not wait for things to happen—they make things happen. They remain proactive rather than reactive. This analysis does import modern management techniques to the tribal community of today, and provides a useful framework to explain the key factors in successful tribal development.

The nation-building model provides a useful approach to leadership for North American indigenous leaders. Nation building is a more holistic approach and does not focus narrowly on business and economic development. Its focus is broadly based, with building the whole nation as its objective. Thus, education and training must be developed simultaneously and in sync with economic development, health, housing, and other areas of reservation life. North American indigenous leaders who seek to revitalize their nations need to have certain modern competencies, knowledge, and skills as well.

Competency Requirements of Leaders

What competencies do North American indigenous leaders need to lead their nations into the new millennium? Besides skills and knowledge about nation building, Indian leaders need the capabilities to deal with the rapidly changing world system. The globalization trend, rapid changes in technology, and the increasingly complex web of economic relations present challenges for indigenous leaders. They will have to learn the competencies of modern managers and leaders on top of traditional knowledge and nation-building skills.

A competency is defined as "any motive, attitude, skill, knowledge, behavior or other personal characteristic that is essential to perform the job and that differentiates average from superior performers."[67] Others have defined competencies as "a cluster of related knowledge, skills, and attitudes that affects a major part of one's job (a role or responsibility), that correlates with performance on the job, that can be measured against well-accepted standards, and that can be improved via training and development."[68]

Competencies are made up of skills, knowledge, experience, attitudes, and our beliefs and values.[69] These collectively make up a competency, which is observable in a leader's behavior. However, being seen as competent in one situation does not ensure competence in another. Thus, we must adjust the observable behavior since each organization or community has its own values or culture and their own expectations of behavior. Therefore, competencies refer to observable behaviors plus values.

Competency maps/charts are used by organizations for the following: to clarify roles and expectations, improve productivity, enhance the feedback evaluation process, adapt to change, and align behavior with organizational strategies and values.[70] The competencies most leaders in the global world need include the following: communication skills, business management, performance management, critical thinking, innovation and creativity, team building, development of others, change leadership, stability, and balance. Technical skills are not sufficient, and leaders must focus on those behaviors that lead to superior performance.

Peter Scholtes argues that "the new leadership" competencies include the following: ability to engage in systems thinking and knowing how to lead systems; the ability to understand the variability of work in planning and problem solving; understanding how we learn, develop, and improve; leading true learning and improvement; understanding people and why they behave as they do; understanding the interdependence and interaction between systems, variation, learning, and human behavior and knowing how each affects the others; and giving vision, meaning, direction, and focus to the organization.[71]

Applying modern management theory on competency maps/charts to the indigenous leadership case, Robert Breaker and I carried out research into indigenous leadership competencies through the Aboriginal Leadership and Management Development Program at the Banff Centre.[72] Through focus group activities, indigenous leaders discussed the competencies they felt indigenous leaders needed today to lead their communities or organizations. The competencies that surfaced repeatedly were knowledge of culture and history of community; spiritual harmony and personal balanced lifestyle; holistic, global worldview; strategic thinker/planner; responsible leader who is accountable to his or her followers; team builder; visionary; risk taker; implement plans and take action; strong integrity; delegates authority/shares power; ability to resolve disputes; strong communication skills; business management skills; objective and open minded; strong indigenous identity, yet understands both worlds; and problem-solving and decision-making skills. When compared with the competencies for business leadership discussed above, many of the same competencies are viewed by indigenous leaders to be necessary for them to lead their communities and organizations. For example, strategic thinking and planning are viewed to be necessary for both sets of leaders.[73] Also, team building, setting a vision, and strong communication skills are also seen as necessary. One interesting difference is the competencies identified by indigenous leaders that deal with their knowledge of the culture and history of their community. This competency seems to be directed to the importance of a strong sense of community and belonging.

If we look again at the generalized characteristics of traditional indigenous leaders I identified earlier from the literature on chiefs and other leaders,[74] we can relate them to the competencies required by the new leadership. We can see overlap or similarities in the traditional characteristics I previously highlighted and the competencies identified by the contemporary indigenous leadership. For example, firstly, the strong sense of community and cultural identity that traditional indigenous leaders exhibited resembles the competency identified by contemporary indigenous leaders regarding having knowledge and understanding of one's culture and the community's history. Secondly, the characteristic of traditional indigenous leaders as being visionaries is similar to the competency identified by the current indigenous leadership about being able to set out a vision and being a strategic, long-term planner. This also fits with the long-term, strategic planning and setting of visions that were discussed as part of the nation-building model. Thirdly, the characteristic of the traditional indigenous leaders being action oriented is similar to the competencies identified by the contemporary indigenous leaders that leaders need to be risk takers and put plans into action. Fourthly, the characteristic of traditional indigenous leadership identified above regarding consensus building and shared decision making has similarities to the competency identified by the contemporary indigenous leaders regarding delegating authority and sharing power. Although contemporary indigenous leaders identified many of the competencies required of leaders of today's indigenous communities, which share similarities with some of the traditional indigenous leaders' characteristics, they do not exhibit such competencies consistently in their behavior as leaders and managers of their nations or organizations.

Much of the competencies required of today's indigenous leadership must incorporate the knowledge, skills, and attitudes of the modern organizational or business leader. However, they should reconcile these modern competencies with some of the principles of the traditional indigenous leadership and governance. Indeed, commentators such as Smith, Begay, Boldt, and Alfred have argued that today's indigenous leaders ought to revitalize traditional governance and leadership processes.[75]

Today's indigenous leaders can learn their cultural and traditional principles of leadership and governance through oral histories, songs, and ceremonies as well as from written historical accounts.[76] They can also learn modern management and leadership competencies by taking professional development courses, attending conferences, continuing their own personal reading, and utilizing other ways of learning the competencies they require.[77] They must become comfortable and competent in both their traditional culture and the modern mainstream world.

Furthermore, nonindigenous leaders could benefit from incorporating some of the indigenous competencies/characteristics into their organizational or business cultures. In fact, much of the newly emerging thinking in leadership and management development literature, such as viewing organizations as part of the "web of life" and bringing "spirituality" and "creativity" into the workplace, resemble traditional indigenous worldviews and values.[78]

Conclusion

Leadership for the indigenous peoples of North America is critical in this age of constant flux and increasing globalization. Indigenous leaders are responsible for leading their communities into a new era where the indigenous peoples will play a more significant role in the mainstream society and economy than they have in the past. With the growing strength of aboriginal and treaty rights through constitutional and judicial recognition and the increase in the settlement of land claims, negotiations of self-government agreements, North American indigenous leaders are assuming increasing amounts of power and responsibility. Furthermore, indigenous peoples in Canada are the fastest growing segment of the population, with a birth rate 1.5 times greater than mainstream society.[79] Half their population is under the age of nineteen and will make up an increasing proportion of the future labor force.[80] The education and skill levels of aboriginal persons are quickly accelerating, which should translate into aboriginal people occupying more meaningful and more decision-making positions in the future. For example, in 1960, there were only 200 First Nations students in Canadian postsecondary institutions; that number increased to more than 28,000 in 2002.[81]

To "survive as Indians," the indigenous leadership must incorporate traditional principles of leadership and governance along with modern management and leadership competencies required for the modern global world. They must weave these leadership qualities together in order to lead their communities and organizations in today's fast-paced world. Although the economic and social environment has changed with the advent of new technologies and the new economy, traditional values can prove invaluable as a means of grounding indigenous peoples in their culture and allow them to better adapt and prosper in the mainstream world. Tradition is not necessarily static, but instead is fluid.

Besides the revitalization of traditional principles of leadership and governance, combined with modern leadership and management knowledge and skills, the contemporary indigenous leadership in North America also ought to utilize the nation-building model as an approach to community development. They must become strategic thinkers, set long-term goals for their communities, set out measurements for evaluating their performance, and be action-oriented leaders. The combination of the nation-building model, traditional leadership and governance principles, and modern leadership and management competencies will assist contemporary North American indigenous leaders in leading through the continuous changes facing their communities in today's global society and economy.

Notes

1. On the concept of imposed law, see S. B. Burman and B. E. Harrell-Bond, eds., *The Imposition of Law* (New York: Academic Press, 1979) and B. Calliou, "The Imposition of State Laws and the Creation of Various Hunting Rights for Aboriginal Peoples of the Treaty 8 Territory," *Lobstick: An Interdisciplinary Journal* 1 (2000): 151.

2. Brian Calliou and Cora Voyageur, "Aboriginal Economic Development and the Struggle for Self-Government," in *Power and Resistance: Critical Thinking about Canadian Social Issues*, ed. W. Antony and L. Samuelson (Halifax, NS: Fernwood, 1998), 115; for a collection of Native American resistance and renewal, see A. M. Josephy Jr., J. Nagel, and T. Johnson, eds., *Red Power: The American Indian's Fight for Freedom*, 2nd ed. (Lincoln: University of Nebraska Press, 1999).

3. I will refer to North American indigenous peoples interchangeably to refer to the original pre-European contact peoples of North America. My use of the term *North American indigenous peoples* would include what is referred to in the United States as Native Americans and Alaska Natives and what is referred to in Canada as aboriginal peoples. In Canada, *aboriginal peoples* is defined in the Constitution Act, 1982, as meaning "Indians" (today generally referred to as First Nations), "Inuit" (previously referred to as Eskimo), and "Metis" (mixed-blood people who formed a distinct identity as a people).

4. See, for example, A. J. Ray, *Indians in the Fur Trade: Their Role as Hunters, Trappers and Middlemen in the Lands Southwest of the Hudson Bay, 1660–1870* (Toronto: University of Toronto Press, 1974); J. E. Foster, "The Indian-Trader in the Hudson Bay Fur Tradition," *Proceedings of the Second Congress, Canadian Ethnology Society*, vol. 2 (Ottawa: National Museum of Man, Mercury Series, Canadian Ethnology Service, Paper no. 28, 1975); W. Swagerty, "Indian Trade in the Trans-Mississippi West to 1870," in *Handbook of North American Indians*, vol. 4 (Washington, D.C.: Smithsonian Institute, 1988), 351; D. J. Wisehart, "Cultures in Cooperation and Conflict: Indians in the Fur Trade on the Northern Great Plains, 1807–1840," *Journal of Historical Geography* 2 (1976): 311.

5. See Sara Carter, *Lost Harvests: Prairie Indian Reserve Farmers and Government Policy* (Montreal: McGill-Queen's University Press, 1990); T. R. Wessell, "Agriculture on the Reservations: The Case of the Blackfeet, 1885–1935," *Journal of the West* 23 (1979): 17; R. J. Stahl, "Farming among the Kiowa, Comanche, Kiowa Apache, and Wichita," PhD diss., University of Oklahoma, 1978; W. D. Pennington, "Government Policy and Indian Farming on the Cheyenne and Arapaho Reservations, 1869–1880," *Chronicles of Oklahoma* 57 (1979): 171.

6. For First Nations' participation in the fishing market, see V. P. Lytwyn, "Ojibwa and Ottawa Fisheries around Manitoulin Island: Historical and Geographical Perspectives on Aboriginal and Treaty Fishing Rights," *Native Studies Review* 6 (1990): 1; J. J. Van West, "Ojibwa Fisheries, Commercial Fisheries Development and Fisheries Administration, 1873–1915," *Native Studies Review* 6 (1990): 31; and P. Gladstone, "Native Indians and the Fishing Industry of British Columbia," in *Perspectives on the North American Indians*, ed. M. Nagler (Toronto: McClelland and Stewart, 1972), 156. For First Nations' participation in fishing and lumbering, see Frank Tough, "Challenges to the Native Economy of Northern Manitoba in the Post-Treaty Period, 1870–1900," *Native Studies Review* 40 (1985): 1.

7. J. A. Kruse, "Alaska Inupiat Subsistence and Wage Employment Patterns: Understanding Individual Choice," *Human Organization* 50 (1991): 317; B. Cox, "Prospects for the Northern Native Economy," *Polar Record* 22 (1985): 393; M. Asch, "The Future of Hunting and Trapping and Economic Development in Alberta's North: Some Facts and Myths about Inevitability," in *Proceedings of the Fort Chipewyan and Fort Vermilion Bicentennial Conference*, ed. P. A. McCormack and R. G. Ironside (Edmonton: Boreal Institute for Northern Studies, University of Alberta, 1990), 25.

8. Calliou and Voyageur, "Aboriginal Economic Development."

9. See, for example, J. Kolby, *Inequality, Power and Development: The Task of Political Sociology* (Amherst, NY: Humanity Books, 1999), 147; W. W. Rostow, *The Stages of Economic Growth:*

A Non-Communist Manifesto (Cambridge: Cambridge University Press, 1964); N. Smelser, "Toward a Theory of Modernization," in *Social Change*, ed. A. Etzioni and E. Etzioni (New York: Basic Books, 1964), 268; Fred Wien, *Rebuilding the Economic Base of Indian Communities: The MicMac of Nova Scotia* (Montreal: Institute for Research on Public Policy, 1986), 88.

10. Howard Dean Smith, *Modern Tribal Development: Paths to Self-Sufficiency and Cultural Integrity in Indian Country* (New York: AltaMira Press, 2000); see also David R. Newhouse, "From Tribal to the Modern: The Development of Modern Aboriginal Societies," in Ron F. Laliberte et al., eds., *Expressions in Canadian Native Studies* (Saskatoon: University of Saskatchewan Extension Press, 2000), 395–409.

11. Although some North American indigenous peoples resisted Western European ideologies, many indigenous persons were subjected to coercive assimilationist policies, such as residential schools, to rid them of their traditional values and culture. See, for example, J. S. Milloy, *A National Crime: The Canadian Government and the Residential School System, 1879 to 1986* (Winnipeg: University of Manitoba, 1999); J. L. Tobias, "Protection, Civilization, Assimilation: An Outline History of Canada's Indian Policy," in *As Long as the Sun Shines and Water Flows: A Reader in Canadian Native Studies*, ed. I. A. L. Getty and A. S. Lussier (Vancouver: University of British Columbia Press, 1983), 39; L. Jaine, "Industrial and Residential School Administration: The Attempt to Undermine Indigenous Self-Determination," *Journal of Indigenous Studies* 2 (1991); Frederick E. Hoxie, *A Final Promise: The Campaign to Assimilate the Indians, 1880–1920* (New York: Cambridge University Press, 1984); W. Cingolani, "Acculturating the Indian: Federal Policies," *Social Work* 18 (1973): 24

12. See, for example, J. Nagel, *American Indian Ethnic Renewal: Red Power and the Resurgence of Identity and Culture* (New York: Oxford University Press, 1996); N. O. Lurie, "Appendix: An American Indian Renascence?" in *The American Indian Today*, ed. S. Levine and N. O. Lurie (Deland, FL: Everett Edwards, 1968), 187; S. Steiner, *The New Indians* (New York: Delta Books, 1968); R. K. Thomas, "Pan-Indianism," in *The American Indian Today*, ed. S. Levine and N. O. Lurie (Deland, FL: Everett Edwards, 1968), 77.

13. M. Willox, ed., *Best Practices in Aboriginal Business and Economic Development: A Report of the Symposium Proceedings September 8–11, 1999* (Banff: Banff Centre, 2000) showcases a variety of successful tribal and First Nations' economic enterprises. See also the section entitled "Models of Community and Individual Enterprise" in the Royal Commission on Aboriginal Peoples, *Sharing the Harvest: The Road to Self-Reliance: Report of the National Round Table on Aboriginal Economic Development and Resources* (Ottawa, ON: Minister of Supply and Services and Canada Communication Group, 1993), 247; P. D. Elias, *Northern Aboriginal Communities: Economies and Development* (North York, ON: Captus Press, 1995); R. B. Anderson, *Economic Development Among the Aboriginal Peoples in Canada: The Hope for the Future* (North York, ON: Captus Press, 1999). For American examples, see Sam Stanley, *American Indian Economic Development* (The Hague: Mouton, 1978); Robert H. White, *Tribal Assets: The Rebirth of Native America* (New York: Henry Holt, 1990).

14. See, for example, C. E. S. Franks, "Indian Policy: Canada and the United States Compared," in *Aboriginal Rights and Self-Government: The Canadian and Mexican Experience in North American Perspective*, ed. C. Cook and J. D. Lindau (Toronto: McGill-Queen's University Press, 2000), 221; James C. Saku and R. M. Bone, "Modern Treaties in Canada: The Case

of Northern Quebec Agreements and the Inuvialuit Final Agreement," *Canadian Journal of Native Studies* 2 (2000): 283; D. Cozzetto, "Governance and Aboriginal Claims in Northern Canada," *American Indian Journal of Culture and Research* 14 (1990): 39.

15. Anderson, *Economic Development*; Colin H. Scott, ed., *Aboriginal Autonomy and Development in Northern Quebec and Labrador* (Vancouver: University of British Columbia Press, 2001); J. R. Ponting, "Economic Development Provisions of the New Claims Settlements," in *Arduous Journey: Canadian Indians and Decolonization*, ed. J. R. Ponting (Toronto: McClelland and Stewart, 1986).

16. For a selective sampling of this literature, see J. M. Burns, *Leadership* (New York: Harper Torchbooks, 1978); A. W. Gouldner, ed., *Studies in Leadership* (New York: Harper & Brothers, 1950); P. Selznick, *Leadership in Administration* (New York: Harper & Brothers, 1957); W. Bennis and B. Nanus, *Leaders: The Strategies for Taking Charge* (New York: Harper and Row, 1985); A. S. McFarland, *Power and Leadership in Pluralist Systems* (Stanford: Stanford University Press, 1969); H. Gardiner, *Leading Minds: An Anatomy of Leadership* (London: Harper Collins, 1996); R. Heifetz, *Leadership without Easy Answers* (Cambridge, MA: Belknap Press, 1994); W. G. Bennis, "Leadership Theory and Administrative Behavior: The Problem of Authority," *Administrative Science Quarterly* 4 (1959): 259; M. K. de Vries, "Leaders Who Make a Difference," *European Management Journal* 14 (1996): 486; S. J. Lilley and G. M. Platt, "Correspondents' Images of Martin Luther King Jr.: An Interpretive Theory of Movement Leadership," in *Leadership: Classical, Contemporary and Critical Approaches*, ed. K. Grint (Oxford: Oxford University Press, 1997).

17. K. Grint, *The Arts of Leadership* (Oxford: Oxford University Press, 2000).

18. Grint, *Arts of Leadership*, 4

19. Grint, *Arts of Leadership*.

20. See, for example, M. S. Wortman Jr., "A Philosophy for Management," in *Issues in Business and Society: Readings and Cases*, ed. W. T. Greenwood (Boston: Houghton Mifflin, 1964), 432; P. F. Drucker, "Potentials of Management Science," *Harvard Business Review* 37 (1959): 25.

21. F. W. Taylor, *Principles of Scientific Management* (New York: Harper & Row, 1911).

22. H. Fayol, *General and Industrial Management* (New York: Pitman, 1949).

23. H. H. Girth and C. W. Mills, eds., *From Max Weber: Essays in Sociology* (New York: Oxford University Press, 1974); M. Weber, *The Theory of Social and Economic Organization* (London: Oxford University Press, 1947).

24. G. Morgan, *Images of Organization.* (Newbury Park, CA: Sage, 1986), 24–25.

25. Max Dupree, *Leadership Is an Art* (New York: Dell, 1989).

26. Dupree, *Leadership Is an Art*, 12

27. Dupree, *Leadership Is an Art*, 12. See also P. Block, *Stewardship: Choosing Service over Self-Interest* (San Francisco: Berrett-Koehler, 1996), who argues leaders need to perform a servant role in a stewardship fashion; Robert K. Greenleaf, *Servant Leadership: A Journey into the Nature of Legitimate Power and Greatness* (Mahwah, NJ: Paulist Press, 1977).

28. Bennis and Nanus, *Leaders: The Strategies for Taking Charge.*

29. Bennis and Nanus, *Leaders: The Strategies for Taking Charge*, 17.

30. Bennis and Nanus, *Leaders: The Strategies for Taking Charge*, 21.

31.   See, for example, W. D. Hitt, *The Leader-Manager: Guidelines for Action* (Columbus, OH: Battelle Press, 1988); and P. Wright, *Managerial Leadership* (London: Routledge, 1996).

32.   J. G. E. Smith, "Leadership among the Indians of the Northern Woodlands," in *Currents in Anthropology: Essays in Honor of Sol Tax*, ed. R. Hinshaw (The Hague: Mouton, 1979), 306; D. B. Smith, *Leadership among the Southwestern Ojibwa* (Ottawa: National Museum of Canada, 1973), 1; J. E. Chute, "Ojibwa Leadership during the Fur Trade Era at Sault Ste. Marie," in *Papers of the Seventh North American Fur Trade Conference* (East Lansing: University of Michigan, 1997); J. H. MacNeish, "Leadership among the Northeastern Athabascans," *Anthropologica* 2 (1956): 131; E. S. Rogers, "Leadership among the Indians of Eastern Subarctic Canada," *Anthropologica* 7 (1959): 263; J. M. Penard, "Land Ownership and Chieftancy among the Chippewayan and Caribou-Eaters," *Primitive Man* 2 (1929): 20; T. Morantz, "Northern Algonquian Concepts of Status and Leadership Reviewed: A Case Study of the Eighteenth-Century Trading Captain System," *Canadian Review of Sociology and Anthropology* 19 (1982): 482.

33.   H. A. Dempsey, *Red Crow: Warrior Chief*, 2nd ed. (Saskatoon: Fifth House, 1995); G. MacEwan, *Sitting Bull: The Years in Canada* (Edmonton: Hurtig, 1973); H. A. Dempsey, *Crowfoot: Chief of the Blackfeet* (Norman: University of Oklahoma Press, 1972); J. Redsky, *Great Leader of the Ojibway: Mis-quona-queb* (Toronto: McClelland and Stewart, 1972); Brigham D. Madsen, *Chief Pocatello* (Moscow: University of Idaho Press, 1999); P. D. Smith, *Ouray: Chief of the Utes* (Ridgeway, CO: Wayfinder Press, 1986); L. M. Urquhart, *Colorow: The Angry Chieftain* (Denver: Golden Bell Press, 1968); M. Sandoz, *Crazy Horse: The Strange Man of the Oglalas* (New York: Alfred A. Knopf, 1942); H. Assu and J. Inglis, *Assu of Cape Mudge: Recollections of a Coastal Indian Chief* (Vancouver: University of British Columbia Press, 1989); D. Kennedy, *Recollections of an Assiniboine Chief*, ed. James R. Stevens (Toronto: McClelland and Stewart, 1972); W. D. Baird, *Peter Pitchlynn: Chief of the Choctaws* (Norman: University of Oklahoma Press, 1972).

34.   A. M. Josephy Jr., *The Patriot Chiefs: Studies of Nine Great Leaders of the American Indians* (London: Eyre and Spottiswoode, 1962); K. Nagelfell, *North American Indian Chiefs* (North Dighton: JG Press, 1995); M. Fielder, *Sioux Indian Leaders* (Seattle, WA: Superior, 1975); E. Brant Monture, *Famous Indians: Canadian Portraits* (Toronto: Clarke, Irwin, 1960); C. Thomas Foreman, *Indian Women Chiefs* (Washington, DC: Zenger, 1976).

35.   H. A. Dempsey, *Jerry Potts: Plainsman* (Calgary: Glenbow Foundation, 1966); M. Dobbin, *The One-and-a-Half Men: The Story of Jim Brady and Malcolm Norris, Metis Patriots of the 20th Century* (Vancouver: New Star Books, 1981); H. A. Dempsey, *The Gentle Persuader: A Biography of James Gladstone, Indian Senator* (Saskatoon: Western Producer Prairie Books, 1986); D. Neel, *Our Chiefs and Elders: Words and Photographs of Native Leaders* (Vancouver: University of British Columbia Press, 1992); F. J. Dockstader, *Great North American Indians: Profiles in Life and Leadership* (New York: Van Nostrand Reinhold, 1977); E. P. Patterson II, "Andrew Paul and the Early History of British Columbia Indian Organizations," in *One Century Later: Western Canadian Reserve Indians Since Treaty 7*, ed. I. A. L. Getty and D. B. Smith (Vancouver: University of British Columbia Press, 1978); G. L. Roberts, "Chief of State and the Chief: Negotiating with the Creek Indians, 1789," *American Heritage* 26 (1975): 28;

G. Miles, "A Brief Study of Joseph Brandt's Political Career in Relation to Iroquois Political Structure," *American Indian Journal* 2 (1976): 12.

36. For a sampling, see P. McFarlane, "Aboriginal Leadership," in *Visions of the Heart: Canadian Aboriginal Issues*, ed. D. A. Long and O. P. Dickason (Toronto: Harcourt Brace, 1996); C. J. Voyageur, "Keeping All the Balls in the Air: The Experience of Canada's Women Chiefs," in *Women and Leadership*, ed. A. MacNevin et al. (Ottawa: Canadian Research Institute for the Advancement of Women, 2002); S. Crowfoot, "Leadership in First Nation Communities: A Chief's Perspectives on the Colonial Millstone," in *First Nations in Canada: Perspectives on Opportunity, Empowerment, and Self-Determination*, ed. J. Rick Ponting (Toronto: McGraw-Hill Ryerson, 1997); F. Jules, "Indian Leadership," unpublished master's thesis, University of British Columbia, 1987; D. M. Prindeville and T. B. Gomez, "American Indian Women Leaders, Public Policy, and the Importance of Gender and Ethnic Identity," *Women and Politics* 20 (1999): 17; P. McFarlane, *From Brotherhood to Nationhood: George Manuel and the Modern Indian Movement* (Toronto: Between the Lines, 1993); D. R. Edmunds, ed., *American Indian Leaders: Studies in Diversity* (Lincoln: University of Nebraska Press, 1980); R. L. Bee, "The Predicament of Native American Leaders: A Second Look," *Human Organization* 49 (1990): 1; M. Boldt, "Canadian Native Indian Leadership: Context and Composition," *Canadian Ethnic Studies* 12 (1980): 15; E. J. Hedican, "On the Ethno-Politics of Canadian Native Leadership and Identity," *Ethnic Groups* 9 (1991): 1; R. F. Berkhofer Jr., "Native Americans," in *Ethnic Leadership in America*, ed. J. Higham (Baltimore: Johns Hopkins University Press, 1978).

37. M. Begay Jr., "Leading By Choice, Not Chance: Leadership Education for Native Chief Executives of American Indian Nations," unpublished EdD diss., Graduate School of Education, Harvard University, Cambridge, MA, 1997.

38. M. Boldt, *Surviving as Indians: The Challenge of Self-Government* (Toronto: University of Toronto Press, 1993); T. Alfred, *Peace, Power, Righteousness: An Indigenous Manifesto* (Toronto: Oxford University Press, 1999); G. R. Alfred, *Heeding the Voices of Our Ancestors: Kahnawake Mohawk Politics and the Rise of Native Nationalism* (Toronto: Oxford University Press, 1995).

39. Boldt, *Surviving as Indians*.

40. Alfred, *Peace, Power, Righteousness*; Alfred, *Heeding the Voices of Our Ancestors*.

41. For example, see C. Voyageur and B. Calliou, "Various Shades of Red: Diversity within Canada's Indigenous Community," *London Journal of Canadian Studies* 16 (2000–2001): 103.

42. See citations in notes 32 to 36. It must also be noted that these characteristics may be illustrated by other leaders worldwide. My point is that the following characteristics/competencies can be extrapolated from the literature on indigenous leaders.

43. See footnote 44 and the text accompanying it.

44. See S. Cornell and J. P. Kalt, "Sovereignty and Nation-Building: The Development Challenge in Indian Country Today," *American Indian Culture and Research Journal* 22 (1998): 187; S. Cornell and J. P. Kalt, "Pathways from Poverty: Economic Development and Institution-Building on American Indian Reservations," *American Indian Culture and Research Journal* 14 (1990): 89; J. P. Kalt, "Sovereignty and Economic Development on American

Indian Reservations: Lessons from the United States," in Royal Commission on Aboriginal Peoples, *Sharing the Harvest: The Road to Self-Reliance—Report of the National Round Table on Aboriginal Economic Development and Resources* (Ottawa: Minister of Supply and Services and Canada Communication Group, 1993), 35; S. Cornell and J. P. Kalt, "Reloading the Dice: Improving the Chances for Economic Development on American Indian Reservations," in *What Can Tribes Do? Strategies and Institutions in American Indian Economic Development*, ed. S. Cornell and J. P. Kalt (Los Angeles: American Indian Studies Centre, University of California, Los Angeles, 1992); S. Cornell and J. P. Kalt, "Where Does Economic Development Really Come From? Constitutional Rule among the Contemporary Sioux and Apache," *Economic Inquiry* 33 (1995): 402. See also the Banff Centre, "Best Practices in Aboriginal Business and Economic Development," Binder of Materials (Banff, AB: Banff Centre, 2001).

45. For example, Stephen Cornell's presentation entitled "Overview of Research Findings of the Harvard Project/Native Nations Institute in Treaty Eight Alberta" at the Banff Centre, Aboriginal Leadership and Management Development program, "Best Practices in Aboriginal Business and Economic Development," January 26, 2004.

46. Banff Centre, "Best Practices in Aboriginal Business," 2.6.

47. Banff Centre, "Best Practices in Aboriginal Business," 2.7.

48. Banff Centre, "Best Practices in Aboriginal Business," 2.8.

49. Banff Centre, "Best Practices in Aboriginal Business," 2.9.

50. See Calliou and Voyageur, note 2, at p. 120 and the citations at note 9.

51. See Calliou and Voyageur, note 2, at p. 120 and the citations at note 9.

52. See Calliou and Voyageur, note 2, at p. 120 and the citations at note 9.

53. Banff Centre, "Best Practices in Aboriginal Business," 2.20.

54. Banff Centre, "Best Practices in Aboriginal Business," 2.23.

55. Kalt, "Sovereignty and Economic Development," 39.

56. Kalt, "Sovereignty and Economic Development," 38.

57. Banff Centre, "Best Practices in Aboriginal Business," 2.15.

58. Cornell and Kalt, "Sovereignty and Nation-Building," 196.

59. Kalt, "Sovereignty and Economic Development," 43.

60. Kalt, "Sovereignty and Economic Development," 45.

61. S. Cornell, "Keys to Nation Building in Indian Country," in *Best Practices in Aboriginal Business and Economic Development—A Report of the Symposium Proceedings September 8–11, 1999*, ed. M. Willox (Banff: Banff Centre, 2000), 12.

62. Kalt, "Sovereignty and Economic Development," 44.

63. Kalt, "Sovereignty and Economic Development," 47.

64. Cornell, "Keys to Nation Building in Indian Country," 13.

65. Banff Centre, "Best Practices in Aboriginal Business," 2.19.

66. Banff Centre, "Best Practices in Aboriginal Business," 2.21.

67. Alberta Public Service Managers, *Core Competencies for Alberta Public Service Managers* (Edmonton: Alberta Public Service Managers, 1995).

68. S. R. Parry, "The Quest for Competencies," *Training* (July 1996): 48.

69. The Banff Centre's Leadership Development division utilizes competency maps/charts and uses this definition and explanation for competencies.

70. A. D. Lucia and R. Lepsinger, *The Art and Science of Competency Models: Pinpointing Critical Success Factors in Organizations* (San Francisco: Jossey-Bass Pfeiffer, 1999). For a sampling of the literature on competencies, see L. M. Spencer and S. M. Spencer, *Competence at Work: Models for Superior Performance* (New York: Wiley, 1993); D. Dubois, *Competency-Based Performance Improvement: A Strategy for Organizational Change* (Amherst, MA: HRD Press, 1993); R. S. Mansfield, "Building Competency Models: Approaches for HR Professionals," *Human Resources Management* 35 (1996): 7; J. L. Eubanks, J. B. Marshall, and M. P. O'Driscoll, "A Competency Model for OD Practitioners," *Training & Development Journal* (November 1990): 85; C. P. O'Neill, "Competencies: A Powerful Tool for Driving Business Results," *Human Resource Professional* (November–December 1996): 22.

71. P. R. Scholtes, *The Leader's Handbook: Making Things Happen, Getting Things Done* (New York: McGraw-Hill, 1998), 21.

72. Robert Breaker, director of the Aboriginal Leadership and Management Program, and Brian Calliou, associate director of the Aboriginal Leadership and Management Program at the Banff Centre, carried out indigenous leadership research and held a number of focus groups with indigenous leaders in Canada and the United States from 1999 to 2001. The research was used in the development of competency maps/charts as part of assessment tools for participants in the courses to focus on a few competencies they wished to improve upon.

73. Literature on strategic planning and analysis is quite extensive. A sampling includes S. Cornell, *Strategic Analysis: A Practical Tool for Building Indian Nations*, Harvard Project Report Series, no. 98-10 (Cambridge, MA: John F. Kennedy School of Government, Harvard University, 1998); J. S. Anderson and D. H. Smith, "Managing Tribal Assets: Developing Long-Term Strategic Plans," *American Indian Culture and Research Journal* 22 (1998): 139; G. Steiner, *Strategic Planning: What Every Manager Must Know* (New York: Free Press, 1979); C. W. L. Hill and G. R. Jones, *Strategic Management: An Integrated Approach*, 4th ed. (Boston: Houghton Mifflin, 1998); F. W. Gluck, S. P. Kaufman, and A. S. Walleck, "Strategic Management for Competitive Advantage," *Harvard Business Review* (July–August 1980): 154.

74. See notes 32 to 36 above.

75. See notes 37 and 38 above.

76. For example, see B. Calliou, "Methodology for Recording Oral Histories in the Aboriginal Community," *Native Studies Review* 15, no. 1 (2003): 73; R. Kugel, "Utilizing Oral Traditions: Some Concerns Raised by Recent Ojibwe Studies, A Review Essay," *American Indian Culture and Research Journal* 7, no. 3 (1983): 65; W. Stevenson, "Narrative Wisps of the Ochekwi Sipi Past: A Journey of Recovering Collective Memories," *Oral History Forum* 19–20 (1999–2000): 113.

77. See, for example, W. R. Lassey and R. R. Fernandez, "Leadership and Community Development," in *Leadership and Social Change*, 2nd ed., ed. W. R. Lassey and R. R. Fernandez (San Diego: University Associates, 1976), 345; W. R. Lassey and A. S. Williams, *Leadership for Community Development: Analysis of an Indian Reservation Area* (Bozeman: Center for Planning and Development, Montana State University, 1971); M. A. Begay Jr., *Designing Native American Management and Leadership Training: Past Efforts, Present Endeavors, and Future Options*, Harvard Project Report Series No. 91-3 (Cambridge, MA: John F. Kennedy School of

Government, Harvard University, 1991); also see more generally J. Hassin and R. S. Young, "Self-Sufficiency, Personal Empowerment, and Community Revitalization: The Impact of a Leadership Program on American Indians in the Southwest," *American Indian Culture and Research Journal* 23 (1999): 265; and S. Mailick and S. A. Stumpf, *Learning Theory in the Practice of Management Development: Evolution and Applications* (Westport, CT: Quorum Books, 1998).

78. For discussion on viewing organizations as living organisms part of a larger web of life, see M. J. Wheatley, *Leadership and the New Science: Discovering Order in a Chaotic World* (San Francisco: Berrett-Koehler, 1999); S. Hegelsen, *Web of Inclusion: A New Architecture for Building Great Organizations* (New York: Currency/Doubleday, 1995); or see more generally F. Capra, *The Web of Life: A New Scientific Understanding of Living Systems* (New York: Anchor, 1996). For discussions of bringing spirituality, meaning, and creativity into the workplace, see K. Cashman (1999) "Pathway Six: Balance Mastery: Leading by Centering Our Life," in *Leadership from the Inside Out: Becoming a Leader for Life*, ed. K. Cashman (Provo, UT: Executive Excellence, 1999), 153; L. Bolman and T. E. Deal, *Leading with Soul: An Uncommon Journey of Spirit* (San Francisco: Jossey-Bass, 1994); B. DeFoore and J. Renech, eds., *The New Bottom Line: Bringing Heart and Soul to Business* (San Francisco: New Leaders Press, 1996); C. Handy, *The Hungry Spirit: Beyond Capitalism—The Quest for Purpose in the Modern World* (New York: Broadway, 1999); R. J. Leider, *The Power of Purpose: Creating Meaning in Your Life and Work* (San Francisco: Berrett-Koehler, 1997); D. White, *The Heart Aroused: Poetry and the Preservation of Soul in Corporate America* (New York: Doubleday, 1994).

79. Statistics Canada 2003, *2001 Census: Analysis Series. Aboriginal Peoples of Canada: A Demographic Profile*, Catalogue Number 96F0030XIE2002007.

80. C. Voyageur, "Keynote Address," *Statistics Canada Aboriginal Strategies Conference*, October 6–9, 2003, Edmonton, Alberta, Canada.

81. Voyageur, "Keynote Address."

Doing Our Share: Employment and Entrepreneurship in Canada's Aboriginal Community

CORA VOYAGEUR

ALTHOUGH ABORIGINAL PEOPLES in Canada remain subject to regulations and policies that can hinder their participation in the Canadian economy, they still actively pursue economic ventures, as they have since European contact. Some groups, like the Canadian Alliance Party[1] and the Canadian Taxpayers Federation, believe that aboriginal people merely draw from the Canadian economy and taxpayers and give nothing in return. This view has resulted in a history of animosity between the Canadian Alliance Party and aboriginal people. To further strain any hopes of a relationship between the two, some Reform Party/Canadian Alliance politicians have made outrageous claims. For example, a Reform MP, Herb Grubel, drew the ire of First Nations across Canada when he said that First Nations people living on reserves "live like spoiled children on a tropical island off the earnings of a rich uncle."[2] Even the party leader antagonizes the Indians. In 2000, then-leader Stockwell Day and his wife, Valorie, had to be ushered out the back door at a political rally when Indian protestors interrupted his speech. Indians were angry about the party's "Aboriginal Policy," which included a proposal for on-reserve Indians to pay "their share" of provincial and federal taxes.[3] One newspaper stated that Stockwell Day encouraged and joined the audience in chanting "We will win, we will win" in response to the Indians' drumming.[4]

Further, the *Benoit*[5] case has kept the Canadian Taxpayers Federation busy trying to ensure that what they call "race-based" taxation (which they say contravenes the Canadian Charter of Rights and Freedoms) does not become part of the Canadian legal landscape.[6] They do not believe the Canadian government should fulfill its promises of tax-free status to Indians as indicated by the treaty commissioners representing the crown at the 1899 signing of Treaty 8. These views are supported by publications like *The Report*[7] that continue to print articles about how the aboriginal people are costing the Canadian taxpayers' money. *The Report* quotes Indian Affairs specialist for the Canadian Taxpayers Federation, Richard Truscott, as saying "'the impact of this [*Benoit*] will not be confined to Treaty 8.' . . . 'Native from other treaties can march into court with hand-picked elders and claim they were promised exemptions.'"[8] Another example from the same issue complains that taxpayers have no say in a land-claim settlement between the government and an Alberta band.[9] Despite all the grumbling, little or no recognition is given to the fact that most aboriginal people (and more First Nations people[10] than not) are also taxpayers. In fact, 55 percent of Canada's First Nations labor force lives off reserve, which means they are potential taxpayers. In addition, if aboriginal people of Canada who do pay taxes—the off-reserve status Indians, the non-status Indians, the Metis, and the Inuit—were compared with those who do not pay taxes (those status Indians who live and work on the reserve or who work for a company with a head office located on a reserve), we find that a very small proportion of aboriginal people have tax-exempt status.[11]

Although this negative sentiment is prevalent among some circles, little is mentioned in these discussions about the source of much of Canada's wealth—its natural resources. These natural resources come from the land surrendered by the Indians under treaty with the crown. Further to this point, many natural resources are actually extracted from Indian land. A 1990 Indian and Northern Affairs Canada inventory[12] states that approximately 30 percent of Canada's 2,267 Indian reserves have either good or moderate resource extraction potential. In fact, of the 564 permits, leases, and agreements issued by Indian Affairs and Northern Development, 406 (72 percent) were issued to the private sector, 79 (14 percent) were given to provincial governments, and 34 (6 percent) were allotted to municipalities.[13] Clearly, someone is getting rich from Indian land! For example, Syncrude Canada Ltd., which operates its oil sands plant on the traditional land of the Fort McKay First Nation in northeastern Alberta, reported pro forma revenues of $3.4 billion and $1.9 billion in 2001.[14]

Despite such negative stereotypes, I argue that Canada's aboriginal population contributes to the Canadian economy through employment and entrepreneurship. Aboriginal people have taken many initiatives to improve their lives and participate in the Canadian economy, sometimes against great adversity. I highlight these initiatives by profiling aboriginal employment, the growth of entrepreneurship in the aboriginal community, and characteristics of the burgeoning aboriginal tourism. However, I will begin by setting out a brief definition and profile of the aboriginal peoples of Canada.

Who Are Canada's Aboriginal People?

Indigenous peoples of Canada are collectively known as aboriginal peoples. They are the descendants of the first inhabitants of North America who lived within the boundaries of Canada. They have eleven language families and speak fifty-three different languages.[15] Within these linguistic categories are many diverse cultures with distinctive identities with varying traditions and cultures. Although there are many commonalties, there are also many differences. These differences can be geographical, linguistic, legal, cultural, and social. For example, First Nations people in Canada (called "Indian" in the Canadian Constitution) are affiliated with 633 Indian bands and reside on more than 2,200 reserves across Canada.[16]

An Indian and Northern Affairs Canada (INAC) report states that 4.4 percent of the Canadian population has aboriginal ancestry.[17] Aboriginal people in Canada are made up of discreet cultural groups, which include Metis, Inuit, non-status Indians, and status Indians. Status Indians are also known as First Nations (also called Indians).[18] Proportionally, the First Nations (Indian) group is the largest of the groups that fall under the aboriginal umbrella. They number 624,200[19] (47.0 percent), while there are 205,800 Metis[20] (16 percent); 57,000 Inuit[21] (4 percent), and 422,600 non-status Indians (33 percent) for a grand total of 1,309,600 aboriginal individuals in Canada.[22]

Various First Nations cultures can be found within any city, province, or territory in Canada. For example, my province, Alberta, has forty-six separate Indian bands among the First Nations population.[23] In Alberta you will find the Blackfoot, Blood, Stoney, Cree, Dene, Saulteaux, and Beaver tribes.[24] Each has its own unique culture and language. For example, the Stoney language is different from the Cree language. Members of linguistic groups cannot understand another group's mother tongue. It seems ironic, but English is the universal language in Canada's aboriginal community.

There has been a rapid increase in the number of aboriginal people in Canada due to changes in legislation such as Bill C-31[25] passed in 1985; a higher fertility rate in the aboriginal community than the non-aboriginal community; and because many people are reclaiming their aboriginal ancestry.[26] The Royal Commission on Aboriginal Peoples (RCAP) forecasts that the aboriginal people's population growth would increase by 52 percent compared to 22 percent for non-aboriginal peoples.[27]

They are a young population. More than half of Canada's aboriginal population is under the age of twenty-five years.[28] Currently, the average age of an aboriginal person in Canada is twenty-five years, making them approximately ten years younger than the average non-aboriginal Canadian.[29] Therefore, Canada's aboriginal population is young and growing rapidly, which means that they will be a growing proportion of Canadian society, the workforce, and the taxpayers who support Canada's social safety net, and the consuming public in the future.

Economic Participation and Canada's Aboriginal Community

Canada's aboriginal peoples had an active trading economy prior to the arrival of Europeans. The archeological record shows extensive trading networks throughout North America. Aboriginal gravesites located in southern Ontario and southern Quebec dating from 6000 BCE contained conch shells from the Gulf of Mexico, copper items from west of Lake Superior, and ground slate points from the Maritimes.[30] These items could only have changed hands through trading since they were not indigenous to the area where they were found. After European contact, aboriginal peoples continued to make valuable contributions to the country's economic development. Scholars in a variety of academic disciplines have recently begun researching this little-known fact. Historian Arthur Ray documented the central role played by aboriginal people as trappers and traders in the fur trade from the mid 1700s. To begin with, they played an enormous role in European explorations and in the fur trade.[31] Geographer Frank Tough found that in northern Manitoba, in the post-treaty period, many aboriginals voluntarily left the fur trade to pursue wage labor in lumbering and fishing, and they geared their diversified economy to seasonal changes.[32] Economist Peter Douglas Elias found that aboriginal peoples' participation in the wage labor market occurred as early as the mid-nineteenth century.[33] He further noted that wage labor was only one component of a complex regional economy, which included market and domestic production components.[34]

Rolf Knight's study *Indians at Work* indicates that aboriginal peoples in British Columbia and elsewhere in Canada have a long history as both wageworkers and independent producers who quickly adjusted to the industrial world.[35] Knight argues that the farming, trapping, and other methods of independent production undertaken by aboriginal peoples were an integral part of the Canadian capitalist economy.[36]

Frank Tough found that aboriginal people successfully integrated into the capitalist labor economy in northern Manitoba despite government policies that hampered their initiatives.[37] Local Indians were active participants in the logging and commercial industries. Indian agents and missionaries commented on the prosperity displayed by the Indians, saying that they were able to purchase sewing machines, buggies, threshing machines, and other consumer goods with their earnings.[38]

Aboriginal people on reserves adapted quickly to farming and many of them became successful, according to Sarah Carter. Eventually, however, the government sabotaged successful aboriginal farming operations by imposing strict regulations prohibiting the commercial sale of the agricultural products from reserves. Government policy also prohibited reserve farmers from using mechanized farming equipment, which further impeded their farming attempts.[39]

In more contemporary times, Stuart Jamieson found west-coast Indians were actively involved in the trade union movement in the 1950s. Although the Indians worked in a variety of industries including fishing, logging, saw milling, farming, trapping, longshoring, railway maintenance, and construction, these industries tended to be of a seasonal nature.[40] Their employment was intermittent only because of the seasonal nature of the industry. Jamieson further stated that union membership gave aboriginal workers equal footing with other workers.[41]

The Royal Commission on Aboriginal Peoples in its comprehensive study of native economic development, found that aboriginal peoples had long coped with social and economic changes in Canada as the land became increasingly settled and industrialization began.[42] The commissioners found that aboriginal people participated in many new industries even in the early twentieth century, finding employment in farm labor, house construction, building municipal infrastructures, road construction, and railroad construction. Native people also worked at logging, milling, mining, shipping, and longshoring. They pursued their own ventures in farming, freighting, and arts and crafts production. Throughout this adaptation to the capitalist economy, most aboriginals continued traditional pursuits and independent production year round. There was never an indication that these workers viewed themselves as being any less aboriginal because they were part of the wage labor force.

The Aboriginal Workforce in Canada

Today, aboriginal workers make up 3.4 percent of the Canadian workforce.[43] Drawing on Statistics Canada data for the 1996 census of Canada, table 6.1 shows the labor participation rates of aboriginal people in Canada in 1999. Statistics Canada data shows that the aboriginal people's labor participation rate in the Canadian labor force is 63 percent; a mere 3 percentage points lower than the non-aboriginal labor participation rate, which sits at 66 percent.[44] However, the Canadian unemployment rate is twice as high for the aboriginal workforce than the non-aboriginal workforce. These high unemployment rates are due to the lack of jobs on reserves—but this situation is improving.

The data show that aboriginal people are participating in the Canada labor force, although at lower rates in some areas. As a rule, labor force participation is

Table 6.1. Labor Force Characteristics Geographic Region, by Aboriginality, Number, Participation Rate and Unemployment Rates, 1996

Geographic Region	Aboriginal Labor Force			Non-Aboriginal Labor Force		
	Number	Participation Rate	Unemployment Rate	Number	Participation Rate	Unemployment Rate
Canada	486.515	63	20	14.326.185	66	10
Newfoundland	11.465	58	33	235.595	56	25
Prince Edward Island	1.210	76	24	69.605	68	14
Nova Scotia	11.685	62	20	427.285	61	13
New Brunswick	8.235	66	26	355.865	62	15
Quebec	69.500	64	19	3.466.700	62	12
Ontario	118.830	66	17	5.468.145	66	9
Manitoba	52.870	57	23	514.955	68	6
Saskatchewan	38.195	53	24	465.305	69	6
Alberta	68.830	66	17	1.418.150	73	7
B. Columbia	88.240	66	21	1.872.420	66	9
Yukon	3.450	73	24	15.480	83	8
Northwest Territories	7.790	64	23	13.635	88	5
Nunavut	7.205	59	21	3.030	94	3

Source: Aboriginal Labor Force Characteristics from the 1996 Census. Ottawa: Indian and Northern Affairs Canada. 2000. Catalogue Number. R21152000. Reproduced with the permission of the Minister of Public Works and Government Services, 2004.

lower on reserve than off reserve for First Nations people. However, other aboriginal groups' equal (as is the case with the Metis) and sometimes exceed non-aboriginals' labor force participation, as with the Inuit.[45]

Table 6.2 compares labor force participation and unemployment rates for geographic areas by aboriginality. Comparisons are drawn between Canadian labor participation rates for aboriginal (63 percent) and non-aboriginal (66 percent) labor forces. The participation rate data shows that the aboriginal labor force involvement ranges from 13 percentage points above the Canadian aboriginal average in Prince Edward Island (PEI) to 10 percentage points below the Canadian aboriginal average in Saskatchewan, for a range of 23 percentage points. The range for the non-aboriginal labor participation rate is even higher. Participation rate data for the non-aboriginal labor force shows a high of 28 percentage points above the Canadian non-aboriginal average in Nunavut to a low of 10 percentage points below the Canadian non-aboriginal average in Newfoundland, for a range of 38 percentage points. In Prince Edward Island the aboriginal labor force participation is not only 13 percentage points higher than the Canadian aboriginal participation rate but 8 percentage points higher than PEI's non-aboriginal labor force participation rate and 10 percentage points higher than the Canadian labor force participation rate.

Table 6.2. Percentage Point Comparisons of Labor Force Participation and Unemployment Rates by Geographic Region and Aboriginality

Geographic Region	Labor Force Participation Rate+/−		Labor Force Unemployment Rate +/−	
	Aboriginal	Non-Aboriginal	Aboriginal	Non-Aboriginal
Canada	63	66	20	10
Newfoundland	58(−5)	56(−10)	33(1.65)	25(2.5)
Prince Edward Island	76(+13)	68(+2)	24(1.2)	14(1.4)
Nova Scotia	62(−1)	61(−5)	20(0)	13(1.3)
New Brunswick	66(+3)	62(−4)	26(1.3)	15(1.5)
Quebec	64(+1)	62(−4)	19(0.95)	12(1.2)
Ontario	66(+3)	66(0)	17(0.85)	9(0.9)
Manitoba	57(−6)	68(+2)	23(1.15)	6(0.6)
Saskatchewan	53(−10)	69(+3)	24(1.2)	6(0.6)
Alberta	66(+3)	73(+7)	17(0.85)	7(0.7)
B. Columbia	66(+3)	66(0)	21(1.05)	9(0.9)
Yukon	73(+10)	83(+17)	24(1.2)	8(0.8)
Northwest Territories	64(+1)	88(+22)	23(1.15)	5(0.5)
Nunavut	59(−4)	94(+28)	21(1.05)	3(0.3)

Source: Aboriginal Labor Force Characteristics from the 1996 Census. Ottawa: Indian and Northern Affairs Canada. 2000. Catalogue Number. R21152000. Reproduced with the permission of the Minister of Public Works and Government Services, 2004.

When comparing labor force participation rate for the aboriginals (63 percent) and non-aboriginal (66 percent) labor forces, we find that a slight majority of the provinces (seven of thirteen, or 54 percent) had either higher or equal labor force participation rates for aboriginals than non-aboriginals.[46]

In only three provinces/territories (Manitoba, Saskatchewan, and Nunavut) does the non-aboriginal labor force participation rate outstrip the aboriginal. In these situations, the provincial/territorial non-aboriginal labor force participation rate is higher than the national non-aboriginal average of 66 percent; while the aboriginal labor force participation rate is lower than the aboriginal labor force participation rate of 63 percent. Another comparison shows the provincial/territorial aboriginal labor force participation rate is at least equal to, or higher than, the national non-aboriginal average of 66 percent in Prince Edward Island, New Brunswick, Quebec, Ontario, and British Columbia. Where both the aboriginal and non-aboriginal labor force participation rates are below the national labor force participation rates, the aboriginal labor force participation deficit is smaller. For example, in Nova Scotia the aboriginal labor force participation rate is 1 percentage point below the Canadian aboriginal average, while the non-aboriginal labor force participation rate is 5 percentage points lower. Further, Newfoundland's non-aboriginal labor force participation rate deficit is twice (10 percent) that of the aboriginal labor force deficit, which stands at 5 percentage points lower. Although higher than the Canadian aboriginal labor force, participation rates in Alberta, Yukon, and the Northwest Territories were still lower than the non-aboriginal labor force participation rates in those locations. Alberta's labor participation rates were 66 percent for aboriginals compared to 73 percent non-aboriginals, while Yukon's labor participation rates were 73 percent for aboriginals compared to 83 percent non-aboriginal, and the Northwest Territories' labor participation rates were 64 percent aboriginal compared to 88 percent for non-aboriginals.

Comparing aboriginal and non-aboriginal unemployment rates across Canada shows the aboriginal unemployment rate to be twice that of the non-aboriginal population. The most pronounced gap occurs in Nunavut were the unemployment rate is seven times higher among the aboriginals at 21 percent than for the non-aboriginals whose unemployment rate sits at 3 percent. This indicates "outsiders" are hired into this region rather than locals.[47] Whenever possible, hiring locals is a smart and economical strategy for employers. Not only are the locals acclimatized to the environment but they also have existing housing, familial ties, support networks, and for the most part, want to remain in the region. These factors are not always considered when employees are brought in from outside the region. After all, locals live in the area and should have an opportunity to earn a living there.

All provinces/territories have aboriginal unemployment rates at least as high as the Canadian aboriginal unemployment rate of 20 percent with the exceptions of Quebec (0.95 percent), Ontario (0.85 percent), and Alberta (0.85 percent). Although below the aboriginal labor force unemployment rate, Quebec, Ontario, and Alberta's aboriginal unemployment is still much higher than the Canadian non-aboriginal labor force unemployment rate, which sits at 10 percent.

There is a growing urban aboriginal population with more than half First Nations people now living off-reserve. Aboriginals can be found working in virtually all facets of the economy but are concentrated in government services (15.2 percent), wholesale and retail trade (14.6 percent), manufacturing (10.3), and accommodation and food/beverage (9.4 percent).[48] There are a number of possible explanations for aboriginal workers choosing (or being chosen by) the above-mentioned industries. If these employers are federally regulated by the Canadian government and have more than 100 employees then they are compelled under the guidelines of the Employment Equity Act[49] to employ aboriginals commensurate with their representation in the Canadian population. For example, if aboriginal people are 4.4 percent of the Canadian population, then companies must strive to have 4.4 percent of their workforce be aboriginal. These industries may be located close to reserves or communities with high aboriginal populations and therefore have a larger aboriginal workforce. Additionally, these industries may require lower educational credentials for their employees and thus matches the lower educational attainment levels of aboriginal people.[50] Aboriginal employees generally work for others but a growing number are now working for themselves.

Aboriginal Self-Employment in Canada

The past two decades has seen tremendous growth in self-employment in Canadian society and this phenomenon has spilled over into the aboriginal community. Aboriginal Business Canada states that there are now about 20,000 businesses owned and operated by aboriginal people in Canada.[51] Industry Canada reports that only a small percentage of aboriginal businesses (15 percent) received government grants or contributions over the past five years.[52] They further state that aboriginal businesses use more equity than debt to begin their ventures.[53] Although aboriginals business is dispersed in virtually every sector of the economy, more than three-quarters of aboriginal businesses fall under four categories: business and personal service (25 percent), retail/wholesale (19 percent), primary natural resources (17 percent), and construction (15 percent).[54]

Based on Statistics Canada data from the 1996 Census of Canada, figure 6.1 shows the average compounded growth of aboriginal self-employment in twelve industrial sectors between 1981 and 1996. The data shows self-employment growth in all industrial sectors.

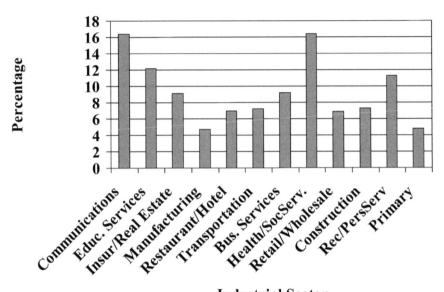

Industrial Sector

Figure 6.1.   Self-Employed Aboriginal Peoples' Compounded Average Growth by Percentage and Industrial Sector, Canada 1981–1996.

The most aboriginal self-employment compounded annual growth was recorded in communications (16.4 percent), manufacturing (16.4 percent), education services (12.2 percent), recreation/personal (11.3 percent), business services (9.2 percent), and insurance/real estate (9.1 percent). Aboriginal entrepreneurs are entering the knowledge industry (such as computer services) and management consulting and professional services industry (such as business-related services, insurance brokerage, and real estate sales). This may a result of the higher level of education credentials obtained by members of the aboriginal community over the past two decades. They are converting this knowledge into employment opportunities that help them serve both the aboriginal and non-aboriginal market.

The data show that aboriginal entrepreneurship is increasing at a greater rate—2.5 times than that of the non-aboriginal community. An Aboriginal Business Canada report states that between 1981 and 1996, self-employment increased by 170 percent for aboriginals and 65 percent for non-aboriginals.[55] However, even with this increase, aboriginals are still less likely to own their own business than non-aboriginals.

Self-employed aboriginal people are found in all parts of Canada, including urban, rural, and in remote locations. The vast majority of aboriginal businesses serve local markets. Industry Canada states that local markets make up 74 percent of aboriginal business.[56] Entrepreneurship in remote locations provides jobs and job-creation opportunities. There are more self-employed aboriginals in British Columbia, Alberta, and Ontario than other areas of Canada. Aboriginal entrepreneurship has created almost 49,000 jobs between 1981 and 1996 according to an Aboriginal Business Canada report.[57]

Métis people have the highest rate of aboriginal entrepreneurs. Aboriginal companies are already trading domestically and abroad in areas such as forest products, knowledge-based services, fine arts, traditional crafts, sculpture, high fashion, technology and tourism.[58]

Figure 6.2 shows the growth in aboriginal self-employment between 1981 and 1996. Between 1981 and 1996, self-employment increased among all aboriginal groups, and especially among youth and among women. The data shows that aboriginal youth are 2.5 times as likely to be self-employed than non-aboriginal youth.[59]

Entrepreneurial growth for aboriginal women was 2.5 times higher than non-aboriginal women.[60] Although self-employed individuals earn less than self-employed non-aboriginals, they still earn more than the average aboriginal income. In 1995, the average aboriginal income was $17,382 while the average self-employed aboriginal person earned $18,947.

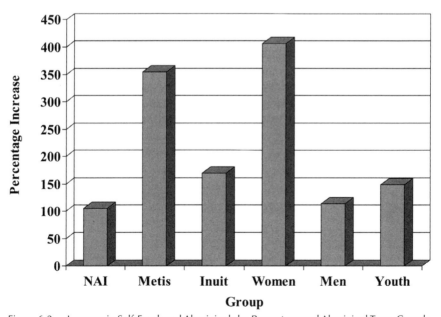

Figure 6.2.   Increase in Self-Employed Aboriginals by Percentage and Aboriginal Type, Canada 1981–1996.

For the most part, aboriginal businesses parallel non-aboriginal businesses in that they are small businesses. A larger proportion of aboriginal businesses employ others (46 percent) than non-aboriginal businesses (40 percent).[61] Community-owned or tribal-owned enterprises are generally larger and employ an average of ten employees.[62]

With this growth in aboriginal business, there is a parallel growth in pride and identity of aboriginal cultures, languages, and traditions taught in schools and universities. These businesses contribute to the Canadian economy. Any off-reserve work or transactions result in taxes being paid. One sector of the economy, the aboriginal tourism industry, is booming. This industry marries aboriginal culture with the economy.

Tourism

In March 1998, Aboriginal Tourism Team Canada (ATTC) was launched to promote aboriginal tourism to the world. Aboriginal tourism is defined by ATTC as all tourism businesses owned or operated by First Nations, Métis, or Inuit people.[63] Aboriginal tourism businesses include transportation/travel tours (air, bus tours, car rentals); hospitality (hotel, motels, B&Bs); culture and heritage (events, cultural sites, experiences, and interpretations); adventure tourism (fishing, wildlife viewing, hunting); and arts and crafts (artists, artisans, and craftspeople, dance, theater, and music).[64]

ATTC believes a successful aboriginal tourism business benefits both the aboriginal and the non-aboriginal community by:

- Sharing aboriginal culture with the rest of the world
- Developing employees front-line and management skills
- Helping dispel negative and stereotypical images of aboriginal people
- Helping employees gain transferable skills
- Allowing new partnerships with non-aboriginal neighbors and businesses.[65]

Heritage tourism is defined as those activities, attractions, facilities, networks, and services that are based upon heritage or cultural elements.[66] Aboriginal cultural products are said to bring tourism dollars to Canada. Tourists are drawn to aboriginal people themselves, their communities, and their cultural traditions. A representative of Canadian National Aboriginal Tourism Association (CNATA) believes that aboriginal tourism is a major growth area. He says, "A resurgence of interest in Native cultures, especially in the United States and parts of Europe, has led to the development of hundreds of companies" and that "Tourists still want feathers and beads rather than the realities of Indian life."[67] Thus, aboriginal groups can celebrate and share their traditions,[68] dances, costumes, foods, stories, and songs with an eager, paying public. According to Alberta Tourism, aboriginal-themed tourist sites are in significant demand.[69] Alberta has 112 aboriginal-themed tourist sites that are expected to host more than 12 million tourists over the next two years, and who are expected to spend $12.880 billion dollars.[70] Currently, about one-third of Alberta's tourist industry earnings derive from heritage tourism, of which aboriginal sites are a large part.[71]

Aboriginal tourism creates both jobs and revenue—both of which benefit the Canadian economy. Aboriginal tourism firms currently have revenues of $270 million annually and are predicted to reach $1 billion. According to Aboriginal Tourism Team Canada, aboriginal tourism employed 14,000 people in 1999.[72]

Aboriginal tourism has proven itself valuable to both the Canadian and the Alberta economies. Aboriginal tourism is important because it brings much-needed jobs and economic development to rural and reserve areas. People can live and work at home. They do not have to move away from their communities, their families, and their support networks to find employment.

Conclusion

Aboriginal people in Canada are doing "their share" to contribute to the Canadian economy. As employees and entrepreneurs, they work to sustain the high standard of living enjoyed by Canadians. Although the labor participation rate is lower for First Nations people than for non-aboriginals, these rates are predicted to increase with increased educational attainment and economic ventures located in rural and reserve regions. Overall, labor employment rates for the Métis and Inuit either equal or exceed non-aboriginal rates. This labor employment rate may be due to the non-reserve environments in which these two aboriginal groups live.[73]

Aboriginal business and entrepreneurship is flourishing in Canada. There are more than 20,000 aboriginal businesses in virtually every aspect of the Canadian economy. In the past fifteen years, they have created about 49,000 new jobs—not only for aboriginals but for the non-aboriginal community.

Aboriginal tourism is big business. It is currently a quarter-billion-dollar in-dustry and is expected to increase threefold. It offers an employment and an op-portunity for aboriginal people to promote culture while participating in economic growth and community development. They have an opportunity to earn a living for themselves and their families. It also promotes partnerships between aboriginals and neighboring businesses and communities. As they all know, relations between the aboriginal communities and their neighbors have not always been positive.

Although there were legislated restrictions on cultural practices and an assault on aboriginal language and tradition, the culture has survived. This culture now serves as the basis for a vast tourism industry.[74]

Since the 1960s, there has been a renewed growth in aboriginal identity and culture.

Aboriginal people and aboriginal culture are not historical relics. Rather, aboriginal peoples are a vital, energetic, and meritorious people. Being aboriginal in Canada today does not mean exclusion from development, the economy, or the cultural fabric of the nation.

A harsh environment has made aboriginal people skilled at adaptation. Joining the wage labor force was simply one more adaptation for aboriginal people in Canada. History shows that aboriginal people of Canada have participated in the country's growth and economy. They have contributed and continue to contribute to Canada's growth and development.

Notes

I would like to thank my research assistant, Sarah Stewart, for her help in gathering materials for this paper. I would also like to thank PhD candidate Sigrid Deutschlander for so generously sharing her research materials with me.

1. The Canadian Alliance Party was created from the remnants of the Reform Party in 2000. Although the Canadian Alliance Party has a new name and a new leader, it still has many of the same party members and many of the same neoconservative ideologies as the Reform Party that includes no "special rights" for aboriginal people.

2. Canadian Press, "Reformer Likens Natives to Overindulged Children," *Calgary Herald*, June 10, 1994, A14.

3. Dan LeMoel, "Alliance Aboriginal Policy Touts Equality," *First Perspective* 9, no. 11 (November 2000): 12.

4. LeMoel, "Alliance Aboriginal Policy."

5. The *Benoit* case deals with taxation of income for an Indian man living and working in the Treaty 8 region of Alberta. Treaty Commissioner David Laird noted that Indians were guaranteed tax exemption in Treaty 8 negotiations. The federal court decision was rendered in March 2002 and has since been appealed.

6. Sheldon Alberts, "Day Cuts Rally Short, Flees Protest: Police Scuffle with Native Demonstrators in Manitoba Trying to Block Leader's Exit," *National Post*, November 18, 2000, A6

7. *The Report* is a western-based publication that espouses right-wing views.

8. Colby Cosh, "Remarkably Long Memories," *Report*, April 17, 2000.

9. Rick Hiebert, "Twice Paid for the Same Land," *Report*, April 2, 2000.

10. First Nations people do not pay taxes if they live *and* work on a reserve or if they work for a company whose head office is on a reserve. All others, including First Nations people who live on the reserve and work off the reserve or who live and work off the reserve, pay taxes—as do all non-status Indians, Metis, and Inuit.

11. There is no definitive number of First Nations people who are tax exempt.

12. This forty-five-volume inventory has 18,000 pages and 10,000 maps. *Indian and Northern Affairs Canada*, Mineral Resource Potential of Indian Reserve Lands: Canada, 1990, available at www.Inac.gc.ca.natres/caada.html.

13. Joyce Green and Cora Voyageur. "Globalization and Development at the Bottom," *Feminists Doing Development: A Practical Critique*, ed. Marilyn Porter and Ellen Judd (New York: Zed Books, 1999), 146

14. Syncrude Canada Ltd., *One Sweet Blend: Sustainability/Annual Report 2002*, at www .syncrude.com/investors/ar02/pdf/SR03_EconomicPerformance.pdf (retrieved May 18, 2004).

15. D. W. Elliot, *Law and Aboriginal People of Canada* (North York, ON: Captus Press, 1992), 11.

16. *Indian and Northern Affairs Canada*, 2002, available at http://esd.inac.gc.ca/fnprofiles/ FNProfiles_Search.asp.

17. *Department of Indian Affairs and Northern Development*, 2002, Fact Sheets: Demographics, available at www.inac.gc.ca/gs/dem_e.html.

18. Some First Nations people insist on being called Indian. Others view the term *Indians* as derogatory and offensive.

19. Undercoverage in the 1996 census was considerably higher among aboriginal people than among other segments of the population due to enumeration not being permitted or was interrupted before it could be completed on seventy-seven (11 percent) Indian reserves and settlements.

20. The Métis are descendants of mixed marriages mainly in the Prairie Provinces and in northwestern Ontario, although the term is often used more broadly to include almost all people of mixed Indian/non-Indian ancestry. Although the Métis have their own distinctive history and culture, non-status Indians have often been described as Métis and vice versa.

21. The Inuit are an aboriginal people in northern Canada who live above the tree line in the Northwest Territories, Northern Quebec, and Labrador. Originally called "Eskimo," the word *Inuit* means "people" in the Inuit language, Inuktitut. They are distinct from "Indians" both legally and culturally. Ernest S. Burch, "The Caribou Inuit," in *Native Peoples: The Canadian Experience*, 2nd ed., ed. R. Bruce Morrison and C. Roderick Wilson (Toronto: McClelland and Stewart, 1995), 115.

22. Indian and Northern Affairs Canada, *Aboriginal Workforce Participation Initiative Employer Toolkit* (Ottawa: Minister of Public Works and Government Services Canada, 1998), 3–11.

23. Indian and Northern Affairs Canada, 2002, http://esd.inac.gc.ca/fnprofiles/ FNProfiles _Search.asp.

24. Hugh Dempsey, *Indian Tribes of Alberta* (Calgary: Glenbow Museum, 1988).

25. Bill C-31 came into effect on April 17, 1985. The Indian Act was deemed to have discriminated on the basis of sex since only Indian women, and not Indian men, lost their Indian status upon marriage to a non-Indian. Bill C-31 was also meant to restore Indian status to those who had been enfranchised for joining military service, joining the priesthood, gaining a university degree, or other reasons.

26. Mary Jane Norris, "Aboriginal Peoples: Demographic and Linguistic Perspectives," *Visions of the Heart: Canadian Aboriginal Issues*, ed. David Long and Olive Patricia Dickason (Toronto: Harcourt Brace, 2000), 176.

27. Royal Commission on Aboriginal People. *Sharing the Harvest: The Road to Self-Reliance*, Report of the Round Table on Aboriginal Economic Development and Resources (Ottawa: Minister of Supply and Services Canada, 1993).

28. Statistics Canada, *Daily*, January 13, 1998.

29. Statistics Canada, *Daily*, January 13, 1998.

30. R. Bruce Morrison and C. Roderick Wilson, *Native Peoples: The Canadian Experience* (Toronto: McClelland and Stewart, 1995).

31. A. J. Ray, *Indians in the Fur Trade: Their Role as Trappers, Hunters, and Middlemen in the Lands Southwest of Hudson's Bay, 1600–1870* (Toronto: University of Toronto Press, 1974). Also see Gerald Friesen, *The Canadian Prairies: A History* (Toronto: University of Toronto Press, 1987) and J. R. Miller, *Skyscrapers Hide the Heavens: A History of Indian-White Relations in Canada* (Toronto: University of Toronto Press, 1989).

32. Frank Tough, "Regional Analysis of Indian Aggregate Income, Northern Manitoba, *Native Studies Review* 12 (1992): 40–66.

33. Peter Douglas Elias, "Wage Labour, Aboriginal Relations, and the Cree of the Churchill River Basin, Saskatchewan," *Native Studies Review* 6 (1990): 43–64.

34. Elias, "Wage Labour."

35. Rolf Knight, *Indians at Work: An Informal History of Native Indian Labour in British Columbia, 1858–1930* (Vancouver: New Star Books, 1996).

36. Knight, *Indians at Work*.

37. Frank Tough, *As Their Natural Resources Fail: Native People and the Economic History of Northern Manitoba, 1870–1930* (Vancouver: University of British Columbia Press, 1996).

38. Tough, *As Their Natural Resources Fail*, 212

39. Sarah Carter, *Lost Harvests: Prairie Indian Reserve Farmers and Government Policy* (Montreal: McGill-Queens University Press, 1990).

40. Stuart Jamieson, "Native Indians and the Trade Union Movement," *Perspectives on the North American Indians*, ed. Mark Nagler (Toronto: McClelland Stewart, 1972), 144.

41. Jamieson, "Native Indians," 155.

42. Royal Commission on Aboriginal People, "Economic Development," *Royal Commission on Aboriginal People* (Ottawa: Minister of Supply and Services Canada, 1996).

43. Indian and Northern Affairs Canada, *Aboriginal Labour Force Characteristics from the 1996 Census* (Ottawa: First Nations and Northern Statistics Corporate Information Branch, 2001), 2. Catalogue No. R21152000.

44. Indian and Northern Affairs Canada, *Aboriginal Labour Force Characteristics*, 2.

45. Indian and Northern Affairs Canada, *Aboriginal Labour Force Characteristics*, 2.

46. These provinces include Newfoundland, Prince Edward Island, Nova Scotia, New Brunswick, Quebec, Ontario, and British Columbia.

47. These "outside" workers may be required to fill positions when local workers lack the skills or training required for the job. However, local people can be trained to replace the "outside" workers in the future.

48. Indian and Northern Affairs Canada, *Aboriginal Labour Force Characteristics*.

49. The Employment Equity Act was legislated by the federal government in 1986 and covers "historically disadvantaged groups" in the labor force. These groups include aboriginals, visible minorities, women, and disabled individuals.

50. The educational attainment level of aboriginal Canadians is increasing but is still lower than that of non-aboriginals.

51. Aboriginal Business Canada, *Success of Aboriginal Business* (Ottawa: Industry Canada, 1998). Catalogue No. C2-301/1988E.

52. David Caldwell, *Aboriginal Business: Characteristics and Strategies for Growth* (Ottawa: Industry Canada, 1998), ii. Catalogue No. C21—25/6-1998.

53. Caldwell, *Aboriginal Business*, 10.

54. Government Assistance at www.ainc-inac.ga.ca/ecdv_e.html.

55. Aboriginal Business Canada, *Aboriginal Entrepreneurs in Canada: Progress and Prospects* (Ottawa: Industry Canada, 2002), L1.

56. Caldwell, *Aboriginal Business*, 8.

57. Aboriginal Business Canada, *Aboriginal Entrepreneurs in Canada*, L6.

58. Aboriginal Business Canada, *Success of Aboriginal Business*.

59. Aboriginal Business Canada, *Aboriginal Entrepreneurs in Canada*, L10.

60. Aboriginal Business Canada, *Aboriginal Entrepreneurs in Canada*, L10.

61. Aboriginal Business Canada, M1.

62. Indian and Northern Affairs Canada, at www.ainc-inac.ga.ca/ecdv_e.html.

63. Aboriginal Tourism Team Canada. 2002. http://www.attc.ca/tourism.htm.

64. Aboriginal Tourism Team Canada. 2002. http://www.attc.ca/tourism.htm.

65. Aboriginal Tourism Team Canada. 2002. http://www.attc.ca/tourism.htm.

66. Alberta Tourism, *Tourism Development Network Bulletin No. 20: Cultural Tourism* (Edmonton: Alberta Tourism, 1990).

67. Alberta Tourism, *Tourism Development.*

68. I expect that only select and more secular traditions would be shared with tourists and that sacred and spiritual practices would not be available for tourist participation. This would limit commercialization of the most important and intrinsic aspects of aboriginal culture.

69. PWC Consulting, *Industry Canada/Aboriginal Business Canada with Support of Alberta Economic Development: Alberta Aboriginal Tourism Product Opportunity Analysis* (Edmonton: Price Waterhouse Coopers, 2002), iv.

70. PWC Consulting, *Industry Canada/Aboriginal Business Canada*, ii.

71. Robert Rock, "Native Tourism: Endangered Species?" *Prairie Forum* (Regina, SK: Canadian Plains Research Institute) 17, no. 2 (1992): 295.

72. Aboriginal Tourism Team Canada, 2002.

73. First Nations people living on reserves have a higher unemployment rate and a lower labor force participation rate than First Nations people living off reserves, non-status Indians, Métis, and Inuit.

74. Care must be taken to ensure that aboriginal traditions are not commercialized to a point that they become caricatures. I do not view ecotourism as a "Disneyland with Indians."

Discussion of Culture and Economics   7

PANEL MEMBERS: BRIAN CALLIOU AND CORA VOYAGEUR;
MODERATOR: JOHN KLOPPENBORG

THE SECOND DISCUSSION took up issues having to do with participation or lack of participation in the wider community: legal, economic, educational, and systemic pathways or impediments. The moderator provided the context:

Kloppenborg: As an undergraduate student in chemistry at the University of Lethbridge, I worked one summer with Alberta Water Resources surveying water quality in southern Alberta. It was the first time I saw the water distribution map for the region, and I was stunned. The reserve was the only part of Alberta that did not have spring water and river water. Suddenly, the enormous economic problems faced by the First Nations people became clearer to me than they had ever been. I also remembered being earlier shocked by the fact that First Nations people in Canada had been prohibited by statute from engaging in mechanized agriculture. Can the panel say a little more about these legal and structural impediments? How might they be overcome?

Voyageur: One legal impediment was the pass system, implemented in 1885, after the Indian Act. Indian agents, known as "reserve baby sitters," were set up on reserves and, in effect, controlled the daily life and the daily running of affairs. They didn't have voting power, but anyone wanting to leave the reservation, even for a few hours, had to go to an agent and tell him their reasons for going and the length of time they planned to be gone. The agent would sit back on his chair and take his time deciding whether or not he would let them off the reserve.

The list of rights the aboriginal people in Canada used not to have is a long one. We did not have universal suffrage, for example, as late as 1960. I was born into a country where I would not be able to vote. It's quite an irony that Canada was seen as a place where people from other countries could go and have religious freedom and opportunities to own land; yet, those rights, and a lot of others, were denied the Indian peoples of Canada. We used not to be allowed, by law, to bring cases against the government. Lawyers were forbidden to represent us in cases against the state. We were segregated from society, put onto reserves, had no freedom of movement. In a very real sense, we were seen and treated as childlike, at best. At worst, we were stereotyped and discriminated against: Indians are poor; Indians are dysfunctional; and even in our modern society, even in the university setting where I work, Indians are assumed not to be meritorious, to have, essentially, very little going for them.

My PhD dissertation was on employment equity and aboriginal people in Canada. I looked at three things: the first was employment equity reports from legislation, published in 1986. Over nine years, I conducted analyses and found that aboriginal people were essentially in job ghettos within the Employment Equity Act. Second, I did a four-week case study of companies that had employment equity/aboriginal-type employment programs to see what was successful and what was unsuccessful in their policies. Third, I interviewed the aboriginal employees themselves about their own experiences in companies that supposedly have fostered "enlightened" environments.

What I found was quite dismal. Aboriginal people, for the most part, are not only ghettoized into certain occupations; they are underemployed, given their credentials. I asked forty aboriginals to compare their educational credentials to those of non-aboriginal people in the same company, doing the same job; and in 70 percent of the cases, the aboriginal person had more or the same education as non-aboriginals in the same job. I then asked the aboriginals to compare their employment experience with the non-aboriginals (I thought perhaps they simply had not been in the job long enough); 73 percent of my respondents said they had more or the same job-related experience as non-aboriginal people who did the same jobs.

Half of those aboriginals interviewed spoke of suffering discrimination on the job. They felt as though they worked in a fish bowl. They were tokens; their credentials were undervalued; they had constantly to prove themselves in what was essentially a chilling work environment. This is structural, systemic discrimination. One work place in northern Alberta, which sees itself as the best thing that ever happened to the Indians, had a restriction on hiring; yet when this company brought its license to operate in the early 1960s, one reason it got the license was a promise to work for the local people. The company also received training money from both provincial and federal governments to support this promise. Well, surprise, surprise, the local people in northeastern Alberta are aboriginal people; and still, after over forty years, there is not one aboriginal manager in this company.

I gave all the organizations where I conducted research a copy of my report. I assured them I had no agenda, that I was simply reporting what employees said about the company and about their experience; but one company, after receiving a copy, vowed never to ask me back to speak with them about anything. I'm not the one needing to do something about the situation.

Calliou: Let me add three more examples of structural, or systemic, impediments: community isolation; economies of scale; and lack of education, training, and, in some areas, experience. I know some aboriginal and tribal organizations are trying to offset economies of scale by forming regional partnerships by which they can buy food, for example, in bulk. The fact of isolation may be difficult to get around but, in some cases, it can be turned into a benefit; for example, in isolating a river, or drawing ecotourists and river rafters to the area. A problem with hunting and dining, however, is that few people are employed in these ventures.

As far as education is concerned, the numbers of educated First Nation people are rising. In my generation, and certainly earlier, our people were forced to work and wait years before being allowed entrance to the universities, but now, a lot of aboriginal students are going into universities right out of high school. More training is also being made available. With the new economy, the need for technical education and training has increased and bands are allocating money to make education and training a priority.

As for legal impediments, certainly there's the Indian Act. One clause in the act talks about the personal property of Indians and of the band being exempt from banks and creditors; but not having collateral is a serious problem when you're trying to raise capital. Without something to secure, banks generally aren't interested in lending. Because of this problem, the government itself began making guaranteed loans. Now Canada has aboriginal banks; but even with the changes, it still isn't always easy for aboriginals to have access to money.

Voyageur: The integration of native peoples is going to take time. In my dissertation research, I found that the native people who made it in a lot of companies were seen as "the exception to the rule": "You're not like any Indian I've ever met before. You're different." The point is, they're not different. They're like everyone else. I am reminded of Oprah Winfrey a couple of years ago talking about moving to a farm in Georgia. She was walking her dog. Her neighbor stopped her and said, "Oh, you're not like those other black people." Winfrey responded, "I'm not like you think those other black people are." It's all about perception. People I interviewed often mentioned how frequently non-aboriginals think of Indians as though it were a hundred years ago: women with braids, treasure troves, little ponies running around. There's this idea that Indians are a historical relic. We need more people in high-profile situations.

Also, in our own communities, we need to start acknowledging that we have our own experts. We don't need experts from the outside. In fact, when experts come into our communities now, they get their information from us, then take their paycheck and laugh all the way to the bank. That money is leaving the community. We need money coming into the community and staying in, supporting our own people. As aboriginal people, we need to get away from this colonization of our minds and away from the idea that we don't have experts in our own community.

A question about how tribes collaborate or create alliances prompted a variety of responses.

Voyageur: The concept of First Nations does not necessarily mean tribe. There can be many First Nations within a single tribe or nation. The Cree nation, for example, spread across much of Canada; they became armed and powerful because of their role in fur trading. As they spread, they displaced other First Nation groups, so that now many First Nations all across western Canada might well be or include Cree.

Calliou: The Lubicon situation in Alberta is another example of structural unfairness. We have spoken briefly about fur trading and treaties generally developing along waterways.

The province of Ontario is a vast track of land with a huge hole in the middle, like a doughnut. The hole covers about two-thirds of the province and is where the Lubicon people live. They were never included in treaties, but were what we call "adhesions" to them. For example, in Treaty 6, around the Rocky Mountain area, an adhesion was made in 1966, although the treaty itself had been signed eighty years earlier. The result of the original exclusion and the later adhesion has been a huge fight between the federal government and the Lubicon. The Lubicons are saying, "You didn't deal with us in 1899. We've got all these people and want you to settle with us now." Since there were so many outstanding land claims, the federal government responded by carving away those people trying to make the claims from the original list of Lubicon. It set up two new bands—the Woodland Cree and the Little River Cree—formed from the dissidents from the Lubicon group. It just created its own bands.

Voyageur: Until recently, no one had really done research on band formation. Now, there's an enormous literature. Generally, nothing exists in the process of land management whereby people can legally inquire into the status of anyone. For example, in northern Treaties 8 and 16, no clear distinction is made as to who was or was not considered Indian. The process has evolved, to be sure, but the Treaty

Commission simply left it up to the people to self-identify, with or without regard to a treaty.

Calliou: A half-breed script commissioner and treaty commissioner traveled the country together identifying people who accepted the treaty land. Descendants of former relations in Alberta traveled with the commission and became enormously wealthy by buying land from people who deemed themselves to be Indian. A person could decide: do you want to be treaty or do you want to be Indian? The choice was between $5 a year in perpetuity, or saying they wanted the land and being told they could sell it to the speculators right there with a trunk full of cash. Essentially, determining whether we were aboriginal or whether we were treaty boiled down to just that. It had nothing to do with cultural identity.

The question was raised about collaboration among First Nation peoples as a means to combat some of the impediments.

Calliou: Some movement has been made among American and Canadian First Nations in developing common policies, but it's uneven. At a recent Indigenous Bar Association meeting, a gentleman now at the University of Arizona Law School presented his work on cross-border trading tax issues that proposed some creative ideas about collaborating. I also know an entrepreneur in Alberta who has involved several native communities and other groups in building resorts and hotels and golf courses. In general, tribal groups, especially in North America, but also around the world, are coming up with hugely innovative ideas relating to telecommunication and Internet. Obviously, borders don't matter in these cases; but I'm not aware of a unified movement.

Voyageur: There are national meetings and organizations. I know in 1999 a joint meeting of chiefs in Vancouver dealt with economics issues across provincial and regional bodies. In eastern Canada, in the Atlantic provinces, there is an association of indigenous fisherman and lobster fishers, which is quite different from fishing co-ops in the west; and efforts are underway to amalgamate and strengthen this type of alliance.

I'd also like to add something about the Lubicon, who have not yet been able to settle their land claim with the government. Until the late 1960s, nobody even knew they existed. They were a self-sufficient band that lived in the back lakes of Alberta. Really, no one knew they were there, until oil was discovered. At one point, over four hundred drilling rigs were drilling within a hundred-mile radius of the community; and the Alberta government was reaping $1 million (Canadian currency) a day in oil royalties, while keeping the people at bay. Absolutely a national scandal.

In response to a question about the number of women chiefs, one panelist offered the following:

Voyageur: Generally, it seems the farther women are away from their home base, the less likely they are to be involved in politics. School trustees and city councils generally have a lot of female representation. On the provincial level, about 25 percent of the NAS in Alberta are women; on the national level, it's 19 percent. Within the entire aboriginal community, about 15 percent of the chiefs are women. It's important to remember that women could not be chiefs before 1951, when changes were made to the Indian Act. (Before 1951, women were not allowed to be in any type of formal or informal governing position.) So, this is still a relatively new phenomenon; but since the mid-1990s, the number of women chiefs has doubled.

Calliou: It's interesting that the higher proportion of educated aboriginal people in Canada tends to be women; and a growing number of women have gone back and gotten their secondary education. Many of them are sitting on some of the local boards and authorities and indigenous groups of chiefs and counselors. One reason that many more women than men are getting educated may be that a man can still get a pretty good paying job, if, for example, he can drive a truck. In northern Alberta, in one of the oil plants there, he can make $60, 70, 80 thousand a year, working six days a week.

Voyageur: One more generalization: with single parenting of families now almost epidemic, women need a way to support their children. Data from 1996 made the shocking revelation that 45 percent of aboriginals under the age of fifteen in Canada are living in major poverty. These children are in single-parent households. Perhaps all the implied questions here about raising a child have something to do with so many women going for postsecondary education.

Calliou: To get back to the subject of collaboration and partnerships, the Banff Centre did several case studies in nation building: one with the White Mountain Apaches; one with the Mississippi Choctaw, both really successful. The visions these nations have are big ones. Their clients are McDonald's, Pepsi, Dodge, Chrysler, Ford.

But then, when Indians get successful, there can be a backlash. In Alberta, in a Treaty 8 territory, our reserve is on one side of Lesser State Lake near the Tahoe First Nation. On the other end of the lake is the Tahoe State Lake, which has a little reserve. For many years, Walter was the chief, before being appointed to the Canadian Senate. He's since passed away, but it was his idea to start ventures with band money. He invested in various businesses; he built a big hotel right on the corner of town. It's the first thing you see when you hit town. He also bought real estate, and he knew the fine line. He would tell us that even though someone's a taxpayer, this band is the largest taxpayer in town; but at a certain point, non-native business people will complain. They're going to argue with the taxpayer's federation and others that Indians are getting subsidies and, therefore, they are tax exempt. That's one of the fine lines.

Whites saw Indians becoming successful in agriculture—and suddenly, Indians were a threat to the economy. We need to share success stories, get them out there. The Mississippi Choctaw are in a very poor area of Mississippi. They bus in blacks and poor whites to work for them. It's like traffic rush hour to and from the reserve every day with all those busloads of people. The Choctaw also invest in the communities where the workers live; they spend money on ball diamonds and recreational facilities and other infrastructure supports because they want to have good relationships with those people who come to the reserve to work. It's possible to build those good relationships and counter the backlash.

The discussion was difficult to close, as people wanted keep talking and adding comments on topics they felt needed serious attention.

Inez Talamantez: What astounds me at every conference I go to is the ignorance about indigenous peoples in this hemisphere. We've all had to learn the Western tradition to get through school, to get to the point where we can begin teaching our own experience. At the same time, mainstream society, unless someone is an anthropologist, or a student of Native American literature, doesn't know anything about us. And how long have we been around?

How much does the Western tradition of knowledge, which compartmentalizes everything, keep us from the indigenous perspective of knowledge, which integrates everything? An Apache can embrace Christianity, but how frequently does Christianity embrace the Apache, other than to proselytize, which means forget your language, your culture, your religious tradition, and become like us.

With all that has been denied us, we continue to look at our reality here as we walk on this land; but we're sharing the experience now. There are nine million non-Indian people who are not native to this land; and all of us have the responsibility to recognize that we're now walking together. My Indian students who come to the university seem to understand this; but my non-Indian students are still shocked to learn American history from a Native American perspective, or to hear about our ecological and environmental concerns, our concepts of reciprocity, of giving back to the natural world and seeing everything in an integrated way, rather than in a compartmentalized way. The New Age spiritual movement makes it romantic and "cool" to be Indian. In Europe, there are societies of red men, weekend Indians. Spiritual fast food. There is, after all, more to being Indian than buying a pipe.

Some people still think that all the Indians have vanished. There are no more pure bloods. Well, there isn't any pure blood anything anywhere, including in the white race; but for some reason, we're supposed to be pure blood. Then there's bifurcation: either you're registered or not; and if you're not, in some academic circles, you're seen as not quite Indian. In other circles, if someone like me who's half Chicana and half Apache is with Chicanas, I'm not Chicana enough: "She's not really Chicana, she's half Apache." But when I'm with native people, I'm not really native, because I'm half Chicana.

Voyageur: Everything started with our being discovered by someone who was lost. The real European doctrine of discovery is European supremacy. Native Americans were not expected to survive because something about the indigenous was inherently inferior. Precisely because we're a dying breed, anthropologists started getting interested in the Indian community for the sake of posterity. In the terms of Charles Darwin's theory of survival of the fittest, we weren't seen to be "the fittest."

Before 1969, in the average Indian community, adaptation was absolutely a way of life. It was survival; but since 1969, there has been a resurgence of interest in aboriginals in Canada. We now have legal precedents. Indian people are being noticed in ways they never have been. We have land. If all the lawsuits go through, we're going to have control over one-third of the Canadian land mass. People will have to start getting to know us, if they don't know us now. Finally, demographically, we are increasing at twice the rate of the rest of the Canadian population. We are not a dying race; we are showing up on the doorstep.

Calliou: One last item. The change in Canadian law is extremely significant. In 1982, an amendment to the Constitution provided our own Bill of Rights. We call it the Charter of Rights and Freedoms. Individual rights were protected; and the state could no longer easily legislate and override them. The Constitution also protected aboriginal treaty rights, the collective rights; the 1962 Bill of Rights is still the law; it was never revoked, but it was a statute. The federal government passed it, but it never became the supreme law of the land, as has the Constitution. Now, judges, lawyers, the courts, take aboriginal treat rights seriously. Industry is dealing with aboriginals now. The First Nations, especially in the north, can say, "Sure, we've entered a treaty on our reserve for this slice of land. But THIS is our original territory. If you're going to run pipelines and cut trees down, we want to know about it; we want to be consulted about it, and we want to reap some of the economic benefits from it." There's been a huge assertion by First Nations, and industry is responding.

With the Liberal Party in power in Canada, and they've been in power for two terms—aboriginal nations and their cultural traits and language have all been recognized, along with treaty rights. Once people are whole and are proud of being whole, things move forward in good ways. In Canada, for such a small population as the aboriginal people are, they have a huge amount of power politically and a national spirit that is quite disproportionate to their numbers.

TRILATERAL DISCUSSIONS: CANADA, THE UNITED STATES, AND MEXICO   III

We Come to Ask for Justice, Not Crumbs 8

SYLVIA MARCOS

O N THE 28TH OF MARCH 2000, at about 10 a.m., a crowd of barefoot Indios (Mexican "Indians") dressed in multicolored garments, wearing hats of different forms and sizes adorned with ribbons, carrying packets wrapped in used plastic bags, entered meekly but triumphantly by the main door of the Mexican Parliament building. They came as invited public speakers and as representatives of many social indigenous organizations. They proceeded to take front seats in our Parliament house.

This unusual sight surprised even the more weathered politicians. What changes are altering the Mexican political landscape? Mexican national policy concerning native inhabitants of the territory has been known for its enforced integrationist strategies. Some renowned anthropologists and statesmen have coined the term *indigenismo* to indicate the kind of relationship that the hegemonic state establishes with the variety of nations of which Mexico is made. In "indigenist" policymaking, the emphasis was on wiping out the differences through several concrete political and educational strategies, and on pretending to build a homogenous social reality in tune with Mexico's Constitution.

Being Indian, showing the signs of this identity (that is, speaking an indigenous language and acting following Indian customs) was—and to a large extent still is—a sign of "backwardness" and "ignorance" and a reason for shame. What new winds are starting to blow over Mexican social reality, inciting Indians not only to enter the House of Parliament but also to publicly address the nation and its legislators?

A major breakthrough was reported in Carlos Monsivais's article "*Todos somos indios*" written in 1994. This slogan was heard in Mexico City's street demonstrations, where more than two hundred thousand people manifested their support of

the Zapatista uprising. Historically, this has been the hint at the possibility to sub-
vert the official integrationist approach, of substituting a proud "We are all Indians" for the shameful "Me? No, I am not Indian." Monsivais was the first to see
that this timely change was a *novedad histórica* (a historical novelty).

The indigenous movements in the Americas are "the transformational force
more visible in the continent."[1] According to Yvon Le Bot, a renowned French sociologist specialized in the study of social movements in Latin America, "they are
claiming both respect for a cultural identity and democratic rights for all Mexicans."[2] They are the most relevant social actors of today. As Yvon Le Bot empha-
sizes, one of their relevances and

> what makes them extraordinarily "modern" is the changes they claim to make in
> the hierarchical system of their communities and in the place of women against the
> exclusive masculine power. . . . The indigenous peoples do not accept any more the
> image that was imposed on them from the exterior, they want to create their own
> identity, they do not want to be objects in the museums. It is not a question of re-
> viving the past, theirs is a live culture. The only way they can survive as a culture is
> to reinvent themselves, to create a new identity, while maintaining their difference.[3]

Closely interlinked with the larger indigenous movement, the women's movement started to create a presence of its own within the Zapatista uprising and later
in the multiple indigenous organizations that sprang up all around the country.

The Indigenous Women: Beyond Zapatismo

On March 3, 2001, the Third National Indigenous Congress of the Congreso
Nacional Indigena (CNI) met in Nurio, Michoacan. The CNI, a network of indigenous political organizations, is the largest and most active of the multiple indigenous organizations that have developed in these last years. The CNI and the
Zapatistas share many political demands and strategies. Zapatismo is inclusive of
several groups, mainly Tzeltal, Tzotzil, Tojolabal, Chol, and Mam. These groups
have a common Mayan (Mesoamerican) ancestry and are close to each other in
worldviews, rituals, symbols, and language.[4] As to the CNI, it includes a larger variety of ethnic groups. To name a few of the forty-seven ethnic groups represented
in the Congress: Purepechas, Amuzgos, Mixes, Mixtecos, Zapotecos, Nahuas,
Raramuris, Ñañus, Huicholes.[5]

Beyond this plurality, and emerging as a new configuration, CNI activists call
themselves "indios" or "indígenas." It is well known that each ethnic group defines
itself by its difference to other ethnic groups and beyond that to the mestizo population in larger Mexico. Nevertheless, as a new outcome of the recent political
upheaval, this new identity has emerged with which they actively identify.

This recovery process has created a new collective subject that struggles to follow the lead of the Zapatistas in their "horizontal" strategies of decision making (public assemblies where everyone participates) and of incorporating the voices and rights of the women. The women within this organization had long been subsumed under the indigenous movement demands. However, in 1997, a group of women within the CNI created a new women's organization—la Coordinadora Nacional de Mujeres Indígenas—with representatives of twenty-six ethnic groups in the country.[6] This organization was founded at the closing of the First National Congress of Indigenous Women, a gathering of more than 560 indigenous women from all regions of the country, to which they invited a handful of nonindigenous women. From then on, a new awareness of the originality and autonomy of discourse of these women began to spread throughout Mexico. Politics joined with poetry, with rhetorical as well as numerical strength.[7] These were the hidden and invisible women, whose identity had been construed as muted and passive! Ramona, spokeswoman of the National Liberation Zapatista Army (EZLN) said, "We are coming from many different indigenous groups to learn how to walk together. The Zapatista movement would be different without its rebellious and renovated women. Let's be united for what we want, because, if there is division, it will not be possible."[8]

The National Political Arena

Both organizations, the Zapatistas and the CNI, have managed repeatedly to attract the political national attention during these last years. Some events merit special attention for the theme that concerns us here. The EZLN Consulta Nacional por la Paz y la Democracia of August to September 1995 is one of them. It reenacted a favored Zapatista strategy of "local decisions to large issues." It convened all the citizens of Mexico to a referendum concerning indigenous rights within the Mexican state. Large sectors of the population helped operationalize this massive national consultation and many citizens responded to the questions. In a Mexico where hardly anything was possible without the acquiescence of the governmental institutions, it was, nevertheless, run entirely on their margins. The Consulta Nacional asked six fundamental questions to Mexico's citizens, all concerned with indigenous rights and acceptance in Mexican society and politics. The last question, the sixth, read: "Should we warrant the presence and participation of women in all the posts of representation and responsibility within the democratic processes in Mexico, as much in civil organizations as in parties, in legislation, and in government?"[9] Of the collected responses, 93 percent were affirmative, 4 percent negative, and 3 percent abstained. The most important point at issue is that, by including such a question, the EZLN manifested the Zapatistas' effort (men's and women's) to inscribe the rights of women on their agenda and, by doing so, to counteract the strong atavistic currents of male supremacy in the Mexican society at large.

In March 2000, the EZLN called the nation to another referendum, the Consulta Nacional por los Derechos de las Mujeres (specifically on the rights of women in Mexico). The *consulta* has been crucial for developing and advancing the need to participate in national decision making for a society that was used to non-involvement. And, once again, the rights of women were at the center.

Zapatistas from Southern Mexico were sent to every city, township, and village where the referendum was held to be witness of it and to assist its organizers. Following a Mayan custom, they all came in couples (*en parejas*, not referring to husband and wife) so that there was exactly the same number of women as of men. Once again, a breath of fresh air was blowing from the south! It was specially relevant to issues that political feminists were trying to get across within their political parties that of quotas, a minimum percentage of women to be elected to participate in the leading positions. The reception of these women and men, their addresses, and their initiative in favor of the rights of women had a lasting national impact. Though the *consulta* was not allowed to take place in some states, in the majority of the states, 94 to 98 percent of the women responded affirmatively to the question about the recognition of their rights.[10] Only 2 to 4 percent thought that it was not necessary. As for men, only 6 to 8 percent defended their "privileges" against the rights of women. The important issue here is the strategic positioning of Zapatismo to generate a wide citizen consensus.

The third example of the huge national mobilization I want to review here is the momentous Marcha Zapatista toward Mexico City in February and March 2001. The main objective of this march was to gather popular support for the approval of a constitutional amendment (Ley Cocopa) that would recognize the rights and values of the indigenous peoples within the national boundaries. These included rights to their culture (*usos y costumbres*), to their citizenship-in-difference, to their territories and their resources. The law project was a call to transform our legislative system so that it could better reflect and include the plurality of peoples that constitutes Mexico.

The representatives of the EZLN in this otherwise called *Marcha por la Dignidad* included four *comandantas* (female commanders): Yolanda, Fidelia, Esther, and Susana. Taking turns to address the hundreds of thousands that gathered to greet and welcome them, they were heard with respectful attention and their discourses were always striking. Their words were full of ancestral references, as well as demands for change in the discriminatory practices toward women. What they want is both the nation's respect for their indigenous custom and their custom's respect for their aspiration as indigenous and as women.

Never before in Mexico was there such a spontaneous, massive, nonparty-aligned congregation of citizens as the one that received the Zapatistas. Governments—the states' as well as well as the Federation—felt threatened by such popular support. Besides the meetings in townships and cities (thirty-three of them), carefully prepared by the Comité Central Revolucionario Indígena, the Zapatista caravan was often asked to stop in this or that village and to improvise a rally. Hundreds of people even stood in the middle of the road to oblige the Zapatistas to make a stop in their place. People wanted to see them, to express their support, saying they understood and subscribed to their struggle. Here is an example of how Zapatista women spoke to the enormous gatherings that greeted them everywhere on their way to Mexico City:

"*Vamos al Distrito Federal a exigir nuestros derechos junto con otros hermanos y hermanas*" ("We are going to Mexico City to demand our rights with our other sisters and brothers"), said Fildelia. "The Cocopa law recognizes our rights as women because as women we have more sufferings, but all the same we are brave. I, as a woman, feel very proud of being as I am. I hope that I will find other women that have my frame of mind and others that have a different thought. We think this is good because in that way an idea grows and gets better and gives us strength to continue struggling for our rights as indigenous and as women."[11]

"Being an indigenous woman is a pride, being indigenous women means that we have thought, that we have dignity, but it is difficult, very difficult, because there is suffering, discrimination and poverty. This is why we want that the constitutional law takes us into consideration, as the Cocopa law does," said Susana.[12]

"We came to spread our word as Zapatistas and we are going to defend our rights as women and as indigenous peoples. As indigenous women, we are not stopping our struggle until we are subjects in our Constitution and we are no longer treated as animals," said Yolanda.[13]

"I am going with my *compañeros y compañeras* to talk to Congress, I am coming as a woman and as indigenous. It is necessary that we mobilize so that legislators listen to us so we recover our dignity. We speak our language, we have our custom, our medicine, our form of praying and our form of dancing. We have our way of respecting our elders, that our grandmothers and grandfathers taught us. They also taught us to resist and to get organized. Not because we are indigenous, and for speaking our language, and for being dark-skinned, can we be looked down. Being Indian is a great pride," affirmed Esther.[14]

In their faltering Spanish—a second or third language for them—they came across as strong Indian women who struggle with both the state and with customary patriarchal norms. Indigenous women have been more defiant than the available literature would lead us to believe.

"The large peace marches," says Yvon Le Bot, "are one of the preferred political actions of the indigenous movements. It sets them apart from the guerrilla tactics and inscribes them in the strategies of Gandhi or Martin Luther King. They ask to be recognized as equal and different within a nation reconstructed on a pluricultural basis."[15]

Defending the Law in Congress

With this experience in the background, the next step was to present the law project, the *iniciativa de ley*, in the legislators' tribune. After many failed negotiations, rebuttals of the indigenous people's claim to address the nation's representatives, and a fierce resistance to their prospective appearance in both chambers, there was finally a last-minute agreement: they would be allowed to speak to the deputies but not to the senators. Of course, all of this was preceded by massive amounts of rallies on the streets of Mexico City to support their appearance in the Deputies' Chamber.[16]

A group of feminists who had been respectfully supporting the indigenous women's movement organized a forum: *"De la ley revolucionaria de las mujeres Zapatistas a la ley de la COCOPA."* (For a full account of the forum, see *Cuadernos Feministas.*[17]) At the closing of this meeting, a "plural commission" was formed.[18] Two indigenous women, a Purepecha and an Amuzga from the Coordinadora Nacional de Mujeres Indígenas, and two nonindigenous feminists were elected to brief Congress on the benefits of the law from the indigenous women's perspective.

This commission also participated in citizenship information forums. They briefed congressmen and congresswomen repeatedly during weeks on the benefits of this law for indigenous women, and on the importance for a plural state, like Mexico should be, to accept it. *"Queremos un mundo donde caben muchos mundos"*: We want a world in which many worlds can fit.

Meanwhile, the most debated issue in the media was whether *Subcomandante* Marcos should be allowed to address the plenum of the Congress. Who else would represent appropriately the Zapatista uprising? Who would have the words and the courage to step up and speak to the highest legislative authority in the country? There was a lot of expectation, a lot of suppositions. The EZLN was silent regarding its representatives. The CNI had already disclosed theirs: María de Jesús Patricio and Juan Chavez.

A campaign of denigration of the Cocopa law project raged in the media, orchestrated by the establishment, politicians, and intellectuals, and amplified by TV programs, newspapers, and periodicals that made a sport of criticizing the "indigenous law." Known for their male chauvinism, they now came up with a new argument: the indigenous people's revindication of their culture was derided as *usocostumbrismo* (customary law-ism) and would, as such, hamper women's rights![19] They were using women—once again—as an excuse for their reactionary political positions!

On March 28, at the parliament building in Mexico City, there were also many invited nonindigenous lawyers, professors, politicians, and supporters who accompanied the indigenous retinue. But, where was *Subcomandante* Marcos? Everyone was looking for him. Minutes later, as the session started, a small figure moved up to take the tribune. She was dressed in white with embroidered flowers. Remindful of the countenance recommended to women and men in the traditional discourses of *ilamatlatolli* and *huehuetlatolli*,[20] she bore herself with indigenous composure, small steps and head covered with a ski mask. Her eyes blinked when she started speaking. It was *Comandanta* Esther. "Here I am. I am a woman and an Indian, and through my voice speaks the Ejército Zapatista de Liberación Nacional." A rumor of surprise raised from the assembly. How dare she—she, a woman and an Indian, she so desperately poor—take this stance? She started shyly, almost faintly. But as her voice progressively raised, her strength came through her words. She made clear that she was there as a commander, that she—along with the other CCRI (Comite Central Revolucionario Indigena) members—gives orders to *Subcomandante* Marcos. He is in charge of the armed forces and, as such, subject to the decisions of the Central Committee.

Those who heard her could recognize in her speech stylistic resources that reminded us of pre-Hispanic poetry. Among them were an "indigenous" syntax in Spanish, certain use of parallelisms and of phrasing.[21] The influences of the indigenous language were present in the choice of words, the nonmatching singulars and plurals, the use of metaphors, and the rhythmic repetition of words.[22] Especially conspicuous was her use of the word *heart* in a context where it did not refer to feelings. Heart in her discourse referred to reason, to history, to truth.[23] All of these characteristics revealed the influence of her Mayan ancestry and *cosmovision* upon her language.

This is not the place to conduct an extended and in-depth analysis of the Mayan cosmological references she echoed.[24] Her words, "*la palabra verdadera*" ("the true word") resounded under Parliament's dome. Six times she was interrupted by roaring applause. In synthesis, she commented on the importance of the law project for the indigenous peoples. She outlined their destitute situation. Then she spoke of the women's situation, the indigenous and the nonindigenous. "It is today's existing law that permits our humiliation and destitution. This is why we got organized to change this situation as Zapatista women. . . . I want to explain the situation of indigenous women as we live it in our communities, today when it is supposed we are guaranteed respect by our constitution. Besides being women, we are indigenous and as such we are not recognized. Yes, the existing law gives us certain rights, but only as women and even that is not satisfactory."[25]

Then, *Comandanta* Esther went on to speak of the situation of Indian women under "traditional" customary rules and of the double discrimination suffered by indigenous women, mentioning many instances where this custom is unjust to them. They treat us "as girls; they think we are not valuable, as women we are beaten. . . . Also women have to fetch water walking two to three hours holding a vessel and a child in their arms. . . . I am not telling you all this so you have pity on us. We have struggled to change this and will continue doing it."[26]

Her discourse proved all those intellectuals removed from the daily life of the indigenous people wrong. In accordance with the multiple indigenous voices heard these last years, she insisted she wanted both to transform and to preserve her culture. "We want recognition for our ways of dressing, of talking, of governing, of organizing, of praying, of working collectively, of respecting the earth, of understanding nature as something which we are part of."[27]

Of the four indigenous representatives to address Mexico's Congress that day, two were women. The second woman to address Congress that day was María de Jesús Patricio ("Marichuy") as a representative of the CNI. In her speech, Marichuy expressed firmly and repeatedly that it is not only in the indigenous communities that women are not respected in their rights. Applauses came from the floor.

"*Que si los usos y costumbres lesionan a las mujeres indígenas en los pueblos en las comunidades, pensamos que es un problema no solamente de los pueblos indígenas, no es de ahí, es de toda la sociedad civil también. Dicen que si se aprueba esta iniciativa de la Cocopa, va a lesionar a las mujeres. Nosotras decimos que no.*" With rhetorical talent, oral eloquence, she started to list the positive *usos y costumbres*, like collective collaboration for communal tasks, political representation as service to the community and not as means of acquiring power and wealth, respect for the wisdom of the elders, and decision making by consensus among others. Then she mentioned some of the influences of the hegemonic legal system that surrounds them and that have impacted negatively the place of indigenous women.

"It is not in our custom that in the documents and institutions a man's name has to appear. It is not our custom, but the dominant law that requires a man— the 'chief of the family'—to sign in the property titles. It is the dominant law that requires to personalize rights, to individualize property and land tenure and it is in this same law that takes women into consideration with different levels of participation, lower than those of men."[28]

"It is the contemporary law that discriminates us as women, not the Cocopa law," insisted both *Comandanta* Esther and María de Jesús Patricio.

With this precision, she was referring to something that several researchers have noted in their writings: "Feminist writing has only just begun to analyze the more interesting problem of how the state inscribes gender difference into the political process in such a way that women are debarred—at least under present state forms—from becoming full political persons."[29]

According to Magdalena León y Carmen D. Deere, in the development projects in Latin America, "Rural women were perceived only as housewives who were responsible for the domestic realm. The state resources directed toward them focused solely on their roles of wife and mother. . . . Programs for agricultural technical assistance and access to credit were directed overwhelmingly toward rural men. Thus, rural extension services reproduced the socially constructed—and idealized—gender division of labor in which men were the agriculturalists and women the housewives."[30] Similar attitudes and situations of hegemonic central power induce the ownership of the land to be in the hands of men exclusively.

Marichuy was thus referring to the state-enhanced social construction of a structure of patriarchal privileges within the indigenous and peasant world. However, as much as Mexican peasant society has become more patriarchal, it remains less so than the hegemonic, urban society. Since the time of contact, the patriarchal styles of the dominator were imposed on the dominated; hence the creation, fortification, and stratification of patriarchal privileges in a world where they were not originally at home. This is a complex issue and one that requires further elaboration. At the moment, it is sufficient to know that historical research into early colonial times has unearthed a wealth of *titulos de propiedad* (land property documents) and inheritance documents where there is ample evidence that women held titles of land property in their own names.[31] It seems that Spanish colonial law and the application of contemporary Mexican law in peasant and indigenous communities have in common the denial of land tenancy rights to women.

But María de Jesús Patricio did not only challenge the application of the law. She was equally critical of certain feminist positions, as exemplified in her use of the family concept: "Women have been participating from within the family, because in indigenous villages, it is not men nor woman, it is the entire family. And women there participate in decision making, getting the ideas together. When the man goes to a communal assembly, in the man's participation goes also the woman's participation. But as I mentioned, it is not only man-woman but the whole family."[32]

As questionable as this might seem from a feminist perspective, it might be of use to revisit some of the ancient Mesoamerican concepts. Both the family and the man-woman couple formed a unity. The concept of the individual was not prevalent.[33] In addition, a pervasive concept of duality still nurtures the vision of most ethnic communities in contemporary Mexico. Was Marichuy referring to this? Most probably, she was trying to get across a concept of collective subjectivity, of feminine-masculine duality that requires a whole epistemological decodification.[34] It's an example of an "indigenous feminist" whose life is a juggling between multiple and contradictory identities, some traditional, some beginning to emerge, and challenging dominant, urban, feminist discourse. Marichuy, however, was also very articulate on the positive aspects of the indigenous communities. She is probably very influenced by the recent writings of indigenous thinkers like Floriberto Díaz, as analyzed by two emerging indigenous scholars: Sofia Robles and Adelfo Regino.[35] "Why do you always mention the 'bad' customs?" she asked. "In our indigenous communities, we have good customs too." Part of her presentation was dedicated to the enunciation of the "good customs."

"For example, one 'good' custom is that of *tequio* (collective voluntary work) and of mutual help. In *tequio*, men get together and give their work to build the houses of everyone in the community. . . . Another 'good' custom is to take decisions by consensus. Our grandparents say 'There has to be 99 percent plus 9.' It has to be the total. It is not voting, it is achieving consensus. . . . Also a positive custom is to do justice by retribution and not by punishing the guilty." To take advantage of the wisdom of the elders is another good custom. "The elders have a privileged place. Political representation is a service, not a privilege. It is a duty, you do not get paid. The whole community is overseeing what you do. This is the true word, the word of our peoples, of our ancestors."[36]

A few days before, on the 8th of March, at a rally for women's rights, *Comandanta* Esther had addressed the massive audience, saying, "We are going to achieve the change we want. Yes, we are going to achieve it because I see many women getting organized. We invited them and like this we are going to be stronger and all together we will succeed."[37]

Notes

1. J. Gil Olmos, interview with Yvon Le Bot, "Moderno y creativo el movimiento de indígenas en América Latina," *La Jornada*, March 26, 2000, 3.

2. J. Gil Olmos, "Mexico en riesgo de caer en el caos y caciquismo: Touraine," *La Jornada*, November 6, 2000, 3.

3. Olmos, "Mexico in riesgo de caer," 3.

4. Alfredo Lopez Austin, "Cosmovision y salud entre los Mexicas," in *Historia General de la Medicina en Mexico*, vol. I (Mexico City: UNAM, 1984); Kirchhoff 1986 [1968].

5. F. Gargallo, "La voz de las mujeres en el Tercer Congreso Nacional Indígena," *La Triple Jornada*, April 2, 2001, 3.

6. Sonia del Valle, "Representantes de 26 pueblos indios conformaron la Coordinadora Nacional de Mujeres Indígenas," in *Las Alzadas*, 2nd ed., ed. Sara Lovera and Nellys Palomo (Mexico City: CIMAC, La Jornada, 1999), 408–11.

7. Sylvia Marcos, "Mujeres indígenas: Notas sobre un feminismo naciente," *Cuadernos Feministas* I, no. 2 (1997): 14–16.

8. "*Pues, 'sta bien, compañeras, venimos varias pueblos indígenas pobres para saber como caminar juntas. El zapatismo no sería lo mismo sin sus mujeres rebeldes y nuevas. Luchemos juntos lo que queremos, porque si hay muchas divisiones no se puede.*" (Marcos, "Mujeres indígenas.")

9. Daniel Cazés, "Consulta o distensión," in *Las Alzadas*, 2nd ed., ed. Sara Lovera and Nellys Palomo (Mexico City: CIMAC, La Jornada, 1999), 310–12.

10. M. Olivera, "La consulta por los derechos de las mujeres en Chiapas," *Memoria*, no. 139 (September 2000): 23–27.

11. *"La Ley sobre derechos de los indígenas que hicieron los de la COCOPA de por si nos reconoce como mujeres, porque como mujeres de por si tenemos más penas, pero igual somos valientes. Yo como mujer me siento muy orgullosa de ser como soy. Yo espero que me voy a encontrar con otras mujeres que tienen mi pensamiento y con otras que tienen otro pensamiento. Pensamos que esto esta bien porque así se hace una idea más buena y más grande y nos da mas fuerza para seguir luchando por nuestros derechos como indígenas y como mujeres."* Perfil de la Jornada, 2001.

12. *"Ser mujeres indígenas es un orgullo. Ser mujeres indígenas representa que tenemos pensamiento, que tenemos dignidad pero también es difícil, muy difícil, porque hay sufrimientos y discriminaciones y hay pobreza. Por eso queremos que se nos reconozca en las leyes de la constitución y que nos respeten nuestra dignidad, como en la ley Cocopa,"* said Susana. (Perfil de la Jornada, 2001.)

13. *"Vamos a difundir nuestras palabras como zapatistas y vamos a defender nuestros derechos como mujeres y como indígenas. Como mujeres indígenas no vamos a dejar de luchar mientras no seamos reconocidas en la Constitución y no seamos tratados como animales,"* said Yolanda. (Perfil de la Jornada, 2001.)

14. *"Voy a ir con mis compañeros y compañeras a platicar con el Congreso de la Unión. Voy como mujer y como indígena, porque es necesaria esta movilización para que los legisladores nos escuchen y porque es necesaria la recuperación de la dignidad. Nosotras somos mexicanas, hablamos nuestra lengua, tenemos nuestra vestimenta, nuestra medicina, nuestra forma de rezar y también nuestra forma de bailar. Nosotros como indígenas hombres y mujeres tenemos nuestro modo de trabajar y de respetar a nuestros ancianos, así como nos enseñaron nuestros abuelos. Desde el tiempo de nuestros abuelos, nos enseñaron a resistir y a organizarnos. No por ser indígenas y por hablar nuestra lengua y por ser morenas nos tienen que despreciar, no por eso ni por nada. Ser indígena es un orgullo muy grande,"* affirmed Esther. (Perfil de la Jornada, 2001.)

15. Yvon Le Bot, "La política según Marcos: Que Zapatismo despues del Zapatismo?" *La Jornada*, March 15, 2001, 19.

16. Le Bot, "La política según Marcos."

17. Comandante Esther, Cdte. Yolanda, Cdte. Susane, Marcela Lagarde, Martha Sánchez, and Nellys Palomo, "De la ley revolucionaria de las mujerres zapatistas a la ley de la Cocopa," *Cuadernos feministas* 3, no. 15 (April–June 2001).

18. Rojas 2001.

19. See Federico Reyes Heroles's exploit in his TV appearance on channel 11, March 22, 2001; see also Juan Pedro Viqueira, "El discurso usocostumbrista," in *Letras Libres* (March 2001).

20. Marcos 1991.

21. Miguel León-Portilla, *Pre-Columbian Literatures of Mexico* (Norman: University of Oklahoma, 1969).

22. Marcos 1997.

23. Perfil de la Jornada 2001, iv.

24. Sylvia Marcos, "Pensamiento mesoamericano y categorías de género: Un reto epistemológico," *La Palabra y el Hombre* (Xalapa, Mexico: Universidad Veracruzana, 1995).

25. *"Es la ley de ahora la que permite que nos marginen y nos humillen. Por eso nosotras nos decidimos a organizar para luchar como mujer zapatista. . . . Quiero explicarles la situación de la mujer indígena que vivimos en nuestra comunidades, hoy que según esto, esta garantizado en la Constitución el respeto a la mujer."* (Perfil de la Jornada 2001, iii.)

26. *"Que somos niñas, piensan que no valemos nosotras como mujer nos golpea también. . . . (Las mujeres) cargan su agua de dos a tres horas de camino con cantaro y cargando a su hijo. . . . No les cuento todo esto para que nos tengan lástima o nos vengan a salvar de esos abusos. Nosotras hemos luchado por cambiar eso y lo seguiremos haciendo."* (Perfil de la Jornada 2001, iii.)

27. *"Queremos que sea reconocida nuestra forma de vestir, de hablar, de gobernar, de organizar, de rezar, de curar, nuestra forma de trabajar en colectivos, de respetar la tierra y de entender la vida, que es la naturaleza que somos parte de ella."* (Perfil de la Jornada 2001, iv.)

28. *"No es nuestra costumbre que ante las instituciones y documentos aparezca el nombre del varón, y no el de la mujer, sino que ha sido por disposición de las propias leyes que exigen el nombre de un jefe de familia, que exigen personalizar el derecho, que exigen individualizar la propiedad o posesión al igual que lo anterior, en donde las mujeres somos tomadas en cuenta con diferentes niveles de participación."* (Triple Jornada 2001.)

29. Henrietta Moore, *Feminism and Anthropology* (Minneapolis: University of Minnesota Press, 1988), 150.

30. Quoted in Stephen 1997, 270.

31. Frances Karttunen, "In Their Own Voices: Mesoamerican Indigenous Women Then and Now," English manuscript for an article in Finnish in Noiden Nuoli (Journal of Finnish Women Researchers), 1983; James Lockhart, "Y la Ana lloro: Cesion de un sitio para caso, San Miguel Tociulan," *Tlalocan* 8 (1980): 22–33; Susan Kellogg, "Cognatic Kinship and Religion: Women in Aztec Society," in *Mesoamerican Studies in Memory of Thelma D. Sullivan* (BAR International Series 402, 1988).

32. *"Así pues la mujer ha venido participando desde la misma familia, porque en los pueblos indígenas no es hombre y mujer sino que son familias enteras. Y ahí la mujer participa desde la toma de decisiones; cuando el marido va a una asamblea comunitaria o a una asamblea ejidal, [la mujer contribuye también] en conjuntar ideas y llevarlas a la asamblea. Pero ya la participación del varón ya va ahí también la participación de la mujer, pero no solamente, como les decía, es exclusivamente hombre-mujer, sino que es de familia."* (Perfil de la Jornada, 2001, vii)

33. Lopez Austin, "Cosmovision y salud."

34. Sylvia Marcos, "Embodied Religious Thought: Gender Categories in Mesoamerica," *Religion* 22, no. 4 (October 1998).

35. Sofia Robles and Adelfo Regino, "Floriberto Dias y el renacimiento indígena," *La Jornada Semanal* 314 (March 2001).

36. *"Por ejemplo, los usos y costumbres positivos son el tequio y la ayuda mutua, cuando se reunen y juntos dan su tiempo para trabajar faenas. . . . Otra de las buenas costumbres es buscar tomar decisiones por consenso. . . . Ahí dicen nuestro abuelos: 'ahí tiene que es el 99% más el 9', ¿verdad?, o sea, que es el total: tiene que haber consenso más que votación. . . . También otra de las costumbres positivas es buscar hacer justicia reparando el daño antes que castigando al culpable."* (Perfil de la Jornada, 2001, vii)

37. *"Creo que vamos a lograr el cambio como nosotras queremos. Sí se va a lograr, porque veo que muchas mujeres se estan organizando, nosotras las invitamos también y así más fuerza vamos a tener, entre todas lo vamos a lograr."* (Memoria 2001, 39)

Competing Narratives: Barriers between Indigenous Peoples and the Canadian State

9

PATRICIA A. MCCORMACK

> *Francis Alexis, Elder from Alexis First Nation, Alberta: "The white people said they were 'developing the land.' The old people called it 'destroying the land.'"*

—PROVINCIAL MUSEUM OF ALBERTA, 2000

IN CANADA WE TALK A GREAT DEAL about building working partnerships between indigenous peoples and a wide array of groups, from individual researchers to government departments, to facilitate indigenous economic, political, and social development, all aspects of decolonization. Yet the process of building partnerships is poorly understood. Too often the term is still used for consultative or advisory relationships, which are far from being true partnerships as they are understood by indigenous peoples or by contemporary researchers working collaboratively with indigenous communities.[1] One useful definition is that "the partners aim to achieve something they could not do alone, by pooling skills and other resources. To do this they need a shared vision of their goals, and a way of working together which realises this ambition."[2] This process can be hampered by "unacceptable inequalities of power and control."[3] However, such inequalities have historically characterized the place of indigenous peoples within the plural society of Canada. Given the persistence of stereotypes and racism directed at indigenous peoples, it seems that we can anticipate a long struggle before they will enjoy relationships of equality in this country.

Mostly, indigenous and nonindigenous people seem to hammer away at one another on multiple fronts. For example, nonindigenous Canadians are typically perplexed by and often angry at indigenous legal initiatives. Indigenous Canadians are similarly perplexed, angry, and hurt by what they often perceive to be bull-headed intransigence on the part of people in power, and the difficulty they experience in having their points of view *heard*, let alone accorded equal weight, even in situations that affect them directly, such as interpretations and representations of their histories and cultural traditions.[4]

Such opposing sentiments were elicited recently by Justice Douglas Campbell's decision in the *Benoit* case, which found that exemption from taxation is a right under Treaty 8.[5] While some editorials and letters to the editors of the *Edmonton Journal* about this judgment provided guarded approval, the tone of most letters was dismay and even outrage. For example, E. G. Brulotte read the decision as "preferential treatment": "With the stroke of a pen he released a specific group of people from any need of obligation, responsibility or duty towards our nation."[6] Most Treaty 8 members, however, feel that their understanding of the obligations of the government under the treaty has at last been vindicated and that they can now participate in the life of the nation with a greater measure of equality.[7]

A conceptual pattern for the development and operation of partnerships with indigenous peoples developed in Canada in the 1990s, in the wake of the controversial *The Spirit Sings* exhibit mounted at the Glenbow Museum during the 1988 Calgary Olympics. The exhibit was contested by a highly visible boycott by the Lubicon Lake First Nations and other indigenous peoples.[8] Nationally, a Canadian Task Force on Museums and First Peoples identified a series of broad principles crucial to establishing partnerships between their respective constituencies, the first of which stated that "Museums and First Peoples will work together to correct inequities that have characterized their relationships in the past."[9] Locally, the Provincial Museum of Alberta in Edmonton introduced a short-lived program intended to implement the recommendations of the task force.[10] This program presumed that the new partners from different cultures striving to work together in a heritage domain would use the dialogue between them to develop an innovative set of meanings that might belong to neither of their respective cultures, a complex process requiring learning done in tandem. The resulting, shared meanings constitute a form of "intersubjectivity," a third space where the partners can interact together to achieve their common goals.[11]

In this paper, I argue that the major barriers preventing indigenous and non-indigenous peoples from building effective partnerships in specific endeavors and as citizens of Canada are, first, the profound differences that persist in their respective *narratives* about themselves as peoples within Canada and, second, the difficulties they have experienced in building third spaces, which are contingent upon building bridges between those narratives. Edward Bruner defines a narrative as a story, "the abstract sequence of events, systematically related."[12] I outline some key features of these competing stories, or narratives, about Canadian history and conclude with some comments about the process and urgency of bridge building.

Canada's Nation-Building Narrative

The nation-building narratives of Canada and the United States are broadly similar. Both national stories construct a heroic past of European settlement, although Canadians construe their treatment of indigenous peoples as more humane than in the United States. In both countries, the national narratives presume an ever-receding frontier, in which the "wild and primitive" were replaced by the "tame and civilized," by "modern" institutions, to the benefit of *all* peoples living within their respective boundaries. In these narratives, indigenous peoples are mostly marginalized as "a once-proud people whose spirit had been broken and who would soon become assimilated into what was then called the 'mainstream' of American [or Canadian] life."[13] At the same time, they are seen as people who have resisted progress, to the ongoing consternation of nonindigenous people.[14] These narratives are deeply embedded in both traditional scholarly analysis and North American popular culture, informing the commonsense understandings of our respective histories.[15] That is, they are "Grand Narratives," the most widely circulated versions of the past, the ones that most people know and that are taught in the schools. They are the dominant stories about how Canada and the United States became nation-states.

Patricia Marchak calls a broad narrative such as this one an *ideology*: "a screen of assumptions, beliefs, explanations, values, and unexamined knowledge" that tells us how to construct and interpret social reality.[16] Canada's nation-building narrative is a dominant ideology, or enjoys hegemony, in that it is "most widely shared and has the greatest impact on social action at any particular time."[17]

One of the reasons for the dominance of this particular story is that in its broadest construction, it speaks of inevitable "modernization," a process of homogenizing cultural change driven by an evolving and expansionary global capitalism, dominated by Europeans who were at the same time "modernizing" into nation-states. It presumed that indigenous peoples drawn into interaction with Europeans would come to resemble them. It was Europeans and European-derived peoples during the nineteenth-century heyday of global colonization who defined themselves as the epitome of "modern" peoples, those "most advanced in technological, political, economic, and social development."[18] As J. A. Hobson wrote from Great Britain in 1902, "We represent the socially efficient nation, we have conquered and acquired dominion and territory in the past: we must go on, it is our destiny." Britain had a "mission of civilization" to the rest of the world.[19] In northwestern Canada, the "modern era" began with the imposition of colonization, in the last quarter of the nineteenth century. By that time, the nation-state of Canada had been created and the form of colonialism was internal.

In Canada, "modernity" translated into a derivative narrative about "progress," a Canadian manifest destiny, which held that Canada developed as a country and achieved its destiny to greatness through the agency of explorers, government agents, and homesteaders—all Europeans—who steadily pushed backward its frontiers between "civilized lands" into the western and northern "wilderness," occupied by "primitive" people—"Indians" and, in the far northern reaches, "Inuit" (formerly, "Eskimos")—who must either disappear or themselves become civilized ("modernize") at which point they will not truly be "Indians" (or "Inuit/ Eskimos") anymore. To historian Sylvia Van Kirk, this account is an example of the "triumphal settler narrative" genre.[20] Indigenous people known as Métis (formerly, "half-breeds") play a marginal role in this story, identified as Indian descendants who were biologically and culturally transforming into non-Indians.[21]

This story of Canada purports to represent the history of us all. Yet it is inherently exclusionary. It constructs some groups—Europeans and their descendants—as prime movers, at the heart of the Canadian success story. It marginalizes others as people who have not only not contributed but who may have blocked the path to progress. These "others" include indigenous peoples: "All too often Native people are treated as if they exist outside the Canadian mosaic rather than as an integral part of it. They are imagined to be leftovers from what was here before Canada began."[22] It is thereby "racializing," defined by the construction of a polarity between groups that enjoy dominance and those that are subordinate, often termed minority groups, who have minimal control over their position within the nation-state.[23] It promotes what J. M. Blaut calls the myth of the European miracle: the idea that Europeans and their descendants achieved what they did because of their own inherent, superior attributes and abilities.[24] Yet this notion flies in the face of decades of global history. We know that European nations and their daughter countries, including Canada, built themselves on the backs of the colonized world and its peoples by appropriating their resources and their labor.

The story of Canada has been more than ideological history.[25] It prescribed a course of action vis-à-vis indigenous peoples and the land, which was elaborated in an evolving set of federal, provincial, and territorial policies, legislation, and regulations. When narratives have direct behavioral implications, and especially when they mandate action, it is useful to call them *paradigms*, in this instance, the *paradigm of progress*. The narrative is the *textual* aspect of a paradigm, and the pattern for behavior is its *operational* aspect.

The concept of paradigm is approached somewhat differently in the social sciences than in the physical sciences, where the concept was developed to account for revolutions in scientific thought and was related directly to experimental testing.[26] In the Kuhnian view, "science is characterized by the existence of a ruling dogma which exercises hegemonic control for lengthy periods."[27] Occasionally there are "upheavals in which accepted wisdom is replaced by a new way of seeing," that is, a "paradigm shift."[28] In this approach, paradigms are incommensurate, with "separate sets of standards and metaphysical beliefs": "rival paradigms cut up the world with different standards, different assumptions, different language."[29] In short, they involve different narratives and discourses, or ways of thinking and talking about a particular subject.

The social sciences do not fit neatly into the Kuhnian framework but are polyparadigmatic, which means that more than one paradigm may be operating at any one time.[30] Because they are derived more from close observation than from experimentation, they are always mediated by culturally influenced human perceptions, including the interests of "elite groups outside of the scholarly field itself."[31] And, when social scientists interact with diverse human populations, they encounter competing narratives and paradigms held by the populations being studied.[32] In situations of power differentials, some paradigms will dominate. That dominance may not be evident. The nature of hegemony is that the dominant interpretation has "come to be taken for granted as the natural, universal, and true shape of social being . . . consists of things that go without saying: things that, being axiomatic, are not normally the subject of explication or argument."[33]

John Hassard has argued that people can be "trained into" new paradigms, just as they can learn new languages and how to translate between them.[34] Moreover, multiple paradigm research offers "several lens for its analytical scrutiny."[35] We can take advantage of this diversity rather than strive to prove one right and another wrong. Part of the process of being "trained into" multiple paradigms is to be able to deconstruct them and understand their implications for political decisions and policy and program development. It also entails a stance of respect and appreciation for what the concepts mean to their respective holders.

This approach is particularly useful for addressing issues of indigenous history as a component of Canadian history. Indigenous and nonindigenous peoples have very different historical narratives. The Euro-Canadian narrative has revolved around concepts of modernization, conquest, and rule of "superior" peoples over "inferior" ones. These narratives are easy to find in the mainstream historical literature, because it is how Canadian historians have explained the growth of Canada as a nation.

Indigenous Narratives

Indigenous narratives have rarely been presented in equivalent fashion, but their essential elements emerge in a wide range of indigenous oral traditions and other literature and in testimony to various commissions and courts, especially concerning their relationship to their traditional lands and their resistance to Euro-Canadian impositions. The "Report of the Royal Commission on Aboriginal Peoples" is an especially useful summary resource.[36]

Indigenous narratives are premised on a belief in the equality of peoples within their homelands and an expectation of their persistent autonomy, both as nations and as individuals within the encompassing framework of their social communities. The indigenous point of view mandates respect for individual choices but resistance to imposed policies and especially to any attempt to interfere with their access to and control over their homeland and its resources. Typically, when indigenous peoples tell their stories of the history of Canada, they divide the long period of contact with Europeans into two broad periods. During the first, they were equals to the incoming Europeans, whom they taught to survive and helped in many ways. This period was not an untroubled "golden age," because indigenous people suffered from new diseases introduced by Europeans and occasionally from other disasters. The second period was marked in western Canada by the signing of treaties and the influx of European settlers. Indigenous peoples lost their autonomy and sovereignty and became subject to the unjust legislation and rule of the nation-state, characterized by policies that fostered assimilation. The "spirit and intent" of the treaties—the formal agreements that were the foundations for sharing the lands of this country—were ignored.[37] As one student wrote in a course paper, "when Native People of today look back on their history they are always going to remember the events that led from contact up until today as major traumatic events that play a key role in the way they perceive the world today."[38] Yet they survived, because "they have an enduring sense of themselves as peoples with a unique heritage and the right to cultural continuity."[39] In Marchak's terms, the indigenous narrative is a counterideology.[40]

Bruner offers a parallel to the indigenous narrative in the new narrative that anthropologists adopted in the late 1960s, when "one story simply became discredited and the new narrative took over."[41] It was a paradigm shift stimulated and signaled by several key events, notably the publication in 1969 of Vine Deloria's book *Custer Died for Your Sins*.[42] In Canada, the single *place* where the opposing nature of indigenous narratives about Canada and their place within it was first clearly articulated, was the reaction in 1969–1970 by a number of Canadian native organizations to the federal government's proposed white paper.[43] Foremost among these was the Indian Chiefs of Alberta, who published their "Red Paper" in 1970.[44] The government's policy paper argued that the cause of Indian problems was their special legal status, which prevented full equality of Indians and integration into Canadian society. The Indian chiefs wanted their special treaty and aboriginal rights acknowledged and recognized, historical grievances addressed fairly, and meaningful participation in any policies that affected them. While this alternate analysis was not new, it represented a unified statement of century-old concerns and issues.

A decade later, the five-hundredth anniversary of Columbus' first voyage to the Americas in 1992 was another landmark for illuminating the persistent distance between the two narratives. Although Columbus barely touched the continent and never reached Canada, he has become the symbol of contact between indigenous and European peoples throughout the hemisphere. From the aboriginal perspective, Columbus' visit signaled:

> the beginning of a five-hundred-year legacy of religious, cultural, social, economic and political intolerance that is still at every level of modern society. . . . From that time on . . . Indigenous peoples have been subordinated in official History, and the denial and erosion of [thousands of years of] Indigenous history by the newcomers has effected lasting damage, rendering Indigenous peoples all but invisible.[45]

Georges Erasmus, then the national chief of the Assembly of First Nations, challenged (Euro-)Canadians to "seriously begin to address the basic relationship they have with this land and the people who were here first."[46]

Building Bridges

Unfortunately, there was little visible response to this challenge. While many smaller partnership projects are being undertaken, in domains as diverse as museums, business, and government, little has been published about them, and they do not seem to have affected public awareness about either indigenous peoples or ways of understanding Canadian history. The shift in narratives, and in paradigms, has not found its way into a broader public discourse.

A decade after the Columbus quincentennial, Georges Erasmus, now a senior aboriginal statesman, restated his original question in the prestigious 2002 La-Fontaine-Baldwin Lecture, which he entitled, "Why Can't We Talk?"[47] He has moved his project along by pointing to points of congruence, similarities in the broadly shared ideals of both aboriginal and nonaboriginal peoples about a "good life." He asks, if we all want similar things, "why is communication between us so difficult, so riddled with misunderstandings and tension?" He argues that semantic differences are part of the problem: "even when the same words were used, aboriginal people and government representatives were often talking about different things." He hopes that Canadians will enter into dialogue with one another, to strive jointly to create that third space where they can agree on a set of meanings that will allow them to work together as equals: "I want to suggest how dialogue with aboriginal people might be framed in different terms, looking for language that expresses aboriginal perspectives and also connects with the aspirations of a wide spectrum of Canadians."[48]

Sadly, there seem to be few substantial efforts in Canada today to build the bridges that Georges Erasmus and other thoughtful commentators are calling for, perhaps because the narratives tend to be represented as mutually exclusive. Accepting one is perceived as rejecting the other.[49] It is here that the idea of multiple paradigms may prove useful. The narrative of modernity and progress may still be meaningful, even in a time of postmodern scholarship for many Canadians whose ancestors immigrated here and constituted the "settler societies." Yet that narrative should no longer be allowed to dominate Canada's national story in official histories. Decentering this story will create a space for alternate narratives. A recognition by nonindigenous Canadians that there is more than one way to understand our collective histories will be a strong first step toward a meaningful dialogue.

The issue is being forced by the court cases and land claims launched by indigenous peoples since the 1970s.[50] These cases call for the settling of outstanding grievances, often stemming from the nineteenth century, and for fair dealings on a nation-to-nation basis. Increasingly, the courts are agreeing, yet the fundamental basis for the oppositions—the competing narratives—are still obscured. Finding ways to make the competing narratives transparent—to decenter the dominant narrative, to legitimize competing indigenous narratives—and to provide a forum for the dialogue that will lay the groundwork for bridges between these competing stories and their constituencies are crucial steps toward dismantling the barriers that restrict opportunities for indigenous peoples and prevent indigenous peoples and other Canadians from living together "in peace and harmony."[51]

Notes

This paper was originally prepared for *Indigenous Peoples and the Modern State*, "Trilateral Discussion: Canada, United States, and Mexico," Claremont Graduate University, April 5–7, 2002. The analysis is still a work in progress, drawn from recent and ongoing research related to the history of the indigenous people of the Treaty 8 region of northwestern Canada (e.g., Patricia McCormack, "The Making of Modern Fort Chipewyan," unpublished manuscript, 2004; Patricia A. McCormack and Gordon Drever, "Treaty No. 8 and Issues of Taxation," report prepared for Karin Buss, of Ackroyd, Piasta, Roth, and Day, in conjunction with *Benoit et al. v. the Queen*, April 20, 1999; Patricia A. McCormack and Gordon Drever, "Treaty No. 8: Rebuttal Report," report prepared for Karin Buss, of Ackroyd, Piasta, Roth, and Day, in conjunction with *Benoit et al. v. the Queen*, March 20, 2001; and Patricia A. McCormack and Gordon Drever, "Imposing Tax: Taxation in the Northwest Territories and Aboriginal Fears in the Treaty 8 Region," selected papers of Rupert's Land Colloquium, compiled by David G. Malaher (Winnipeg, MB: Centre for Rupert's Land Studies, 2002). Opening quote taken from the Provincial Museum of Alberta, *Syncrude Gallery of Aboriginal Culture: Research Guide* (Edmonton: Provincial Museum of Alberta, 2000).

1. There are strong parallels between this approach to partnership and the development of community-based participatory research (e.g., Joan Ryan and Michael P. Robinson, "Implementing Participatory Action Research in the Canadian North: A Case Study of the Gwich'an in Language and Cultural Project," *Culture* 10, no. 2 (1990): 57–71; Verna St. Denis, "Community-based Participatory Research: Aspects of the Concept Relevant for Practice," *Native Studies Review* 8, no. 2 (1992): 51–74; and Susan Guyette, *Community-based Research: A Handbook for Native Americans* (Los Angeles: American Indian Studies Center, University of California, 1983).

2. David Wilcox, "A Short Guide to Partnerships," *Partnerships Online*, 2002, at www.partnerships.org.uk/part, p.1 (retrieved May 11, 2004).

3. Wilcox, "A Short Guide to Partnerships."

4. John Ralston Saul, "Rooted in the Power of Three," *Globe and Mail*, 2002, at www.globeandmail.com/, p. A15 (retrieved March 11, 2002). Saul, who speaks about Canada's unique, "non-monolithic foundation," ("aboriginal, francophone, anglophone"), claims "that Canadian society is all to eager to limit the contribution of aboriginals to questions that directly concern them. If Canada does have a triangular foundation, I personally want to hear what that first party has to say about the whole of our society."

5. Douglas Campbell, "Reasons for Judgment in *Benoit et al. v. the Queen*," Federal Court of Canada Trial Division, Court no. T-2288-92, March 7, 2002.

6. E. G. Brulotte, "Respect Lost," *Edmonton Journal*, March 13, 2002, A16.

7. Justice Campbell's decision was overturned by the Federal Court of Appeal a year later (Federal Court of Appeal, *Canada v. Benoit*, FCA 236, June 11, 2003), and on April 29, 2004, the Supreme Court of Canada announced that it would not hear the case.

8. Assembly of First Nations and Canadian Museums Association (AFN and CMA), *1992 Task Force Report on Museums and First Peoples* (Ottawa: CMA and AFN), 1; cf. Julia Harrison, Bruce Trigger, and Michael Ames, "Museums and Politics: The Spirit Sings and the Lubicon Boycott," *Muse* 6, no. 3 (1988): 12–16.

9. AFN and CMA, *1992 Task Force Report*, 7. There is a broad literature about historical and contemporary relationships between indigenous peoples and museums in North America and elsewhere that is beyond the scope of this paper. It documents former practices of appropriation and representation and current efforts to construct partnerships in which indigenous peoples contribute in meaningful ways to representations of their histories and cultures in museums. Examples of recent endeavors can be read in self-representations, such as the book that accompanies a new Blackfoot gallery at the Glenbow Museum (Blackfoot Gallery Committee, *Nitsitapiisinni: The Story of the Blackfoot People* [Toronto: Key Porter Books, 2001]) and in analyses such as Huhndorf's unsettling interpretation of the reconstituted Museum of the American Indian, now the New York Heye Center, under the auspices of the Smithsonian Institution (Shari M. Huhndorf, *Going Native: Indians in the American Cultural Imagination* [Ithaca, NY: Cornell University Press, 2001], 199–202).

10. Patricia A. McCormack and Arthur J. Sciorra, "Building Partnerships: Canadian Museums, Aboriginal Peoples, and the Spirit and Intent of the Task Force on Museums and First Peoples." Paper presented at the Canadian Association for the Conservation of Cultural Property, Whitehorse, YT, May 29–31, 1998.

11. McCormack and Sciorra, "Building Partnerships; cf. also McCormack, "The Making of Modern Fort Chipewyan," chap. 2; Johannes Fabian, *Time and the Work of Anthropology: Critical Essays 1971–1991* (Chur, Switzerland: Harwood Academic Publishers, 1991), 92; and Richard F. Salisbury, "Transactions or Transactors? An Economic Anthropologist's View," in *Transaction and Meaning: Directions in the Anthropology of Exchange and Symbolic Behavior*, ed. Bruce Kapferer (Philadelphia: Institute for the Study of Human Issues, 1976), 42.

12. Edward Bruner, "Ethnography as Narrative," in *The Anthropology of Experience*, ed. Victor W. Turner and Edward M. Bruner (Urbana: University of Illinois Press, 1986), 145.

13. Bruner, "Ethnography as Narrative," 141; cf. Deborah Doxtator, "The Home of Indian Culture and Other Stories in the Museum," *Muse* 6, no. 3 (1988): 26.

14. A substantial scholarly literature addresses the ways in which the historical relationships between indigenous peoples and European settlers/colonizers have been represented by racialized and stereotyped understandings of a conceptual category of "Indian-ness" (or "Inuit/Eskimo-ness"), constructed to serve multiple European goals, from definitions of "whiteness" and identities of European immigrants to Canada and the United States, to justifications for conquest of the continent and its indigenous populations, to ongoing reproduction of contemporary racial hierarchies. Cf. inter alia Berkhofer 1978; Daniel Francis, *The Imaginary Indian: The Image of the Indian in Canadian Culture* (Vancouver: Arsenal Pulp Press, 1992), a popular Canadian book; Patrick Brantlinger, *Dark Vanishings: Discourse on the Extinction of Primitive Races, 1800–1930* (Ithaca, NY: Cornell University Press, 2003); Huhndorf, *Going Native*; and Audrey Smedley, *Race in North America: Origin and Evolution of a Worldview* (Boulder, CO: Westview Press, 1999). This literature has been remarkable in part for its lack of influence on popular understandings about indigenous peoples.

15. Marlene Shore, "Introduction," in *The Contested Past*, ed. Marlene Shore (Toronto: University of Toronto Press, 2002), 5. Shore has argued that Canadian historians have never constructed a national chronicle, or at least not one on which everyone agrees. The online debate between Jack Granatstein and Michael Ignatieff illustrates some of the arguments between historians about what could or should be taught. However, the appreciation of professional historians for the complexities and nuances of Canadian history has not informed a broader public or "popular" understanding of Canada's past. See Jack Granatstein and Michael Ignatieff, "Does History Matter? Four Articles," *Canadian Questions, GCQ Home*, 1999, at www.schoolnet.ca/greatquestions/e/q6/ (retrieved May 16, 2004).

16. M. Patricia Marchak, *Ideological Perspectives on Canada*, 3rd ed. (Toronto: McGraw-Hill Ryerson, 1988), 1. In Bruner's words, "the narrative structures we construct are not secondary narratives about data but primary narratives that establish what is to count as data" (Bruner, "Ethnography as Narrative," 142–43).

17. Marchak, *Ideological Perspectives*, 5.

18. C. E. Black, *The Dynamics of Modernization: A Study in Comparative History* (New York: Harper & Row, 1966), 6; cf. J. M. Blaut, *The Colonizer's Model of the World: Geographical Diffusionism and Eurocentric History* (New York: Guilford Press, 1993).

19. J. A. Hobson, *Imperialism*, 3rd ed. (London: George Allen & Unwin, 1948), 156–57, originally published in 1902.

20. Sylvia Van Kirk, "Competing Visions: Integrating Aboriginal/Non-Aboriginal Relations into Canadian History," 2002, 3; unpublished paper used with permission of the author.

21. The ambiguous position of Métis in the Canadian national story can be seen as early as 1880, when Alexander Morris identified at least three "classes" of "half-breeds," which represented three distinct paths of cultural development. At one end of an evolutionary continuum were those who had become farmers and lived in permanent homes, while at the other end were those "who are entirely identified with the Indians." Between these extremes were the half-breeds "who do not farm, but live after the habits of the Indians, by the pursuit of the buffalo and the chase"; see Alexander Morris, The Treaties of Canada, facsimile ed. (Toronto: Coles, 1971), 294; originally published in 1880 in Toronto by Belfords, Clark. The third adaptation, which involved a form of independent commodity production, has been romanticized in Canada, though not by Morris. Morris did not consider the important economic role that Métis played in freighting as independent contractors.

22. Trigger in Harrison, Trigger, and Ames, "Museum and Politics," 13.

23. Cf. Bonnie Urciuoli, *Exposing Prejudice: Puerto Rican Experiences of Language, Race, and Class* (Boulder, CO: Westview Press, 1996).

24. Blaut, *The Colonizer's Model of the World*.

25. John Comaroff and Jean Comaroff, *Ethnography and the Historical Imagination* (Boulder, CO: Westview Press, 1992), 19; cf. Bruner, "Ethnography as Narrative," 144.

26. T. S. Kuhn, *The Structure of Scientific Revolutions* (Chicago: University of Chicago Press, 1962).

27. J. Hassard, *Sociology and Organization Theory: Positivism, Paradigms, and Postmodernity* (Cambridge: Cambridge University Press, 1993), 79.

28. Kuhn, *The Structure of Scientific Revolutions*.

29. Hassard, *Sociology and Organization Theory*, 78.

30. J. A. Barnes, *Models of Interpretation* (Cambridge: Cambridge University Press, 1990); Hassard, *Sociology and Organization Theory*.

31. Blaut, *The Colonizer's Model of the World*, 37.

32. See, for example, Patricia A. McCormack, "Native Homelands as Cultural Landscapes: Decentering the Wilderness Paradigm," in *Sacred Lands: Aboriginal World Views, Claims and Conflicts*, ed. Jill Oakes, Rick Riewe, Kathi Kinew, and Elaine Maloney (Edmonton: Canadian Circumpolar Institute, University of Alberta, and Department of Native Studies, University of Manitoba, Occasional paper no. 43, 1998), 25–32.

33. Comaroff and Comaroff, *Ethnography and the Historical Imagination*, 28–29.

34. Hassard, *Sociology and Organization Theory*, 86–87.

35. Hassard, *Sociology and Organization Theory*, 88.

36. Royal Commission on Aboriginal Peoples, *People to People, Nation to Nation: Highlights from the Report of the Royal Commission on Aboriginal Peoples* (Ottawa: Minister of Supply and Services Canada, 1996).

37. See, inter alia, Royal Commission, *People to People*, 1; Richard Price, *The Spirit of the Alberta Indian Treaties* (Montreal: Institute for Research on Public Policy and Indian Association of Alberta, 1979); Treaty 7 Elders and Tribal Council, with Walter Hildebrandt, Sarah Carter, and Dorothy First Rider, *The True Spirit and Original Intent of Treaty 7* (Montreal: McGill-Queen's University Press, 1996).

38. Richelle Badger, "Culture Clash and the Loss of Identity: Looking to the Past for Visions of Tomorrow," research paper done for NS210, School of Native Studies, University of Alberta, April 2 2003, p. 8.

39. Royal Commission, *People to People*, x.

40. Marchak, *Ideological Perspectives on Canada*, 5–6.

41. See Bruner, "Ethnography as Narrative," 139; cf. Doxtator, *The Home of Indian Culture*, 27. It is not always clear whether Bruner is discussing indigenous narratives or those of anthropologists *about* indigenous peoples. While they are related, they serve different purposes and are not synonymous. This fascinating dimension is not explored here.

42. Vine Deloria, *Custer Died for Your Sins* (New York: Macmillan, 1969).

43. Department of Indian Affairs and Northern Development, *Statement of the Government of Canada on Indian Policy 1969* (Ottawa: Queen's Printer, 1969), white paper; cf. Sally Weaver, *Making Canadian Indian Policy: The Hidden Agenda, 1968–1970* (Toronto: University of Toronto Press, 1981); Royal Commission, *People to People*, 17–18.

44. Indian Chiefs of Alberta, *Citizens Plus: The Red Paper* (Toronto: New Press, 1970).

45. Gerald McMaster and Lee-Ann Martin, "Introduction," in *Indigena: Contemporary Native Perspectives*, ed. Gerald McMaster and Lee-Ann Martin (Douglas, QC: Canadian Museum of Civilization, 1992), 12.

46. George Erasmus, "Statement," in *Indigena: Contemporary Native Perspectives*, ed. Gerald McMaster and Lee-Ann Martin (Douglas, QC: Canadian Museum of Civilization, 1992), 8).

47. Georges Erasmus, "Why Can't We Talk? The 2002 LaFontaine-Baldwin Lecture," *Globe and Mail*, March 9, 2002, F6.

48. Erasmus, "Why Can't We Talk?" F6.

49. As well, analysts such as Hugh Brody, Elizabeth Furniss, and Shari Huhndorf demonstrate the powerful countervailing forces that reproduce the status quo, especially the racial hierarchies that underlie much public perception. See Hugh Brody, *The People's Land: Eskimo and Whites in the Eastern Arctic* (Markham, ON: Penguin Books, 1975); Elizabeth Furniss, *The Burden of History* (Vancouver: UBC Press, 2000); and Huhndorf, *Going Native*.

50. Some commentators have also pointed to the demographic incentives to address these issues, as the percentage of indigenous peoples increases in the overall population in some regions of Canada (e.g., Saul, "Rooted in the Power of Three"; Gerald Friesen, "White Law, Frontier Justice," *Globe and Mail*, March 7, 2002, A17). The new northern territory of Nunavut was a remarkable political experiment, established April 1, 1999, with an Inuit majority.

51. Royal Commission, *People to People*, ix.

The Mayan Quest for Pluricultural Autonomy in Mexico and Guatemala 10

JUNE NASH

THE GLOBALIZATION OF PRODUCTION and exchange in an expanding world market has brought with it countercurrents challenging the domination of capital and the exclusionary terms of entry in a single world order. Indigenous peoples of the American hemisphere have been able to gain a wider audience for their voices in the new spaces opened up by global communication networks and an expanding civil society. The democratizing tendencies, aided by United Nations conventions, provide the basis for consolidating indigenous autonomy. Thus these internationalizing currents are concurrent with grassroots movements for the cultural rights of distinctive cultures.[1]

The resurgence of ethnicity witnessed by anthropologists throughout the Western Hemisphere—particularly since the organization of the celebration of five hundred years of resistance in 1992—places what Darcy Ribeiro calls the testimonial people in the vanguard of resistance and protest to many of the globalization processes that concern anthropologists.[2] Many continue to practice collective lifeways and to relate to cosmic powers in ways envisioned by their ancestors. These normative practices are not the result of passivity, but rather the product of resistance by those who have experienced the trauma of conquest and colonization. This ritual reinforcement and daily enactment of their sacred ties with the land cultivates an environmental ethic of conservation and sustainability among testimonial peoples. In recognition of the unique contribution they can make because of this, participants at the Conference on Environment and Development at Rio de Janeiro in 1992 adopted a comprehensive program for sustainable development with indigenous stewardship.

Mayas are among the indigenous peoples of the Western Hemisphere, defined by the United Nations Inter-Commission Task Force on Indigenous People as

"those which, having a historical continuity with pre-invasion and pre-colonial societies that have developed on their territories, consider themselves distinct from
other sectors of the societies now prevailing in those territories or parts of them."[3]
In their five hundred years of contact and colonization, Mayas have resisted assimilation to the dominant European and mestizo (mixed blood) society by holding on to the small plots of land they cultivate. Yet they have also adopted new
crops and responded to new opportunities in order to "remain the same."[4] When
forced to move, they have cultivated ways of reestablishing their own community
and cosmic orientations.[5]

Mayas on both sides of the border are now confronting the threat of disloca-
tion brought about by neoliberal trade and economic policies. The resurgence of
ethnic identification challenges assumptions about the inevitability of cultural ho-
mogenization and the loss of local control.[6] They have done this in distinct ways
that conform to different levels of indigenous autonomy in each country. In Mexico, following the Revolution of 1910 and its belated realization in Chiapas in the
1930s, the Party of the Institutional Revolution (PRI) pursued policies designed
to integrate highland pueblos in a national project premised on mestizo identity.
Following the first Chiapas National Indigenous Congress in 1974, *campesinos*
(small plot cultivators and agricultural labor) formed independent agrarian organizations that broke away from official PRI confederations. These regional organizations were the organizational basis for an increasingly independent role of
indigenous campesinos of Chiapas that provided the impetus for the 1992 celebration of "Five Hundred Years of Resistance to Conquest and Slavery." When
feudal coffee plantations on the Pacific coast declined in the 1970s, indigenous
colonos (indentured labor) migrated to the Lacandón rain forest. As the government
withdrew its support for semisubsistence cultivation in the 1980s, campesinos
moved from a position of the right to land for those who work it to the right for
indigenous people to govern themselves in the regional territories in which they
constitute a majority.

Like the Mayas of Chiapas, Guatemalan Indians bore the brunt of liberal
trade policies adopted in the 1870s that opened their borders to investment in
commercial crop cultivation, cattle raising, and tourism. In *municipios* of the western highlands of Guatemala, where the Mayas constitute a majority of the population, they were able to maintain their cultural identity while migrating seasonally
to coastal plantations. Their marginalized economic and political position persisted until the revolution of 1944 brought Juan José Arévalo came to power. He
replaced the ladino *intendentes* with local, indigenous leaders in the pueblos. Their
success in developing cooperatives and unionizing wage workers was countered by
government repression backed by the military after the U.S.-instigated coup in
1954. Small plot cultivators of the western highlands of Guatemala migrated to

the Ixcán rain forest contiguous with the Lacandón rain forest on the northern border with Mexico, where they were promised title to the land. Practicing a communal form of life, they organized cooperatives linked in a loose network called Communities of Populations in Resistance (CPRs).[7] Even in these newly constituted communities, indigenous people of Guatemala could not escape the internal class conflicts endemic in a nation structured in racist as well as classist terms.[8] Following the militarization of the northern frontier and western highlands in 1975, the Guatemalan Mayas were caught in a near genocidal conflict.

The colonizers of both the Lacandón rain forest and of the Ixcán rain forests took a stand against deterritorialization when the promises to the lands they colonized were revoked. This happened first in Guatemala in 1975 when oil was discovered and the oil companies—Getty Oil, Texaco, Amoco, and Shenandoah Oil—extended their drilling into settled areas of Ixcán. The army and paramilitary forces backed up the companies against the settlers when they tried to defend their lands.[9] Some joined the Committee of Campesino Unity (CUC), a broadly based community action organization of indigenes and mestizos. Others joined the Guerrilla Army of the Poor (EGP), especially after the massacre in Rio Negro in 1982 when the Guatemalan Army killed over half the villagers because they opposed the damming of a river for an international hydroelectric company.[10] The concerted attempt by the federal army to destroy the spatial and symbolic boundaries in the church, community, and home through state terror failed to eradicate the identity maintained by indigenous people to these sanctuaries.[11]

The contest for control of the Lacandón area that began with the Zapatista Army of National Liberation (EZLN) on New Year's morning of 1994 intensified after what some called "an ocean of oil" was discovered beneath the forest cover, the same ocean that flowed beyond the border into Guatemala.[12] Clearly, this was a known factor when President Zedillo ordered the invasion of the Lacandón rain forest on February 9, 1995, in a military operation that increased the troop buildup from 12,000 during the twelve-day war after the uprising to 60,000 soldiers. Zedillo referred to the invasion simply as the apprehension of Subcommander Marcos and other "terrorists" identified as guerrillas of the 1968 insurrection, but many civil society activists considered that this was an excuse to militarize the Lacandón. It may even have been prompted by the oil discoveries since the EZLN had not violated the conditions of the ceasefire agreement signed twelve days after the uprising. In the ensuing protests against military occupation, Maya colonists of the jungle are putting into practice the autonomy they seek.

Following the decades of war in which Guatemalan Mayas were entangled as combatants or victims, Maya organizations emerged during the peace process in the mid-1980s. They have called for control over educational programs, the official use of Mayan languages, participation in election debates.[13] The growing demand for control of their lands among Mayas in both nations set off broader demands for territorial autonomy that will be discussed below.

Autonomy in Mayan Procedural Culture

The practice of autonomy is deeply embedded in indigenous societies throughout the Americas.[14] Autonomy goes far beyond the demands for "equality" and "liberty" that are the rallying cry of Western democracies from the time of the French Revolution and its reverberations in independence struggles of the hemisphere. Rather, autonomy is a dimension of interpersonal as well as intersocietal relations expressed in behavior among all members of a social group.[15]

In order to comprehend Mayan precepts of governance, it is important to consider the cultural and moral commitments in all their diversity. I learned in my fieldwork in Amatenango that celebrations for Christian saints and preconquest spirits and divinities are important venues for cultivating the flowery language, *nichinal k'op,*[16] of their ancestors. The couplets of the *patotán*, literally "behind the heart" or ritual prayer, carry a double meaning for each phrase that officeholders learn as they take on the burden of celebrations for the saints. The imagery and metaphors that abound in Mayan languages survive in their Spanish rendition. There is no sense of contradiction in these syncretic expressions that seem to gain strength in assimilating the dual tradition. Many indigenous people who have turned to the Protestant churches that have grown in numbers in the decades since the 1970s are seeking the same communal values they feel are lost in their communities of origin.[17]

The shared Mayan traditions in myths and prayers contain some of the enduring templates for their behavior. The adventures of the twin gods who mediate relations between gods of the upper world and the lower world that are recounted in the *Popol Vuh*, the Quiché origin myth, provide a model of confrontation and opposition to forces that are part of the cosmic unity. The cycles of resistance and conquest contemplated in indigenous myths respond to generative cycles of human reproduction and finding a new balance with cosmic forces. Death is only an episode encountered in the continual regeneration of new forms. Contained in local cultures that differ in details but share common elements, Mayan traditions helped preserve a sense of distinctive roots and their own autonomy that was disrupted by ethnocidal attacks undertaken by the national governments in both Mexico and Guatemala in the late twentieth century.[18]

Rituals, even though they were enacted ostensibly for Catholic saints and deities, were one way of retaining their link with a preconquest identity. In the *patotán* the officeholders announce repeatedly that they are doing what they do just as the ancestors did, here in the eyes of the ancestors. Stories of past and contemporary encounters with authorities reveal the telescoping of time that attunes them to the cycle of life and death. They also show the humor, wit, and insights into power contained in the epic tales of the *Popol Vuh* that enabled them to conserve their culture over the centuries.

Mayas recognize the energy of ants and of bees in myths that recount how the collective strength of these small creatures overcomes formidable opposition. They also recognize the fact that ants, like bees, are able to proceed about their business because their actions are often not detected. The cell-like organization of the honeycomb provided an ideal model for their resistance movement during the colonial and independence period. It exemplifies Mayan ideals of governance, with each unit acting autonomously in accord with a collective organization. This strategy maximized flexibility, allowing them to reconnoiter their forces when threatened with annihilation. The activities of myriad protagonists, each pursuing autonomously an agenda agreed upon by the group, have enabled Mayas to escape detection during centuries of resistance and protest. Two of the major civil society organizations in which Ch'oles of the Northern Frontier and contiguous Tzotzil hamlets of Chenalhó relate call themselves the Bees (*Ab'u Xú Tzeltal* or *Abejas Spanish*).

These strategies are still central to the practice of autonomy. Operating within existing organizations, campesinos develop opposition positions that then become the basis for new organizations in an ever-renewing cycle. This is expressed in the Tzeltal phrase *Kiptik ta Lecubtesel,* meaning "Applying our Strength for a Better Future," the name of producer unions that developed in the Ocosingo area after the First Indigenous Congress, called by the bishop in San Cristóbal de las Casas.[19] The name evokes the collective action of ant and bee colonies that clearly inspires the unremitting determination of campesinos to gain justice in the face of massive repression.

Another common orientation in the "procedural culture"[20] of Mayas that contributes to their exercise of autonomy is their belief that humans share collectivity responsibility for maintaining the balance between the sun, or Tatik K'ak and the moon, Me'tikchich U. In Amatenango, for example, having sexual relations in the *milpa* is so abhorrent to the sun, Tatik K'ak, that he would refuse to follow his diurnal course to the underworld and would remain in orbit, causing the crops to dry up. The rains brought by the Grandmother Moon, Me'tikchich U, are also the responsibility of all people, who must behave so that she will return. This gendered complementarity is implicit in the many traditions in folk Catholicism that attempt to retrieve the female principle that is systematically undermined in orthodox Christianity.[21]

The Mayan rule of governance, command while obeying, implies a dialogue, so that listening becomes an important aspect of the qualifications for leadership.

When I did my first fieldwork in Amatenango del Valle in Chiapas in 1957, I asked civil officials what were the duties of each office; for judges, it was to sit and listen, for policemen to sit and watch. This would probably never be the response given to such a question in Western culture, where the verb "to govern" is taken to be an expression of the will of the sovereign, and where the role of police is active intervention. There is little or no reflection on what Westerners assume to be passive roles of sitting, watching, or listening that are so intrinsic to Mayan governing practice. The dialogic approach to governing is also part of the procedural culture continuously evoked during assemblies when leaders may raise issues but listen attentively to the responses of people. The central importance of dialogical interaction in the emergence of all culture is particularly important in nonhierarchical exchanges that try to promote the autonomous engagement of participants.

Implementing Autonomy in Indigenous Relations with the State

Mayan linguistic groups of both Mexico and Guatemala were united in the governance of the province of Guatemala. Indians on both sides of the border were subject to tribute payments that forced them out of self-sufficient agriculture and into the market, to sell their products or labor.[22] Lands granted to indigenous populations were expropriated by the Spanish, who thereby acquired a labor force of the expropriated Indians for their haciendas and *obrajes*, the eighteenth-century equivalent of textile mills.[23] In both areas, the liberal period, especially after 1870, brought about the loss of communal lands, forced labor, and pressure for Latinization. Communities in the more isolated areas of the highlands on the slopes of the Sierra Mountains were able to retain their traditional culture until the revolutionary period, but the price was seasonal labor in coastal plantations.[24] Rebellions occurred when indigenous people were pressed beyond their ability to sustain the culture of their ancestors or when corruption of Spanish and Ladino *mediaries* exceeded the norms. Thus the Rebellion of Cancuc broke out in Chiapas in the township of Cancuc in 1712 when tributes rose in a declining economy, during the droughts that affected the townships of Yajalón, Petalcingo, Tila, and Tumbala in 1771, and in 1867–1869 in Chamula. As capital-intensive exploitation intensified in Guatemala, revolts occurred in the mid-nineteenth century in Ixtahuacán, in 1876 in Momostenango when liberals seized the lands of Indians, and in Ixcoy in 1898.

Since colonial times, the township was the basis for distinctive ethnic groups to cultivate a sense of autonomy. Endogamy within these boundaries and a hands-off attitude of Ladino (nonindigenous or mestizo) officials at departmental and national levels permitted the illusion of local control to flourish. But since in-

digenous peoples did not enter into the political and economic circuits that determined the structural conditions for survival, autonomy limited to the community also engendered strife. Envy and the competition for "limited goods" were
promoted by the governments of both Mexico and Guatemala.[25] In Mexico, in-
tracommunity conflicts actually increased with the "institutionalization" of the
1910 Revolution since the federal government favored the *cabeceras*, or head towns,
in the distribution of resources that never reached the hamlets. As the inequality
between elite residents in the cabeceras and the outlying hamlets progressed in the
1970s, the latter began to contest the rule of the *caciques*, or indigenous leaders allied to the ruling PRI. Regions differentially favored by the land reform policies
of the central government began to participate in breakaway campesino—rural
cultivators—organizations. The migration of many highland indigenous peoples
and of coastal plantation workers to the Lacandón forest in the 1970s created a
dynamic center freed from the caciques' claims to traditional leadership.

In Guatemala the revolution brought about by the democratic election of
Juan José Arévalo in 1945 provided a decade of democratic experimentation in
indigenous relations with the state. The advances made in land reform and greater
local autonomy were cut short in a U.S.-engineered coup in July 1954.
Guatemala then became an arena for fighting the Cold War against communism,
with ever-increasing repression of agricultural and industrial unions.[26] Protestant
evangelizing and Catholic Action groups contested the power of traditionalists
who held offices in the civil religious hierarchy, providing ideological formulations for a war between ethnic groups, political parties, and social classes. Falla
saw a diminishing of ethnic conflict with the resurgence of class antagonism after 1954, but his last period of field research ended in 1970 before the genocidal policies of the Guatemalan army began to escalate.[27] Multiple, coexisting
models of world creation allowed indigenous people to maintain a vision of autonomy, while paradoxically perpetuating their subordination to Ladino domination, as Kay Warren suggests.[28]

Mayas on both sides of the border between Mexico and Guatemala constitute themselves as actors in the national and global settings. Yet, at the same time,
they are demonstrating their ability to reconstitute traditions in territories occupied by their predecessors since the first millennium. I shall examine several mo-
ments in the crisis precipitated by neoliberal policies that were countered by
distinct responses among differentiated sectors of Mayas living on both sides of
the border. The withdrawal of support for subsistence cultivators by neoliberal
governments on both sides of the border has promoted various forms of resistance, protest, and ultimately the practice of autonomy. In Mexico, settlements of
the Lacandón rain forest were the first to declare war in the January 1, 1994, uprising when the Zapatista Army of National Liberation (EZLN) declared an end

to the marginalization and impoverishment caused by neoliberal policies of the Salinas government. Migrants into the area were drawn by promises of land that were revoked by the passage of the "reform" of the Agrarian Reform Law of the 1917 Constitution. In 1992 the PRI-dominated Congress passed a "reform" of Article 27 of the Constitution, making it possible for individual *ejidatarios* (shareholders in communal lands) to sell land or to engage in commercial ventures going beyond the community. The repudiation of the government's commitment to land for those who work the soil, combined with the passage of the Tratado de Libre Comercio (North American Free Trade Agreement) that was to go into effect on the eve of the uprising, ended the social contract that had sustained the PRI in the seventy-one years of monopoly control of power. Communities of the northern frontier were the first in proclaiming their autonomy as a Pluricultural Autonomous Region on October 11, 1994. As a result, they have experienced the brunt of state military repression often extended in paramilitary attacks. Triggered by the 1994 uprising, support groups for the EZLN developed within municipalities of the highlands and the northern frontier. This occurred particularly in outlying hamlets that turned against caciques—corrupt local officials co-opted by the PRI—in the cabecera, or head town (much like a county seat). Communities within the highland and lowland regions are now enacting the premises of autonomy to various degrees.

The harsh attack on indigenous communities that accelerated in Guatemala from 1978 to 1985 left little ground for the expression of autonomy. The terror began with the Panzos massacre in 1974. Located in the Ixil triangle in Alta Verapaz on the border with the Lacandón rain forest, the area was occupied by colonizers far from the locus of guerrilla activity in the east. Called the "Zone of the Generals," it was the site where General Lucas and other army generals were grabbing land where transnational oil explorers discovered oil.[29] The highly publicized massacre of settlers in 1975 was committed in broad daylight rather than in secrecy, perhaps to inspire fear and withdrawal. Indigenous youths were forced to join patrols in search of dissidents, and their complicity out of fear for their own lives reinforced the militarization of society. Cultural revitalization came with the peace process of the 1990s, when teachers and educators of Maya descent began to challenge the legacy of colonial and nineteenth-century state formation.[30]

The autonomy movements on each side of the border differ in the processes set in motion and the directions they are pursuing. In Guatemala, an impressive group of Mayan intellectuals are exploring cultural resources of Mayas, integrating them in the educational system of Guatemala. The movement is tied to transnational nongovernmental organizations that are inspired by United Nations declarations, especially the 1983 "Elimination of All Forms of Racial Discrimination" and the 1989 "Universal Declaration of Rights." Although vitalized by grassroots organizations that derive from the five hundred years of resistance to assimilation, Guatemalan Pan Mayanism is clearly giving priority to the production of cultural distinctiveness.[31] In Mexico, the movement for autonomy is more strongly rooted in grassroots activists in producer and distribution cooperatives, land struggles, and social services. The Zapatista Army of National Liberation is a symbolic show of armed force to back up the demands for the right to autonomy that are set in practice in the colonized area of the Lacandón rain forest and in Christian-based communities in support of these. Mexican intellectuals have played an important role in integrating local discourses with national and international currents, but with few exceptions such as Margarito Ruiz Hernandez, they are not of Mayan descent. Some supporters of the autonomy movement, such as Pablo Gonzalez Casanova and Hector Diaz-Polanco, have reversed earlier formulations of indigenous peoples' separate and distinct relation to the state as "internal colonialism" that perpetuated exploitation.[32] Their direct involvement along with Bishop Samuel Ruiz, in the dialogues that led to the San Andrés Agreement in February 1996, has promoted respect for the autonomy movement as a harbinger of pluricultural coexistence.

Although the forms of activism differ across the border, the objectives of Mayas in both Chiapas and Guatemala are similar. Guatemala public intellectuals contest the representation of Mayas in national culture, both of the colonial and independence period. Mayan intellectuals such as Demetrio Cojtí Cuxil and Enrique Sam Colop reject the "discourses of concealment" that speak of a humbled and ignorant population overawed in their view of the Spaniards as gods.[33] The terminology of "icon," translated by Spaniards as "god," is not necessarily a divine figure but may be an alien or even evil image. These intellectuals, as Kay Warren points out, create larger identifications and counterhistories in ways that enable Mayas to see themselves as agents of their own history.[34] This serves, like the narrative histories of the Chiapas Mayan campesinos, to reaffirm their agency and ability to transform their destiny. I have seen this in the chalkboard chronologies of assassinations of campesino leaders written on the walls of the Casa del Pueblo in the embattled township of Venustiano Carranza, which campesinos point out to visitors to cue them in to their history. The same urgency is expressed in the Acteal chapel where the names and photographs of the forty-five victims of the massacre carried out by paramilitaries trained by the Mexican government in December 1997 are posted above the massive cement mausoleum constructed in their memory.

The premises of autonomy and dialogue are the ideal, not always realized in the day-to-day governance of people. References to these traditions in the San Andres Accord cosigned by government representatives and the EZLN on February 16, 1996, include self-governance of regions in which the indigenous population constitutes a majority, with the right to designate culturally appropriate educational, social, and economic programs in accord with ancestral practices. The Zapatistas have emphasized the rights of indigenous peoples to control at least 10 percent of the revenues from natural resources within their regions for collectively designated programs. Since an "ocean of oil"[35] has recently been discovered beneath the lands occupied by the settlers of the Lacandón, this could put a sizeable part of federal revenues directly under the control of indigenous peoples. Chiapas is the state with the highest capacity for generating hydroelectric power, supplying 2 percent of national needs, and exporting power to Guatemala, yet few of the settlements are connected to the high-power transmitters that pass overhead. The accord includes provisions for pluriethnic representation and coordination in municipal councils, regional general assemblies, and executive commissions. The communities in the autonomous territories would select representatives who would participate in state representative organizations and in the Congress of the Union. Within the territories that would be affected, indigenous forms of government by consensus and communal sharing of the proceeds from collective production activities are called for along with a general claim to govern by "traditional uses and customs."

Women in the National Indigenous Congress and the EZLN conventions have made a significant departure from liberation movements of the past by developing an internal critique of the everyday practice of politics in the movement. They have objected to the unqualified acceptance of "uses and customs," particularly those involving sexist status relations. They insist that there are bad traditions as well as good, and that the tradition of forced marriages at an early age, alcoholism, wife abuse, and other premises of gender inequality should be drastically altered. I shall consider the transformations they are making later on.

Combining preconquest powers with saints and spirits from the Christian religion, Mayas of both countries still maintain a cosmogony that holds humans responsible for the balance in the universe. This has profound consequences for their preference for collective projects in development and for their daily behavior. During the 1990s as Guatemalan Mayas entered into peace negotiations with their government, they focused increasingly on issues of indigenous land claims, evoking *Ruwach'ulew* (The Earth/the World), or *Quate' Ruwach'ulew* (Our Mother the Earth) in what Kay Warren calls "an indigenous ecological discourse in overlapping ways to interconnect Maya cosmology, agricultural rituals, strategies for socioeconomic change, land issues, and rights struggles."[36] Chiapas Mayas have always invoked preconquest cosmic powers as they try to achieve a balance with nature. Zapatistas often contrast this reverence for nature in opposition to neoliberal policies of death, as during the Intercontinental Convention for Life and against neoliberalism in late July and early August 1996. When many fires blew out of control during the planting season in March 1998, Tzeltal-speaking Zapatista supporters in the highlands attributed the loss of forest lands in the Lacandón to an upset in the balance between the sun and the moon caused by the raping and pillage carried out by the army and paramilitary troops in full view of the Tatik Sol. In the Lacandón rain forest, Tojolobil residents of towns hard hit by the fires asserted that they were lit by the army as a means of clearing the forest cover to improve their visibility in combat.

With the advent of the millennium and the newly elected President Vicente Fox promising to resolve the conflict, Zapatistas and their supporters planned a campaign to bring their demands to the federal capital. In January 2001, Zapatistas congregated in San Cristóbal in the Plaza of the Cathedral, where they had protested on so many occasions the presence of the army in the Lacandón rain forest in the years after the uprising. The plaza had become the contested arena for civil society to articulate their sentiments where peace marchers and the national consultations with civil society congregated to speak. There had been clashes between the ranchers calling for the hanging of Bishop Samuel Ruiz and the Zapatista supporters calling for resumption of the dialogue and peace with dignity after the army invasion of the jungle in 1995. It was an appropriate place for Zapatistas and their supporters to congregate as they announced their departure to Mexico City. They arrived in late afternoon as the winter sun set the ochre tones of the cathedral ablaze. They were still masked but bearing banners with their messages clearly articulated: President Fox should carry out his promises to withdraw troops from the rain forest, to implement the Agreement of San Andrés, and to release Zapatistas incarcerated without charges brought against them.

After many stops visiting with indigenous groups en route, the Zapatista convoy with foreign supporters arrived in Mexico City in March. There they were hosted by the Institute of Anthropology and History in the Universidad Nacional Autónoma de Mexico where *Subcomandante Insurgente* Marcos addressed the community of scholars and activists in his inspired poetic vein. The leaders of the EZLN high command spoke in the public squares of the city that were filled with tens of thousands of their supporters. Commander Esther asserted there would never again be a Mexico without women. Commander David inveighed against the continued military posts in indigenous zones, calling upon President Fox to fulfill his commitments to meeting the conditions for resuming the dialogue interrupted in 1996.

On March 11, for the first time in the history of the republic, indigenes spoke in the federal congress. Many of the congressmen of President Fox's own Party of National Action (PAN) boycotted the meeting and the autonomy bill they approved was gutted, leaving indigenous peoples even more subject to state control than before. President Fox admitted that they were justified in their position, although he had at first acclaimed the bill as a historic victory.

Commander Tacho's message to the congress acclaiming the roots of the resistance and survival in the past five hundred years will probably become a refer-
ence point in Mexico's history:

> We fled far to defend ourselves from the great oppressor in order not to be ex-
> terminated unjustly. Given their intelligence and knowledge, our first grandparents
> thought that they would find refuge in the farthest mountains where they could
> promote their resistance and where they could survive with their own forms of
> government politically, socially, economically and culturally, so that our roots
> would not be ended, so that our mother land would never die, nor our mother
> moon, nor our father sun. And so our roots could never be torn out and die, these
> deep roots that survive in the deepest heart of these lands that take on the color
> that we are, the color of earth.[37]

In the last year of the second millennium, the PRI deployed all the skill with
which they constructed the hegemonic accord that sustained them in power for
seventy years in order to fragment indigenous organizations that have escaped
from their control. In its waning days, the PRI is still able to promote fratricide
within indigenous communities by allotting the same parcels of land to contend-
ing factions, or by allowing local caciques to expel their neighbors and even kin on
the premise that they are of an alien religious group. In the 1997 massacre carried
out in Acteal, a hamlet of Chenalhó that supported the EZLN, the PRI government provided the Protestant PRI mayor with guns and ammunition with which
he armed youths of the town to kill forty-five women, children, and men while
they prayed in their makeshift chapel. Armed gunmen of the paramilitary Paz y
Justicia group in Tila continue to threaten their neighbors who support the
EZLN, even after the election of an alliance governor in Chiapas and the decline
in direct financial support.

Mexico's strong civil society may have saved the country from the genocidal
attacks of the army experienced by Guatemalan Mayas. With the growing repression of the EZLN after the cessation of the dialogues in August 1996, the
coordination of the interactions of campesinos and indigenes as a working-class
and civil-society sector was undertaken by the Independent Center of Agricultural Workers and Campesinos (CIOAC). This national organization originated
in the Independent Campesino Center (CCI) formed in 1963, which split into
two wings, one "official" party organization and the other Communist. The
Communist wing was renamed CIOAC in 1975 but was later expelled from the
Maoist Política Popular party along with leaders of campesinos in the rain forest.[38] This expulsion probably freed the energies of these rural workers and
farmers to pursue the uniquely indigenous practices and goals that characterize
CIOAC's actions. CIOAC counts about 300,000 heads of families as members,
predominantly in the poorer states of the southeastern part of the country.

They were among the first to engage in the takeover of land claims that had not been adjudicated by the government in the year following the uprising. Disdaining the PRI tactics of trucking in campesinos for their demonstrations, the CIOAC members walk hundreds of kilometers to bring their claims to state and national capitals.

CIOAC, along with other contemporary campesino organizations, put into practice autonomy during the turbulent years of the 1970s and 1980s. Some, like the National Plural Indigenous Assembly for Autonomy (ANIPA), developed out of the mobilization for the quincentennial celebration of indigenous resistance. All of these organizations embody the aspirations and strategies of the Bees and Ants as they rebuild society from the bottom up. Each unit has responsibility for its actions, yet all act in concert to undermine unjust authority and to construct the base for a new society. The regional indigenous and campesino organizations provide a civic network that fed into broader political actions throughout the state of Chiapas. This introduced a plurality of visions that posed new modes of civic action through a collective strength that can overcome formidable opposition. Through these organizations, Mayas of Chiapas are attempting to regain autonomy not only as an abstract principle in collective life, but for individuals— women and children as well as men—operating within the collectivity.

Participating in regional groups, indigenous campesinos forged the groups that enabled them to raise the level of solidarity in pluriethnic and multicultural regional levels. CEOIC, a group representing a wide array of mestizo and indigenous *ejiditarios, comuneros,* and agricultural laborers, was the first organization to respond to the claims of the rebels. They were successful in their call for cessation of the armed conflict, and amnesty for EZLN in the early weeks of the uprising, and their call for a political resolution of the conflict gained wide support. The organization included both moderate as well as confrontational organizations during the tumultuous years following the uprising. Their presence as a pluriethnic regional representation of indigenous and campesino interests maintained support for the autonomy of indigenous communities and the municipalities and regions in which they constitute a majority.[39]

The very diversity of interests and origins resulted in fissures within CEOIC. The pro-EZLN group within the organization joined with 120 other social organizations to create the State Democratic Assembly of the Chiapas Pueblo (AEDPCH). This organization was the driving force for the candidacy of Amado Avendaño in 1995. When his campaign faltered after an accident that nearly cost his life, the PRI candidate Robles was declared a victor. Upon his recovery from the severe concussion that he had sustained, Amado Avendaño set up a parallel government in the old San Cristóbal INI headquarters where he put into practice the autonomy called for by the Zapatistas and their supporters. AEDPCH served as the major group coordinating civil-society groups of campesinos, professionals, and merchants in the actions taken by the parallel government in the months following the rebellion.

The principle of autonomy was intrinsic to the indigenous movement before the Zapatista uprising, but it was months before an agenda was worked out between leaders in the EZLN with campesino and indigenous leaders. The EZLN opened spaces for existing indigenous movements, but it took over a year of mobilization and dialogue to persuade the revolutionary forces to adopt the ideas developed by ANIPA on autonomy for indigenous pueblos. ANIPA drafted the initial proposals for autonomy that were presented in the federal congress by Margarito Ruiz Hernández, as PRD representative, in 1990. The parallel government of Amado Avendaño worked with the State Council of Indigenous and Campesinos Organizations (CEOIC) and the State Democratic Assembly of Chiapas (AEDPCH) to establish the legal basis for the autonomy of indigenous pueblos.

Concomitant with this process of mobilizing civil society in the parallel government were the distinct but coordinated activities of the Zapatistas and the indigenous campesino organizations. The Zapatistas, working with the National Democratic Convention (CND), convoked the huge convention of Zapatistas and their supporters in Chiapas and throughout the world in the rain forest in August 1994, promoted an international support group that probably contributed to their survival in the months following rebellion. The indigenous groups modified and deepened their proposal for a new pact between indigenous pueblos with the nation. They defined three levels of government that would operate simultaneously at the levels of community, municipality, and regional.[40] Some of these proposals became incorporated in the San Andrés Accord, but indigenous organizations that had fought for regional representation for autonomous entities were disappointed that this proposition was not included.

The parallel engagement of indigenous women in constituent organizations of ANIPA deepened the meaning of autonomy in their assertion of the rights of gender. Three organizations of women, which united women in the Lacandón rain forest and communities of support in the highlands, formed an umbrella organization called Xi' Nich', which included the Committee for the Defense of Indigenous Freedom, Reunion to Resolve Our Problems, and the Union of Communities of the Chiapas Selva. The association with women from many different pueblos was even more dramatic a change for women than for men, yet they adapted to the new organizations, still retaining their independence. Their statement formulated at the fourth assembly of ANIPA in December 1995 demonstrates the importance of defining autonomy in instrumental terms:

> Autonomy for us women implies the right to be autonomous, we, as women, to train ourselves, to seek spaces and mechanisms in order to be heard in the com-

munal assemblies and to have posts. It also implies facing the fear that we have in order to dare to take decisions and to participate, to seek economic independence, to have independence in the family, to continue informing ourselves because understanding gives us autonomy. To be able to participate in this type of reunion enables us to diffuse the experiences of women and animate others to participate.[41]

Women show a clear awareness of their responsibility in cultivating the practice of autonomy in society as well as in the home and family, since it is there that children are enculturated in the patterns that define future behavior. Women who live in fear of abuse, who accept subordination in the home, diffuse sentiments that reproduce subordination and marginalization. This is nowhere more evident than in the devastated communities of Guatemala, where women as widows are trying to reconstitute their families and communities after the devastation wreaked by the Guatemalan army. They must address the immediate needs of their children as single parents as well as overcome the *susto* (fear illness) instilled by arbitrary acts of violence.[42] Always figured as the repository of tradition, women became the guardians of those traditions as they resisted the concerted attempts by the army to destroy the territorial base for cultural regeneration.[43]

Indigenous women have unified their movement at a national level in the National Coalition of Indigenous Women of Mexico (CONAMIM), which also belongs to the continental organization of indigenous women. The militarization of the conflict with the federal troops invading the jungle in 1995 further united women, who became the most vocal opponents of the war. Women distributed leaflets bearing their denunciation of the military in their communities during their March for Peace on March 8, 1995. Looking more like a religious procession than a political movement, as they carried flowers and candles along with babies on their backs, and with their leaders wafting incense to mark their way, the women from throughout the diocese marched throughout the city of San Cristóbal de las Casas. They protested the invasion of their communities and the deployment of troops in the rain forest in their leaflets and speeches, as the following statement shows:

Women relate their oppression to its root cause in the indigenous cultural setting: We are educated to serve in house and communities. Families give preference to boys while girls leave school to work in the house. The government does not give credit or land to women. We do not work for wages, and we have nothing to pay for cultivation. When we ask for legal aid, officials ask for a marriage license, and if we are not married, they say they will not write a warrant. Women cannot be officials in their communities, and do not have the right to a voice, and our word is not worthwhile in court. With the bad treatment we receive, we see rage and suffering as something normal. We seek democratic and harmonious relations with equality and without discrimination and the sharing of household responsibilities.[44]

As a result of the discrimination they have experienced within male organizations, women have formed separate groups to establish their own agenda as protagonists for change. Margarita Gutiérrez and Nellys Paloma, representatives in the Women's Indigenous Convention, clarify the reasons why they have followed this course:

> So we are convinced that the relations of our lives are also determined by the relations that we establish with men (those of our ethnicity and those who are not indigenes), and that these relations . . . have oppressive consequences for us and ought to be transformed. Therefore, the spaces that we value and that we seek to construct are the organizations of women, where we construct our own identity that marks and defines the gender condition and permits the flow and interaction with both male and female "others" and allows us to establish a dialogue of reentry with our own pueblo, with our customs, and to make alliances and actions with women in general to demand a recognition as indigenous women.[45]

In these public consciousness-raising groups, the women tried to overcome the timidity that was part of their socialization. Indigenous women on both sides of the Mexican-Guatemala border can state with pride, as they did in the Convention of Indigenous Women in 1997, that "The great cultural richness of our pueblos has been maintained, reproduced, and enriched by we women." They have defined as a future objective the prevention of the exploitative use by outsiders of "this richness used in a manner foreign to our view of life."[46]

Women's involvement in political action is promoting a greater consciousness of their own rights as human beings. Because of their responsibilities in the family and community, changes of the sort women are experiencing can radically change expectations of what behaviors are acceptable, not only in the intimate spheres of the home, but also in public life. As the repositories of indigenous culture in indigenous communities that relied on their exclusion from the dominant sectors of political and social life, women's demands for full participation in the emergent civil society is a premonition of the end of cacique co-optation and other features of male hegemony during the PRI monopoly of power. It has at the same time threatened some sectors, particularly the male youth of indigenous communities, who sense a loss of their control over women's labor and bodies at the same time that they are losing a sense of their own future in a declining agrarian economy. In this transition, youths can still be recruited into paramilitary operations. Nonetheless, women's assertion of autonomy is crucial for the attainment of indigenous autonomy.

Conclusions

In reaction to state policies that ignore, marginalize, or exploit them, Mayas of Chiapas and Guatemala are attempting to regain autonomy at the regional and national levels. In Guatemala, Mayan intellectuals are revitalizing Mayan languages and culture in order to promote indigenous self-awareness as a basis for self-governance and to overcome racist biases in the dominant culture.[47] Seeking the roots of Mayan ways of governance and behavior, leaders in the Pan Mayan movement such as Demetrio Cojtí Cuxil, Enrique Sam Colop, and Irma Otzoy study Mayan origins in order to unite those of distinct language groups and separate communities. Their principle avenue for mobilizing and disseminating a new status of indigenous people is through education in the schools and public arenas. Other Mayan activists work through Campesino Unity Councils to promote unity of indigenous and non-indigenous people in presenting demands for self-determination on the national agenda. A leading spokesperson for this approach is Rigoberta Menchu, who embodies the presence of indigenous peoples in national and international arenas.

In contrast with Mayan leaders of Guatemala, Chiapas Mayas seek autonomy not only as an abstract principle but also in the daily practice of individuals—women and children as well as men—operating within the collectivity of indigenous people governing themselves in their traditional territories. This collective ethic can be perceived in the ethnographies written before the 1970s. It is also manifested in indigenous campesino mobilizations of some of their organizations during the turbulent years of the 1970s and 1980s. The indigenous movement parallels and draws strength from regional unions and cooperatives to promote indigenous claims to autonomy in regional territories. It has culminated in the indigenous women's movement that charts out the universal claim for the right to autonomy of women as well as men, and even that of children.

The cellular structure of organizations such as the Bees, formed during the mobilization for the quincentennial celebration of 1992 in Acteal, allows for maximum flexibility. This enables the constituent organizations to shift arenas, modifying their strategies in response to attacks by federal and state police and paramilitary forces. It permitted the collective mode of organization that had prevailed within communities to extend into regions. Indigenous people in the self-constituted autonomous regions of the northern frontier and the Lacandón rain forest as well as in bordering hamlets of highland municipalities are in fact engaged in the practice of autonomy while waiting for the government of President Fox to implement the San Andrés Agreement.

The demand for land as a means of work and subsistence receded as land as a territory generating new symbolic and cultural imaginaries for a change in governance became central to the objectives of a conjuncture of diverse social entities. The new, more complex conjuncture of interests and motivations relate the gathering struggle of indigenes and campesinos to a national level, as they became the core for even larger groups that constituted the civil society opposition to the PRI government.

The kind of flexible networks of shifting alliances and diverse interests that originated in indigenous campesino organizations in the northwest region and in the colonized area of the Lacandón rain forest became enmeshed with regional organizations, some of which were sponsored by the Catholic church and others by the PRI government. These movements developed increasing autonomy as they successfully confronted the PRI monopoly of power. The carefully documented criticisms and disciplined objections by CIOAC members recall the centuries of protests by Morelos campesinos that Warman documented in the twentieth century.[48] A major difference in the presentation of their case in the turn of the millennium from that of the past two centuries is the campesinos' explicit rejection of the racism implicit in the official behaviors they confront. This consciousness, along with the women's rejection of gender marginalization within indigenous society, fosters demands for personal dignity and autonomy that are the distinctive characteristics of the current rebellion. It draws upon the roots of rebellion among marginalized groups of the northern and Lacandón region. It spread to the hamlets of indigenous municipalities where women became the principal movers in their demands for dignity.

Following the rejection by Congress to implement the San Andrés Agreement signed between COCOPA and the Zapatistas in February 1996, and the failure in 2001 of resolving differences, Zapatista autonomous communities in the Lacandón rain forest have been practicing autonomy in their everyday life. They are implementing new curricula in their schools, and adjudicating land disputes that have been left suspended in the decade since the uprising. Some of the unity that characterized the communities during and after the uprising has been lost, but in the process of exercising autonomy those who have remained faithful to the agreements have found ways of reaching consensus in the *Juntas de Buen Gobierno*. They are drafting the basis for development projects that depart from the federal government's neoliberal programs in Plan Puebla Panama. Rejecting export-oriented assembly production and major hydroelectric energy projects for commercialization, the Zapatistas are trying to pursue a mixed agricultural and artisanal economy that will enable them to retain their position in the lands they have colonized.[49]

Comparative analysis of the autonomy movement in Guatemala and Chiapas, Mexico, enables us to pinpoint some common strategies that emerged:

- Recourse to primordial strategies of multicellular organizations coordinating actions through consensual principles exemplified by the Abejas

- Continuous engagement of civil society in the actions of regional groups protesting corruption and arbitrary power of officeholders
- Appeals to transnational NGOs, such as with SIPAZ, Global Exchange, and human rights organizations that help maintain open spaces for democratic exchanges
- Insistence on women's participation in decision making at all levels

Concurrent strategies put into action by indigenous activists and a broadly mobilized international civil society in the turbulent decades of the 1980s and 1990s reveal these underlying premises of Mayan protagonists for a new relation with the state. Whether these collective strategies based on the flexible organization of autonomous local groups and relying on consensual decision making can withstand the co-optive strategies and military control exercised by the government remains uncertain. The significance of women as a defining force within the autonomous communities may make the difference between the Zapatista and preceding rebellions that came to reinforce the old hierarchies. The shift in the arenas of struggle to households and communities places human survival rather than the global accumulation of capital at the center of development goals.

In Guatemala where indigenous people have only recently emerged from a genocidal war, Mayas are not yet sure enough of their fragile position to fight strictly in terms of ethnicity outside of the relatively protected environment of schools and transnational study institutes. The CUC draws strength from campesino unity rather than ethnic roots, and they phrase their demands in terms of shared needs with nonindigenous peoples. The relatively small group of people who relate to the Pan Mayan movement responds to foreign rather than domestic audience. Yet in their "creation and redistribution of 'cultural capital,'" these scholars create the resources for political activists to invigorate their movement.[50]

As Mayas strengthen their ties with international agencies, they pose the potential alternative of pluricultural coexistence in global settings. Whether they can withstand the divisive tendencies within their own societies as these are played upon by the state and international capital is still a question. The dialogue among Mayanists on both sides of the border will hopefully contribute to an analysis of the comparative advantages of such collective approaches for pluricultural survival in a globalized world.

Notes

1. For a comparative study of indigenous movements, see Jens Brosted et al., *Native Power: The Quest for Autonomy and Nationhood of Indigenous Peoples* (Bergen: Universitetsforlaget AS, 1985).

2. Darcy Ribeiro, *The Americas and Civilization* (New York: Dutton, 1971).

3. The Intercommission Task Force on Indigenous Peoples (IUCN), *Indigenous Peoples and Sustainability: Cases and Actions* (Utrecht: International Books, 1997), 27.

4. Robert S. Carlsen, *The War for the Heart and Soul of a Highland Maya Town* (Austin: University of Texas Press, 1997).

5. Minor Sinclair, "Faith, Community and Resistance in the Guatemalan Highlands," in *The New Politics of Survival: Grassroots Movements in Central America*, ed. Minor Sinclair (New York: Monthly Review Press, 1995), 75–108; Kathlene Sullivan, "Religious Change and the Recreation of Community in an Urban Setting among the Tzotzil Maya of Highland Chiapas, Mexico," PhD diss., Graduate Center of the City University of New York, 1998.

6. Edward F. Fischer and R. McKenna Brown, "Introduction: Maya Cultural Activism in Guatemala," in *Maya Cultural Activism in Guatemala* (Austin: University of Texas Press, 1996), 1–18; June C. Nash, "The Reassertion of Indigenous Identity: Mayan Responses to State Intervention in Chiapas," *Latin American Research Review* 30, no. 3 (1995): 7–42; June C. Nash, *Mayan Visions: The Quest for Autonomy in an Age of Globalization* (New York: Routledge, 2001); Kay B. Warren, *Indigenous Movements and Their Critics* (Princeton, NJ: Princeton University Press, 1998).

7. Sinclair, "Faith, Community and Resistance," 75.

8. Susanne Jonas's structural analysis of the intersection of ethnic and class antagonism reveals the persistent tendencies toward violence to ensure the rule of a narrow elite in Guatemala. See Susanne Jonas, *The Battle for Guatemala: Rebels, Death Squads, and U.S. Power* (Boulder, CO: Westview Press, 1991).

9. Sinclair, "Faith, Community, and Resistance," 85 et seq.

10. Rolando Alecio, "Uncovering the Truth: Political Violence and Indigenous Organizations," in *The New Politics of Survival: Grassroots Movements in Central America*, ed. Minor Sinclair (New York: Monthly Review Books, 1985), 26.

11. Linda Green, *Fear as a Way of Life* (New York: Columbia University Press, 1993), 9.

12. *El Financiero* 1995.

13. Fischer and Brown, "Introduction," 15.

14. Missionaries often commented with astonishment on the latitude for self-expression and the exercise of will allowed to all members of societies that lived outside of American empire states; see Eleanor Leacock, "Montagnais Women and the Jesuit Program for Colonization," in *Women and Colonization*, ed. M. Etienne and E. Leacock (New York: Monthly Review Press, 1980). They used their observations of egalitarian behavior to indicate the level of barbarity of the people they encountered, and as proof of their need to be civilized. The notion that there could be alternative visions of how humans can relate to society would have been, and still is among some observers, regarded as abhorrent. The importance of these early ethnographic relations lies in the light they cast on the potential for autonomy in the human species.

15. Jorge Santiago Santiago, who has worked in development projects in the communities in resistance in the Lacandón rain forest, has made this distinction between the practice of autonomy and submitting to the state as dependents in his interview with Hugo Isaac Robles and Gaspar Morquecho (February 2002). Responding to their question,

"What are the communities seeking in the months they have been silent after the congressional rebuff to the 2001 mobilization for the San Andrés Accord?" he replied, "They seek autonomy in practice; autonomy as a concrete realization of the communities. It is a continuing exercise, it is an everyday task of the communities as they are involved in relating to their bases of support, that are organized, that have the capacity to command, and that have a long range perspective. They are working on how to construct themselves, after reconstructing themselves, from a disadvantaged position imposed by the political and economic structure. They are working to survive and to resist, in the presence of the militaries and paramilitaries."

16. Christine Eber indicates the importance of tradition embedded in the flowery word of Cenalhó; see Christine Eber, *Women and Alcohol in a Highland Maya Township* (Austin: University of Texas Press, 1995). The ability to pass on the *pa'otán* from elder to younger in Amatenango confirmed the gender and age priorities of the Amatenangueros in the 1960s. June C. Nash, *In the Eyes of the Ancestors: Belief and Behavior in a Maya Community* (New Haven, CT: Yale University Press, 1970).

17. Sullivan, "Religious Change."

18. Kay Warren proposed that in these regenerative struggles for autonomy in San Andres Semetebaj, Guatemala, indigenous philosopher-leaders proposed mythic solutions that resolved ethnic conflict at the local level; see Kay B. Warren, "Creation Narratives and the Moral Order: Implications of Multiple Models in Highland Guatemala," in *Cosmogony and Ethical Order: New Studies in Comparative Ethics*, ed. Robin W. Lovin and Frank E. Reynolds (Chicago: University of Chicago Press, 1985), 251–78. As she demonstrates in her book *The Symbolism of Subordination*, that resolution negated wider spheres of interaction, and it was only when the Civil War threatened them with cultural annihilation that the pan-Mayan movement bridged the self-constituted boundaries of indigenous identity; see Kay B. Warren, *The Symbolism of Subordination: Indian Identity in a Guatemalan Town* (Austin: University of Texas Press, 1998), originally published in 1978. John Watanabe provides innunerable instances of how Guatemalans draw on collective local traditions to restore their sense of self and community after the trauma of war; see John Watanabe, *Maya Saints and Souls in a Changing World* (Austin: University of Texas Press, 1992). Esther Hermitte's memorable account of indigenes' recuperation of their cargo system in Pinola after their civil religious officials were banished from the town hall in the 1950s reveals the resolve with which they guard traditions under assault; see M. Esther Hermitte, *Poder Sobrenatural y Control Social en un Pueblo aya Contemporaneo* (Tuxtla Gutiérrez: Instituto Chiapaneco de Cultura, 1992).

19. Andres Aubrey, "La historia inmediata: Una lenta acumulación de fuerzas en silencio," *Revista Cihmech* 4, no. 12 (1991): 43.

20. John Watanabe denotes the "procedural culture" as the everyday behaviors that are the taken-for-granted ways of being in the world; see John Watanabe, "With All the Means that Prudence Would Suggest: Procedural Culture and the Writings of Cultural Histories of Power about Nineteenth-Century Mesoamerica," *Journal of Latin American Anthropology*, forthcoming.

21. June C. Nash, "The Fiesta of the Word: The Zapatista Uprising and Radical Democracy in Mexico," *American Anthropologist* 99, no. 2 (1997): 261–74.

22. Murdo McCleod, "Ethnic Relations and Indian Society in the Province of Guatemala ca 1620–ca. 1800," in *Ethnic Relations and Indian Society in the Province of Guatemala*, ed. M. McCleod (Austin: University of Texas Press, 1983), 189–214.

23. McCleod, "Ethnic Relations and Indian Society," 194; Robert M. Carmack, "Spanish-Indian Relations in Highland Guatemala, 1800–1944," in *Ethnic Relations and Indian Society in the Province of Guatemala*," ed. M. McCleod (Austin: University of Texas Press, 1983), 214; Robert Wasserstrom, "Spaniards and Indians in Colonial Chiapas, 1528–1790," in *Ethnic Relations and Indian Society in the Province of Guatemala*, ed. M. McCleod (Austin: University of Texas Press, 1983), 92–126.

24. Carmack, "Spanish-Indian Relations," 217; Wasserstrom, "Spaniards and Indians"; Jan Rus et al., *Abtel ta pinka* (San Cristobal, Chiapas: INAREMAC, 1986).

25. Foster 1965.

26. Carol A. Smith, *Guatemalan Indians and the State: 1540 to 1988* (Austin: University of Texas Press, 1990); Jonas, *The Battle for Guatemala*.

27. Ricardo Falla, *Quiché Rebelde* (Guatemala City: Editorial Universitaria de Guatemala, 1978), 44.

28. Warren (1982, 272).

29. Jonas, *The Battle for Guatemala*, 128.

30. Warren, *Indigenous Movements and Their Critics*, 11.

31. Warren, *Indigenous Movements and Their Critics*, 13.

32. Hector Diaz-Polanco, "Indian Communities and the Quincentenary," *Latin American Perspectives* 19, no. 3 (Summer 1992): 6–24; Hector Diaz-Polanco, *La Rebelión Zapatista y la Autonomía* (Mexico City: Siglo XXI, 1997).

33. Dimitrio Cojtí Cuxil, "The Politics of Maya Revindication," in *Maya Cultural Activism in Guatemala*, ed. E. F. Fischer and R. McKenna Brown (Austin: University of Texas, 1983).

34. Kay B. Warren, "Reading History as Resistance: Maya Public Intellectuals in Guatemala," in *Maya Cultural Activism in Guatemala*, ed. E. F. Fischer and R. McKenna Brown (Austin: University of Texas Press, 1996), 89–91.

35. I had seen teams of oil explorers in outlying hamlets of Chamula in the early 1990s, a phenomenon that a former PEMEX engineer explained as an attempt to verify the extent of oil reserves in the lowlands by assessing the appearance in higher altitudes. The first public acknowledgment of the extent of these oil reserves was, to my knowledge, stated in an article in *El Financiero*, February 26, 1995, 57.

36. Warren, *Indigenous Movements and Their Critics*, 65.

37. "¡Ya basta!" EZLN, March 17, 2001, available at www.ezln.org; my translation.

38. Neil Harvey, *The Chiapas Rebellion: The Struggle for Land and Democracy* (Durham, NC: Duke University Press, 1998).

39. Harvey, *The Chiapas Rebellion*, 211–12.

40. Margarito Ruiz Hernández, "México: Experiencias de Autonomía Indígena," in *México: Experiencias de Autonomía Indígena*, ed. Aracely Burguete Cal y Mayor (Copenhagen: Documento IWGIA no. 28, 1999), 33.

41. Margarita Gutiérrez and Nellys Paloma, "Autonomía con Mirada de Mujer," in *México: Experiencias de Autonomía Indígena*, ed. Aracely Burguete Cal y Mayor (Copenhagen: Documento IWGIA no. 28, 1999), 83.

42. Green, *Fear as a Way of Life*, 122 et seq.

43. Green (1992, 10).

44. Gutiérrez and Paloma, "Autonomía con Mirada de Mujer."

45. Gutiérrez and Paloma, "Autonomía con Mirada de Mujer."

46. Gutiérrez and Paloma, "Autonomía con Mirada de Mujer," 71.

47. Warren, *Indigenous Movements and Their Critics*, 169.

48. Warman (1980).

49. For an inspiring account of how the autonomy process is being implemented, see Duncan Earl and Jeanne Simonelli (2004).

50. Warren, "Reading History as Resistance," 178.

Indigenous, Cosmopolitan, and Integrative Medicine in the Americas

I I

BARBARA TEDLOCK

> *Herbs are shared by everyone and belong to no one. How can a scientist patent our plants?*
>
> —TALÍN PERUCH, MAYAN HERBALIST

GLOBALIZATION, OR THE PROCESS of integrating the world economy in key investment and production locales, has had unexpected results in many areas of social life, including medicine: Until 1940 new drugs of plant origin were discovered at the rate of only one every two or three decades. Today, with the AIDS and cancer epidemics, the global search for new biologically active agents to treat these and other diseases is accelerating. Thus the primary mission of the field of pharmacognosy is now directed almost exclusively toward the discovery of new biologically active substances from natural sources, most especially from the higher plants. As a result, dozens of new plant drugs are now being "discovered" each year.[1]

The selection for initial screening of a plant as potentially useful is determined either by random sampling or else by targeting specific vegetation for testing, based on indigenous medicinal and botanical knowledge. The latter approach, which is rapidly becoming the predominant one, is based on the hypothesis that broadly held knowledge of the use of a particular plant species over many generations provides an indication of its efficacy.[2]

Indigenous healers worldwide have not only passed down an ancient and valuable heritage but they also continue to discover new herbal tonics and blends for strengthening the immune system. The identification, collection, preparation, and use of herbs for health and healing involves a combination of institutional and inspirational intelligence. Within the institutional worldview, reality is revealed only when we are in total control of our faculties, while within the inspirational worldview, reality is revealed during dreaming, meditating, and other alternative forms of consciousness. Indigenous healers routinely combine these worldviews into a holistic-synthetic mode of practice that is difficult to understand from within the narrow linear-rational framework of cosmopolitan science.

Because of their combination of rational and spiritual approaches to healing, shamans, midwives, bonesetters, masseuses, and herbalists were once dismissed as naïve, silly, superstitious, and even neurotic. This began to change in the mid-1970s when the World Health Assembly requested the director general of the World Health Organization (WHO) to initiate programs designed to evaluate and utilize traditional medicine in order to meet world health needs by the year 2000. Scientists and politicians were aware that high-technology, high-cost cosmopolitan medical treatments could never function as a pervasive global health intervention. They passed a series of resolutions recommending that all member-nations study, encourage, and facilitate collaboration between practitioners of cosmopolitan or biomedical and indigenous or local medical systems. Shortly thereafter, scientists reviewed publications noting the lack of methodological and theoretical work. They also noted the frequency of an approach in which traditional medicine is considered prescientific, with connotations of inferiority to biomedicine. They suggested that biology and culture mutually determine the overall phenomenology of illness and concluded that studies constructed from the perspective of a researcher's own predetermined categories and characterized by a Western naturalist view of disease had made no significant contribution to world heath.[3]

In Mexico, the policy of the Indigenous Affairs Office (INI) soon shifted from condemnation of indigenous healing strategies to respect for and even recuperation of local medical knowledge. The deepening global economic crisis encouraged Mexico, together with a number of other nation-states with large heterogeneous populations, to guarantee health care for all based on indigenous rather than cosmopolitan medicine. This was a radical change in policy from the earlier antitraditional healing campaigns of the 1950s and 1960s during which people were encouraged to discard indigenous medicine as superstitious and unscientific practices dangerous to human health.[4]

Trade Competition

In order to comprehend the context in which such sweeping reforms in health care were made, a brief review of cosmopolitan medicine is in order. Today, as in the recent past, the American Medical Association (AMA) claims a monopoly on most forms of healing. There also exist dozens of statues severely limiting the practice and transmission of traditional holistic medicine due to AMA lobbying.

Since the turn of the twentieth century, there has been a unified effort on the part of government regulatory agencies in the Americas to punish individuals who either recommend or practice alternative therapies intended to maintain health and prevent or treat illness. Medical boards censured and, in a few cases, even revoked the licenses of physicians who practiced such medicine because their treatments did not conform to "accepted standards of care," even though many of these treatments actually worked. Insurance companies refused to pay for what they considered alternative treatments such as acupuncture, chiropractic, Swedish massage, homeopathy, and nutritional medicine, labeling them "unapproved therapies." In the early 1990s, manufacturers of nutritional supplements and herbs, together with health food stores where they were sold, became the target of Food and Drug Administration (FDA) seizures in an attempt to block the manufacture and sale of natural substances used in holistic healing.[5]

Critics have noted that the FDA waged health-fraud campaigns against alternative products, practitioners, or treatments while ignoring obvious health violations by major pharmaceutical companies. One recent example is Bristol-Myers, who was caught selling unapproved cancer drugs through illegal promotions but escaped criminal charges. Another was Pfizer, who produced and sold a defective heart valve which resulted in over three hundred deaths. The heart valve was eventually removed from the market but no fraud charges were ever filed by the FDA. This situation came about because the FDA is now partially supported by the industry it regulates and thus it must cooperate with the drug companies it oversees. This unfortunate conflict of interest was established in 1992 when Congress passed the Prescription Drug User Fee Act that required drug companies to pay a user fee to the FDA for every drug the agency reviewed. Such fees currently amount to approximately half the budget of FDA's drug review center. Since the FDA immediately doubled the number of drugs it reviewed annually and cut in half the time spent on each review, the quid pro quo is obvious. This is clearly not in the public interest.[6]

In 1993 the FDA proposed regulation requiring companies that manufactured herbal supplements to prove that these remedies did what they claimed. To demonstrate efficacy, these manufacturers would have to conduct expensive studies. Since herbs that have been used for centuries would be difficult to patent, these companies would never recover their expenses. When the public heard about this, they wrote their congressional representatives in large numbers. Then, in 1994, the U.S. Congress responded by passing the Dietary Supplement Health and Education Act (DSHEA), which states that manufacturers of dietary supplements did not have to prove safety or efficacy of their products before they put them on the market. This legislation also created the National Center for Complementary and Alternative Medicine whose mandate is to coordinate research on dietary supplements. In November of 2001, a nongovernmental medical research group, U.S. Pharmacopoeia (USP), was set up to verify nutritional supplements ensuring that they were manufactured appropriately, contained the ingredients they claimed on the label, and that accurate doses were listed.[7]

Recently the competition between the pharmaceutical and the dietary supplement industries for market share of the drug business exploded into a negative advertising campaign against herbal supplements. In a series of infomercials, paid for by the pharmaceutical industry, that were released in 2002 on CNN, listeners learned that "while one-third of all Americans are taking some form of herbal supplement, many of them are unaware of possible interactions with prescription drugs such as birth control pills." And "that the most popular of all herbs, kava, has been shown to cause liver damage." The details of any scientific studies backing up these assertions were not mentioned in the infomercials, which aired throughout the months of March, April, May, and June of 2002.

When I checked into the situation, I found that in Germany the euphoriant tranquilizer kava (*Piper methysticum*) was introduced into the national herbal register in the 1970s because of its muscle-relaxant and endo-anesthetic activity. Kava-root crystal substances, known as kava-pyrones, are the key ingredient of an herbal sedative called "kavo sporal" in Germany and "kavaform" in Switzerland. However, it was not until 2002 that cases of liver damage were actually reported. Since no prior health warning had ever come from the islands of the South Pacific where kava is native and has been safely used for centuries, these recent European reports appear to be connected to the method of extraction rather than to kava root itself.[8]

If it does turn out that there are serious problems with this herbal drug, it would hardly be surprising—given that side effects of prescription drugs are currently the fourth-leading cause of death in the United States. However, this has not stopped the pharmaceutical industry from overstating the benefits of their drugs in advertising campaigns. In a recent article appearing in the *New England Journal of Medicine*, we learn that "media reports on new medications tend to exaggerate their benefits, ignore their risks, and fail to disclose their cost."[9]

The Emergence of Integrative Medicine

In spite of ridicule and repression by members of religious, academic, political, medical, and scientific orthodoxies, indigenous healing modalities have managed to survive and even flourish. The recognition and demand for holistic healing has contributed to a heightened profile for indigenous healers and this public presence necessitated interaction with the biomedical health care system. In Canada, the National Aboriginal Health Organization (NAHO) is working toward ensuring access to culturally appropriate health services. As Dr. Judith Bartlett, chair of

NAHO, recently said, "I believe that moving towards aboriginal culturally based, not culturally sensitive, but culturally grounded approaches is really going to be the future of Aboriginal health care . . . that it will go beyond the Aboriginal community, and it will improve the health care of *all* Canadians."[10]

Indigenous healers in Canada and the United States currently know and use more than 1,500 plants with hypoglycemic and antidiabetic properties including American barberry, Canada flea bane, alum root, bilberry, goat's rue, fenugreek, nopal, bitter melon, garlic, mulberry leaves, olive leaves, wild ginger, and ginseng. Most of these plants are indigenous to the North American continent. In 2002 the Chehalis Indian Reservation hosted the "Salish & Sohaptan Cultures, Foods and Medicine Workshop," which drew on the extensive knowledge and authentic food and medicines of the Salish nations along the Pacific Coast in British Columbia, south to southern Oregon. This historic workshop in which indigenous and cosmopolitan healers participated as equals could only take place in a state such as Washington that had passed a "freedom of practice" statue, allowing health care providers to practice alternative forms of healing without fear of retribution from the state medical board. The statute declares that "failure to conform to standards of care shall not by itself be considered incompetence unless patients are exposed to unreasonable risk or are actually harmed."[11]

A recent outgrowth from freedom-of-practice legislation is the field of "integrative medicine," which combines cosmopolitan medicine with alternative therapies including massage, herbal medicine, acupuncture, yoga, aromatherapy, homeopathy, and chiropractic. Dr. Andrew Weil, the founder of the Program in Integrative Medicine at the College of Medicine, University of Arizona, has brought the concept of integrative medicine into the mainstream. Today a new Integrative Medicine Center has opened in New York City at the Memorial Sloan-Kettering Cancer Center, the bulwark of the cancer establishment. Its advertising features a middle-aged woman in a bandanna (hiding her hair loss) saying, "My fight against cancer includes chemotherapy, Swedish massage, and relaxing to the muffled rhythms of Tibetan drums."[12]

An increasing number of health care institutions that are associated with medical institutions are implementing integrative medicine techniques. In 2001 the Integrative Medicine Foundation (IMF), a nonprofit organization located in Santa Fe, New Mexico, set up a clinic called "Sanctuary." It was designed as a place where Native American, Anglo, and Hispanic oncology patients could receive complementary medicine recommendations including spiritual help. The care givers at Sanctuary believe that coordinating alternative techniques with traditional ones can not only improve a patient's quality of life but can also decrease health care costs by lessening some of the side effects from conventional cancer treatments.[13]

Bioprospecting and Biopiracy

The dark side of this new openness to indigenous medicine is found in the field of drug discovery or "bioprospecting." As a result of the enormous profits now available to pharmacological firms and universities, scientists have fanned out across the globe to interview herbal healers and shamans in order to collect plant specimens and test them for biologically active ingredients. This embrace of indigenous plant knowledge would not have occurred just a few years ago when neither herbal remedies nor plants hybridized generations ago could be patented because they were considered to be in the public domain.[14]

This changed after pharmaceutical corporations lobbied Congress for a reinterpretation of "intellectual property rights" that would allow private ownership of living beings that were modified through breeding or genetic engineering. It also allows ownership of plant medicines that were scientifically augmented by the isolation of their active ingredients. In 1994 the Trade Related Aspects Intellectual Property Rights Agreement (TRIPS) was ratified requiring nations to create patents for life-forms found in their territory. Under this agreement, bioprospecting became a growth industry for pharmaceutical firms who claimed information that they gained from talking with indigenous peoples as their own property to do with as they pleased.[15]

Immediately upon ratification of the TRIPS agreement, Colorado State University (CSU), together with the nation of Peru, patented an Andean cereal grain known as "Apelawa Quinoa." It was named after a village on Lake Titicaca where scientists first picked seed samples. Because the patent covered a method of hybridizing quinoa, it subsumed forty-three other traditional varieties named after villages stretching from Ecuador to Chile.[16]

This case, along with several others, demonstrates that under this agreement scientists can take a plant hybridized for generations by indigenous peoples and with the agreement of the nation-state, but without the knowledge of the local community, patent it. In so doing, they claim ownership of the entire species and receive all future profits from it. Universities together with bioprospecting firms and the governments of various nation-states are now in the business of transferring knowledge from one public domain—indigenous cultures where it is well known—to another domain—university laboratories and transnational pharmacological corporations—where it is unknown.[17]

Indigenous healers have employed lawyers to protect their communities from what is now called "biopiracy." The concept of biopiracy was coined by a Canadian NGO, Rural Advancement Foundation International (RAFI), to cover the unauthorized and uncompensated expropriation of traditional knowledge. This includes patenting of healing herbs and the selling of human tissue.[18]

A particularly egregious example of biopiracy took place in August of 1996 when U.S. researchers obtained authorization from the Brazilian National Indian Foundation (FUNAI) to conduct research on a giant sloth. Hunters from the Karitiana tribe took a group of scientists into the forest to show them the animal. There the team's doctor casually asked the men for samples of their blood, saying that he wanted to see if they had anemia, AIDS, or other diseases. The men were surprised by the request but complied. Later, when the doctor was questioned by authorities, he claimed that he had obtained the hunters' blood because they appeared malnourished. When questioned further, he said that he did not intend to commercialize the blood. Since international biomedical science already knew that Karitiana plasma was very valuable because it is a highly resistant to malaria, his statement was dubious. That it was commercialized is revealed by the fact that Coriell Cell Repositories, a not-for-profit scientific institution located in Camden, New Jersey, soon began selling human tissue on the Internet. Among the items for sale, costing $500 per sample, was Karitiana blood. There are today more than seventy-five commercial and academic human tissue depositories in the United States.[19]

That there is a great deal of money to be made through biopiracy is further demonstrated by the work of another American company, Sequana Therapeutics, who recently sold DNA samples taken under false pretenses from indigenous people for $70 million to Boehringer, a German pharmaceutical laboratory. The DNA in this transaction is believed to contain the key to curing asthma.[20]

Intellectual Property Rights vs. Indigenous Heritage

In the Western intellectual property rights system—consisting primarily of patenting, trade secrets, trademarks, and copyright—individuals and groups who claim to have discovered or invented something are given a monopoly for a limited period of time (usually twenty years) over the commercial development of their innovation. Anything that is not protected by intellectual property rights is considered to be in the public domain. This means it can be exploited by anyone without concern for the wishes of the original knowledge holders and without sharing any monetary or other rewards with them. Intellectual property rights legislation focuses on the material and commercial aspects of knowledge at the expense of the immaterial cultural and spiritual aspects.[21]

Indigenous organizations have sharply criticized intellectual property rights legislation as fundamentally biased against traditional knowledge systems that developed most of the world's food crops and herbal medicines. They point out that the definition of "innovation" within Western intellectual property rights discourse excludes knowledge systems that have been handed down over many generations and note that the forms of protection offered by trademarks center on commercial exploitation rather than ensuring respectful use of sacred knowledge. Since plants present the life energy of the universe and, according to native and First Nations people, are the hair of Mother Earth, they must be spiritually cared for and shown respect if we are to benefit from them.[22]

In order to develop alternative understandings and protections for indigenous people's rights, the United Nations created a new agency in 1998 called the World Intellectual Property Organization (WIPO). It was put in charge of the development, revision, harmonization, and application of international norms and standards for intellectual property rights. While this is encouraging, it is unlikely to outweigh the competing commercial interests of the signatories of the TRIPS agreement backed by the World Trade Organization.[23]

The goal of working toward the establishment of a more general framework for the protection of indigenous heritage offers an opportunity for deeper reflection on the nature of the quest for knowledge, as well as the relationships between rights and duties. It has been noted that the professionalization of knowledge together with the notion of knowledge for knowledge's sake gave industry a boost. For indigenous peoples, on the other hand, wisdom has long been the primary goal.[24]

Conclusions

Despite the attempt to legitimize indigenous medical and botanical knowledge, the ongoing process of globalization has ensured the dominance of cosmopolitan medicine. As a result, the spiritual dimensions of healing are absent in the political, economic, and health-related discourse of nation-states and indigenous understanding reemerges at the local level. This is so because cultural globalization places different forms of knowing side-by-side, creating a relativization of all cultural forms and, in so doing, cosmopolitan culture cannot silence local cultures. As a result of globalization, indigenous health care providers throughout the Americas have been able to garner recognition for their healing knowledge as well as for their combination of spiritual and pragmatic healing practices. This process has helped to create a synthesis now generally known as integrative medicine.

Notes

1. For more about the effect of globalization on indigenous peoples, see J. Nash, "Global Integration and Subsistence Insecurity," *American Anthropologist* 96 (1994): 1–31; J. Rus, "Local Adaptation to Global Change: The Reordering of Native Society in Highland Chiapas," *European Review of Latin American and Caribbean Studies* 58 (1995): 71–89; J. Nash and C. Kovic, "The Reconstitution of Hegemony: The Free Trade Act and the

Transformation of Rural Mexico," *Globalization: Critical Reflections*, ed. J. Mittelman (Boulder: Lynne Reiner, 1996), 165–86; I. Nobutaka, *Globalization and Indigenous Culture* (Kokyo: Institute for Japanese Culture and Classics, Kokugokuin University, 1997); S. Sassen, *Globalization and Its Discontents* (New York: New Press).

2. B. Berlin et al., "The Maya ICBG: Drug Discovery, Medical Ethnobiology, and Alternative Forms of Economic Development in the Highland Maya Region of Chiapas, Mexico," *Pharmaceutical Biology* 37 (1999): 127–44.

3. R. Katz, "Utilizing Traditional Healing Systems," *American Psychologist* 37 (1982): 715–16; D. Pedersen and V. Baruffati, "Health and Traditional Medicine Cultures in Latin America and the Caribbean," *Social Science and Medicine* 21 (1985): 5–12; B. Tedlock, "An Interpretive Solution to the Problem of Humoral Medicine in Latin America," *Social Science and Medicine* 24 (1987): 1069–83; L. Foss, "The Challenge to Biomedicine: A Foundations Perspective," *Journal of Medicine and Philosophy* 14 (1989): 165–91.

4. Indigenous peoples are those who have maintained a collective identity, even within repressive states, and have continued to struggle to preserve control over their own identities and sovereignty over their own territories. There are today more than 300 million indigenous people living in over seventy countries worldwide. B. Hyma and A. Ramesh, "Traditional Medicine: Its Extent and Potential for Incorporation into Modern National Health Systems," *Health and Development*, eds. D. R. Rhillips and Y. Verhasselt (London: Routledge, 1994), 65–82; S. I. Ayora-Diaz, "Globalization, Rationality and Medicine: Local Medicine's Struggle for Recognition in Highland Chiapas, Mexico," *Urban Anthropology* 27 (1998): 165–95.

5. K. Ausubel, *When Healing Becomes a Crime* (Rochester, VT: Healing Arts Press, 2000); J. Duke with M. Castleman, *Anti-Aging Prescriptions* (New York: Rodale, 2001), 283.

6. B. Goldberg, *Alternative Medicine* (Fife, WA: Future Medicine, 1993), 25–26; M. Angell and A. Relman, "Patents, Profits and American Medicine: Conflicts of Interest in the Testing and Marketing of New Drugs," *Daedalus* 131 (2002): 102–11.

7. Mayo Clinic, "Using Herbal Supplements Wisely," 2002, at www.MayoClinic.com.

8. R. Gatty, "Kava—Polynesian Beverage Shrub," *Economic Botany* 10 (1956): 241–49; R. Hansel, "Characterization and Physiological Activity of Some Kava Constituents," *Pacific Science* 22 (1958): 293–313; J. Cawte, "Psychoactive Substances of the South Seas: Betel, Kava and Pituri," *Australian and New Zealand Journal of Psychiatry* 19 (1985): 83–87; L. Garner and J. Klinger, "Some Visual Effects Caused by the Beverage Kava," *Journal of Ethnopharmacology* 13 (1985): 307–11; P. Cox and L. O'Rourke, "Kava (*Piper methysticum*, Piperaceae)," *Economic Botany* 41 (1987): 451–54. For a balanced discussion of the current kava controversies, see A. Weil, MD, "Can Kava Harm the Liver?" January 29, 2002, at www.drweil.com.

9. For more about media coverage of scientific medicine, see D. Nelkin, *Selling Science: How the Press Covers Science and Technology* (New York: Freeman, 1987). Some of the media tactics practiced by the pharmaceutical industry are revealed in J. Abraham, *Science, Politics and the Pharmaceutical Industry: Controversy and Bias in Drug Regulation* (New York: St. Martin's, 1995); "Deadly Rx: Why Are Drugs Killing So Many Patients?" *USA Today*, April 24, 1998. 18A; Mayo Clinic, "New Drugs and the Media," 2000, at www.MayoClinic.com.

10. J. Bartlett, "Healthy Lifestyles: NAHO," *Aboriginal Times* 6 (2002): 30.

11. E. Barrie Kavash and K. Baar, *American Indian Healing* Arts (New York: Bantam, 1999), 261; B. Goldberg, *Alternative Medicine* (1999): 261.

12. The quote is from K. Ausubel, *When Healing Becomes a Crime* (2000, 1). There are many websites with information about herbal, integrative, and alternative medicine, including Father Nature's Farmacy (USDA database) at www.ars-grin.gov/duke; Health World Online at www.healthy.net; The Eclectic Physician at www.eclecticphysician.com; Center for Complementary and Alternative Medicine at www.camra.ucdavis.edu; and the University of Texas Center for Alternative Medicine Research at www.sph.uth.tmc.edu/utcam/default.htm. Key journals include *Alternative Therapies in Health and Medicine, Integrative Medicine*, and *The Journal of Naturopathic Medicine*.

13. R. Macintosh, "The Sanctuary: Cancer Patients Say Therapy Center Provides a Retreat from Grueling Treatments," *Santa Fe New Mexican*, May 20, 2002, B1.

14. S. Brush, "Bioprospecting the Public Domain," *Cultural Anthropology* 14 (1999): 35–55; RAFI, "Messages from the Chiapas 'Bioprospecting' Dispute," *Geno-Type*, December 22, 1999, at www.rafi.org; R. Nigh, "Bioprospecting Research as Herbal Fetishism," *Current Anthropology* 43 (2002): 451–77.

15. T. Simpson and V. Jackson, "Protección efectiva para el conocimiento cultural indígena: Un desafio para el próximo milenio," *Asuntos Indígenas* 3 (1998): 44–56; Nigh, "Bioprospecting Research," 451–77.

16. C. Benjamin, "The Pirating of Quinoa?" *Native Americas* 14 (1997): 24; C. Benjamin, "Amazonian Confrontation: Native Nations Challenge the Patenting of Sacred Plants," *Native Americas* 15 (1998): 24–33; ETC group, "Quinoa Patent Dropped: Andean Farmers Defeat U.S. University," 1998, www.etcgroup.org.

17. Brush, "Bioprospecting the Public Domain," 35–55; RAFI, "Messages from the Chiapas 'Bioprospecting' Dispute."

18. For more about biopiracy, see C. Benjamin, "Biopiracy and Native Knowledge: Indigenous Rights on the Last Frontier," *Native Americas* 14 (1997): 22–31; RAFI, "Maya Indian Organizations Denounce Biopiracy Project in Chiapas," 1999, at www.rafi.org; RAFI, "Captain Hook, the Cattle Rustlers, and the Plant Privateers: Biopiracy of Marine, Plant, and Livestock Continues," RAFI Communiqué 65, 2000, at www.rafi.org; S. Ribeiro, J. Delhanty, and P. Mooney, "Stop Biopiracy in Mexico! Indigenous People's Organizations from Chiapas Demand Immediate Moratorium," *Geno-Type*, October 23, 2000, at www.etcgroup.org; S. Ribeiro and H. Shand, "Mexico Biopiracy Project Canceled," *Geno-Type*, October 23, 2001, at www.etcgroup.org; RAFI, "Biopiracy + 10," 2002, at www.rafi.org.

19. J. Hanna, "Indian DNA for Sale," *Native Americas* 14 (1997): 4.

20. J. McEwen, "DNA Sampling and Baking: Practices and Procedures in the United States," paper at the First International Conference on DNA sampling, Montreal, September (1996); J. Forbes, "Indigenous Americans: Spirituality and Ecos," *Daedalus* 130 (2001).

21. M. Manek and R. Lettington, "Indigenous Knowledge Rights: Recognizing Alternative Worldviews," *Cultural Survival* 24 (2001): 8–9. Note that according to the *Oxford*

English Dictionary, the phrase "intellectual property" first appeared in the English language in 1845. See C. Hesse, "The Rise of Intellectual Property 700 BC–AD 2000: An Idea in the Balance," *Daedalus* 131 (2002): 26–45; E. I. Daes, *Protection of the Heritage of Indigenous People* (New York: United Nations, 1997); R. Posner, "The Law and Economics of Intellectual Property," *Daedalus* 131 (2002): 5–12.

22. V. Deloria Jr., "Tribal Colleges and Traditional Knowledges," *Tribal College* 5 (1992): 32; J. Barden and P. Bayer, "Ways of Knowing," *Tribal College* 4 (1993): 12–15; G. Cajete, *Native Science: Natural Laws of Interdependence* (Santa Fe: Clear Light Books, 2000); Manek and Lettington, "Indigenous Knowledge Rights," 8–9; M. Riley, "The Traditional Medicine Research Center (TMRC): A Potential Tool for Protecting Traditional and Tribal Medicinal Knowledge in Laos," *Cultural Survival* 24 (2001): 21–24; T. Low Dog, "Inequity in the Health-care System," *El Dorado Sun*, June 2002, 21.

23. Information about the World Intellectual Property Organization (WIPO) and its work can be found on the Internet at www.wipo.int/traditionalknowledge/report/.

24. R. Proctor, *Value-Free Science? Purity and Power in Modern Knowledge* (New York: Basic Books, 1991); F. Apffel-Marglin, *The Spirit of Regeneration: Andean Culture Confronting Western Notions of Development* (London: Zed Books, 1998).

Discussion of Trilateral Exchanges between Canada, the United States, and Mexico   12

PANEL MEMBERS: SYLVIA MARCOS, PATRICIA MCCORMACK,
JUNE NASH, INEZ TALAMANTEZ, AND BARBARA TEDLOCK;
MODERATOR: KAREN TORJESEN

*T*HE FINAL DISCUSSION *focused around change and the role of discourse in change. How can you get people to listen to a new discourse?*

McCormack: Work for change around projects. If you try to attack anything on a global level, you will fail; but if you attack it particular project by particular project, you basically build something. It also takes a remarkable amount of commitment on both sides. Rather than two sides introducing two different models, when they learn to work in tandem, they learn to build a third space. Several experiments, especially in business, are now going on where First Nations are involved with corporations in joint ventures, often on a long-term basis. Both sides have had to figure out how they can reconcile different positions, different cultures, and work together. The models are there; but no one appears to be publishing anything on them. Unless someone actually does the research systematically and disseminates that information, it will be very difficult for anyone to grasp the range of possibilities.

The necessity of getting information out, of publicity, was reinforced by others in the room. As one panelist said: We found it necessary to stage a war, a wake-up call to get this publicity going because you try other means, like protest marches; and nobody is listening.

Calliou: That's the problem with court cases, too. We just had a major decision in the treaty litigation case. I'm conscientiously clipping letters to the editor and sending them out; almost without exception, people are outraged. It is forcing people to pay attention and think about what the issues are. The dominant discourse is still what we call basic redneck. We need to get people to rethink, and there is really no opportunity. Whatever education is going on is still, with a few minor exceptions, lower education. There's no great sign about that changing in the near future, at least not in most schools.

One audience member told of teaching a course at Claremont Graduate University Claremont called the "Frontiers of North American Literature." Class discussion actually got into many different frontiers, and they had to choose to concentrate on one. They chose transformation. The point here is to address issues with many voices. Change of consciousness comes through multiplying the number of voices. Leslie Silke's Ceremony, *James Welch's* Billy *are very powerful novels about Native America. We need more Native American voices, more major works. The idea is to think of a plurality of modes beyond just the political. The real problem with the political realm is that it is adversarial; you're locked into my truth versus your truth. If you separate the contestants and, to use a football metaphor, do a more circuitous end run with multiple voices, then you invite others to participate and to become part of the solution.*

McCormack: Certainly at the University of Alberta we invite students in class to do just that. And we see them going out after they graduate and being part of the group of people who, in their own careers, provide support. They have at least some understanding that alternative ways of thinking may occur around the same issues.

Calliou: The Banff Centre has a one-week program on negotiation skills. It's based on the Harvard model of inner space and negotiating that within communities. At the beginning we ask people to dialogue. Rather than sit around a table, insisting on positions and rights, we want people to learn to put those aside and work to set up some common goals and objectives. When we approach problems as common, as something we can work at together, most people are already talking before they get to that last stage.

Talamantez: I start my classes with a novel because, especially a novel like *Water Lily*, it gives students a really good idea of Indian culture, in this case, prior to contact; but contact was coming. Students then get into a frame of mind to read other things and to start comparing. I must have taught *Ceremony* three times. It's an extremely complex book; students will get some parts of it, but not all. They do see the veteran coming home and trying to work his way back into the native culture. They see that "okay, there are two different cultures at work here," but mostly they see the basic ideas about purity and coming into contact with death; they don't see that in mainstream culture, even though the Native American fought to protect American values, he is still treated as a second-class citizen.

McCormack: I try to get students to use their critical analysis skills. I show two videos. One was made to commemorate the treaty and the creation of the Hudson Bay Company and their exploration in Canada. Everybody's happy, all the Indians and the white men, everybody. The second video I show is called *The Other Side of the Ledger*, which was done by National Indian Brotherhood. This film looks at the fur trade in terms of how the Indians are essentially being ripped off by the Hudson Bay Company; the markup on one fur coat was more than most Indians made the entire year. We look at the same issues from two perspectives. They are asked to think not just about right and wrong but about multiple realities.

Marcos: Mostly I work at the grassroots level. I have to use language that indigenous people on the reservation can understand. The women ask me to give seminars on gender. How can I talk about this very complicated, political, and theoretical topic so they can understand? I try to say things simply, in a language that doesn't rely on political terms. Because they have their own ideology and their own way of grasping things, I start with metaphorical phrases and then elaborate. It works because it mirrors the way the women grasp life. Through metaphors; they grasp religion through metaphors. I try to follow their own style of knowing, their own style of approaching the world.

Talamantez: I think there is such a thing as indigenous theory. The problem we have is really the terminology of mainstream culture. I'm out there and I think "Why, I have a theory for this." Nobody said it or wrote about it. It isn't called a theory, but in fact it is theory.

Nash: This is the core issue. I don't think we need to transform Native Americans to be something else, or teach them. They will eventually pick up whatever they want; they will and they do. They pick it up, reformulate and reorganize, and then relate back again. I don't think the way to proceed is to teach them to dress nicely, for example. In Mexico, women are being trained on how to do makeup and dress so they can negotiate with other people. It's stupid. It sounds ridiculous, but it's happening all over the world. I have read that American companies are training nonprofit people so they can make a good impression—to dress in suits in order to make an impact when they negotiate.

There are two ways of being Indian. Rigoberta Manchu can say by her own example, they are always dressed in traditional Indian dress; I dress in whatever.

As a final question, the panel was asked about creating an indigenous identity, how to go about nation building, for the next century, the next millennium, within the trilateral context of Canada, the United States, and Mexico? Are Native Americans in the United States coming to the Banff Centre for training? And what does that process look like ultimately in the Mexican context?

Calliou: We don't actually get very many Americans coming into our program, though there have been a few over the years. We have two people on the Aboriginal People Advisory Council who are from the United States. This is an advisory body of business leaders across Canada, and it does include two people from the University of Arizona. We also have sort of "best business practices" people come from the United States to have conversations around thinking about the big picture.

Marcos: The situation in Mexico is difficult, given the historical tradition and the issues of traditional people. In Mexico, we have autonomy. We are not asking for sovereignty, though I don't think it has been accepted because the other Mexicans didn't want to think about the possibilities of self-government. It has been very political, very misogynist; and the fighting is everywhere; but never just between sovereignty and autonomy.

McCormack: There is also in the United States a sense of fear, I think that's an argument made in Alberta, that the many nations of indigenous people will try to assert themselves. The fear is of national separation, something like Bolivia or Ecuador. I believe the Canadian government has followed along. It has something to do with the nation-state not being stable enough, not institutionalized enough to deal with the diversity of culture and self-governance. The United Nations lobby for nation-states was ultimately designed to protect them. So there is indigenous protection whether it is working or not: you could argue both ways.

Index

About the Contributors

Brian Calliou is the program director for the Banff Centre's Aboriginal Leadership and Management. Brian is a member of the Sucker Creek First Nation in north-central Alberta. He holds memberships with the Canadian Bar Association, the Indigenous Bar Association, and the Legal Archives Society of Alberta. He was appointed by the Alberta Minister of Community Development to chair the Alberta Historical Resources Foundation Board, which adjudicates matters relating to the preservation of Alberta's heritage. Brian holds a bachelor of arts in political science, a bachelor of laws, and a master of laws from the University of Alberta. He has published works in various academic journals and books and has coauthored "Aboriginal Economic Development and the Struggle for Self-Government" in *Power and Resistance: Critical Thinking about Canadian Issues.*

Duane Champagne is professor of sociology and member of the Native Nations Law and Policy Center at the University of California, Los Angeles. He is a citizen of the Turtle Mountain Band of Chippewa from North Dakota. Professor Champagne was director of the UCLA American Indian Studies Center from 1991 to 2002, and former editor of the *American Indian Culture and Research Journal.* Professor Champagne's research focuses primarily on issues of social and cultural change in both historical and contemporary Native American communities. He has focused on a variety of Indian communities including the Cherokee, Tlingit, Iroquois, Delaware, Choctaw, Northern Cheyenne, Creek, California Indians, and others, and has authored and edited more than one hundred publications, including *Native American Studies in Higher Education: Models for Collaboration Between Indigenous Nations* (2002), the *North American Almanac* (2001), *Contemporary Native American Cultural Issues* (1999), *Native America: Portraits of the Peoples* (1994), and *Social Order and Political Change: Constitutional Governments among the Cherokee, Choctaw, Chickasaw and Creek* (1992).

Steven Crum is a member of the Western Shoshone tribe with enrollment on the Duck Valley Indian Reservation in Nevada. He is a professor of Native American Studies at the University of California, Davis. His PhD is in history from the University of Utah. He is the author of the book *The Road on Which We Came*, which is a history of the Western Shoshone people of the Great Basin. Additionally, he is the author of several journal articles.

James Dempsey is an associate professor at the University of Alberta and the director of their School of Native Studies. The independent structure of the school, which is unique among Canadian universities, attracted James to move to Edmonton and accept the position. The school is not formally a part of the Faculty of Arts and, as such, has been able to create its own identity within the University of Alberta. James is a member of the Blood Tribe.

Sylvia Marcos is a Mexican scholar specializing in the study of gender in Mesoamerican religions. An activist in the struggle for the rights of indigenous peoples, Dr. Marcos for years has combined her scholarly research, teaching, and writing with an active participation in the indigenous women's movement in Mexico. Dr. Marcos has taught at several U.S. universities and lectured all over the world, as well as in her native Mexico. She is the author of several books and articles, among them *Gender/Bodies/Religions*.

Patricia McCormack is an associate professor with the School of Native Studies at the University of Alberta. She received her PhD in anthropology for research conducted in Fort Chipewyan, Alberta, a community with which she has been involved since 1968. Pat served for ten years as the curator of ethnology at the Provincial Museum of Alberta and prepared several exhibits, including a major display about Fort Chipewyan, *Northwind Dreaming*. She has published widely about Fort Chipewyan history and culture and about First Nations representation in museums. Her northern experience extends to the Northwest Territories and the Yukon, where she lived for five years, and she subsequently introduced an interdisciplinary course on northern studies at the University of Alberta. In recent years, she has done fur-trade-related research in Scotland and begun projects in partnership with members of the Blood and Peigan First Nations about horse traditions and ranching. Her involvement in the Blackfoot research led her to learn to ride and acquire a horse, which she is now training. She is particularly interested in how aboriginal peoples represent their cultures and histories and draw upon their traditions to maintain their distinctive identities in today's world.

June Nash is distinguished professor emerita at the Graduate Center and City College of the City University of New York. She has done fieldwork in Chiapas,

Mexico, where she studied Mayas engaged in small-plot cultivation in the 1950s and 1960s, returning in the 1990s to see the development of conditions that led to the 1994 uprising. Her early work is recorded in a monograph, *In the Eyes of the Ancestors, Belief and Behavior in a Mayan Community*, and her work in the 1990s in *Mayan Visions: The Quest for Autonomy in an Age of Globalization*. She has also worked in Bolivian tin mining communities, publishing *We Eat the Mines and the Mines Eat Us*, as well as an autobiography, *I Spent My Life in the Mines*. She has worked with industrial workers in Pittsfield, Massachusetts, publishing *The Clash of Community and Industrial Cycles*. She has collaborated with Helen Safa in two anthologies on women in Latin America, and one with M. Patricia Fernandez-Kelly on women in the global division of labor. Another anthology, *Crafts in the World Market*, shows the growing importance of artisan production in the peasant economies of Middle America. Her anthology *Social Movements: A Reader* will soon be published by Blackwell Publishers.

Susan Steiner, PhD, is associate vice president of research at Claremont Graduate University. With degrees in religion and in literature, she has taught and consulted at universities throughout the United States. Actively involved for many years in civil rights and other social issues in the United States, she has written a book on the 1960s Berkeley Free Speech Movement, been on the Steering Committee after the 1983 Los Angeles civil unrest, initiated multiple university/community development projects, served on the Board of PEN USA West, and cofounded a Latino theater company to work in the schools. She is presently involved in a number of writing as well as development projects.

Barbara Tedlock is distinguished professor of anthropology at the State University of New York at Buffalo and research associate at the School of American Research in Santa Fe, New Mexico. Her ongoing research centers on indigenous scientific and spiritual knowledge systems including ethnomedicine, spiritual healing, ethnobotany, astronomy, and calendrics. Among her many publications are *The Beautiful and the Dangerous: Zuni Indian Encounters*, *Dreaming: Anthropological and Psychological Interpretations*, and *Time and the Highland Maya*.

Karen Jo Torjesen is the dean of the School of Religion at Claremont Graduate University and Margo L. Goldsmith Professor of Women's Studies. Professor Torjesen's research interests include constructions of gender and sexuality in early Christianity, authority and institutionalization in the early churches, hermeneutics and rhetoric in late antiquity, and comparative study of Greek and Latin patristic traditions. During her tenure as assistant professor of patristic theology at the University of Goettingen (Germany), her book *Hermeneutical Procedure and Theological Structure in Origen's Exegesis* was published by de Gruyter. Her most recent book is *When Women Were Priests: Women's Leadership in the Early Church and the Scandal of Their Subordination in the Rise of Christianity.*

Cora Voyageur is an associate professor of sociology at the University of Calgary. Her research explores the aboriginal experience in Canada and includes aboriginal employment, economic development, and politics. She is a member of the Athabasca Chipewyan First Nation from Fort Chipewyan, Alberta.